LIVING ABROAD
Spain

FIRST EDITION

Nikki Weinstein

© Jessica Chesler

AVALON
TRAVEL

C O N T E N T S

INTRODUCTION 1

DAILY LIFE 69

PRIME LIVING LOCATIONS 185

RESOURCES 295

About the Author

© Nancy Nowacek

Nikki first went to Spain when she was 20 years old. She arrived in the country on an overnight train and as soon as she bit into her first *jamón* sandwich, she knew she was home.

Against her instincts, Nikki returned to the United States, graduated from Kenyon College, and moved to New York City. She made multiple trips back to Spain, and at 28, decided to move to Madrid. Once she settled in, Nikki made a valiant attempt to try every restaurant in town and practice yoga in Spanish (note: the word *om* remains the same) and was witness to a traditional pig slaughter.

She enjoyed spinning her lunches into lengthy, multi-course affairs and leaving town for weekend trips whenever she could. On past excursions, she skied Sierra Nevada, took in the Semana Santa procession in Seville, discovered Basque Country's incredible surf, and experienced sheer terror when she learned to drive a stick shift car on a winding, hilly road outside Madrid.

Nikki started her career at CBS News and has contributed written pieces and commentary to NPR. She's written on everything from mock rockers to real rockers, travel to urban bird watching. She now divides her time between Madrid and New York City and continues to write about Spain.

Preface

The moment I set foot into Spain, I was enamored with the place. The ham was to-die-for good, the streets were twisted, cobbled, and charming, and the museums were some of the best I'd seen—but what *really* got me were the people. On my first morning in Spain, the friend with whom I was traveling and I emerged from a metro station, bewildered and squinting at a city map. Strangers helped us with directions and people engaged us in conversation, praising our weak Spanish skills and offering tips on what to see while we were in the city. After a few days filled with such experiences, I was hooked on the country.

That first trip was nearly a decade ago, and in the following years I'd loudly insist to people that I'd move to Madrid . . . eventually, but the truth is I never really thought that I would. However, when I quit my job at a magazine to begin freelance writing fulltime, I realized that if I was going to make a move, I'd have to do it then or I likely never would. Looking at it that way, the decision wasn't so hard, and within months I was set up in Madrid.

While moving to Spain was one of the best decisions I've made, it wasn't as easy as I had expected—especially in the beginning. My language mix-ups ranged from the hilarious to the frustrating, and it was a few months before I felt comfortable leaving home without a translation dictionary. Contrary to the image some people have of living overseas, I didn't land in some movie-set version of Spain in which I spend my days wandering through sun-dappled olive groves. I ended up in a real place that's now full of friends and neighborhoods that I've come to know well. It's a place where I've grown to know by name the guy who sells me a newspaper every morning, where I spend summer evenings over beers and tapas in local plazas, and where I find myself staying out until dawn more often than I ever had before.

Today, my map of Madrid no longer looks like the one I pulled out when I first arrived in the city. Mine is far more personal and it's constantly changing. Its landmarks are beloved restaurants, favorite hangouts, and friends' homes rather than historical monuments and museums. Madrid's layout no longer bewilders me because it's now my city. It's where I live. It's finally home. And as I've settled into life in Spain, I've discovered something I didn't expect. Living abroad, when you come right down to it, is life as usual—it just happens somewhere else.

—Nikki Weinstein

Introduction

Welcome to Spain

The Andalusian poet and dramatist Frederico García Lorca once noted that in Spain, the dead are more alive than the dead of any other country in the world. When I read that line, I mulled it over for a while and eventually repeated the quote to a Spanish friend. She laughed. "That's great. It so perfectly describes Spain!" But she was stumped when I asked her to explain exactly why she thought so. Finally, she summed it up with a triumphant smile. "It just *feels* right."

Perhaps that really is why Lorca's description of Spain is so fitting—because it elicits a feeling that is even more important than the actual words. It often seems that what binds Spain together is a collective feeling. Emotion is the unifying glue in a culture awash with contradictions, rife with regional differences, and alive with the past. From Galicia to Ibiza, the Spanish jump into life heart first.

Spain is a passionate country where people have an enormous appetite for absolutely everything—parties, wine, familial love, political sparring, and oh yes, food. God, do the Spanish love food. This is a country where lunch can last for three hours, legs of *jamón* (ham) hang in nearly every restaurant and home, and when you order paella, what lands on your table can be so huge that it leaves no room for your wine glass. That enormous platter says it all. Dig in but take it slowly and savor every bite—there's no rush.

Spain is fully modern today and its teeming city streets reveal the country's commitment to commerce, but something old-world still prevails. The union of tradition and forward-looking vision might strike Americans as incongruous, but in Spain it works. The siesta is a perfect example of that. Sure, the Spanish may no longer snooze during midday, but lunch is often a long meal accompanied by a glass or two of wine. In order to take that leisurely break—one that many view as a necessity more than a luxury—the Spanish will work into the evenings to accommodate their ample, afternoon rest.

> Most people who visit Spain remember the passionate temperament of the Spanish more than anything else. Those who are really smitten return because they want more than just a small dose of that culture.

When one of the country's many annual fiestas rolls around, the revelry pulls out the entire town. Grandmother to teenager, everyone stops what they're doing to stroll through the streets, eat *churros y chocolate* (fritters and hot chocolate), and celebrate with their neighbors. Work is important but it revolves around life rather than the reverse, and that says something important about the Spanish: what matters here is what you're doing with your time when you're not working. Family is everything, the bonds of friendship are ironclad links that often date back to childhood, and ample vacation is paramount.

I suspect that so many people fall in love with Spain at first visit because of the country's enormous enthusiasm for life. Of course the strong, Andalusian sun is also a powerful draw, the verdant mountains in the north are beautiful, Madrid oozes charm, and Barcelona woos visitors with a culture that is both avant-garde and rooted in thousands of years of history. But most people who visit Spain remember the passionate temperament of the Spanish more than anything else. Those who are really smitten return because they want more than just a small dose of that culture—they want to become a part of it. Some of those visitors return to the country over and over, until they finally decide to stay and make Spain home.

I still wonder what Lorca really meant by his statement about Spain's dead being so alive. It probably refers to the country's long history; one marked by bloody battles, shifting kingdoms, and romantic myths. But when I think about the Spanish appetite for life, I change my mind about the writer's intention. Maybe Lorca was commenting on the Spanish character, and he figured that a fire so strong couldn't be snuffed out. Ultimately I just don't know—but still, his quote somehow feels so right.

IS SPAIN RIGHT FOR YOU?

It's often said that Spain is different, and indeed it is—especially for foreigners. Spain won't feel like home for the first few months, but isn't that the point of moving abroad? For most people who pick up and leave the United States—be it for a semester, a year, or for life—they're specifically looking to encounter a new culture, different customs, and to master another language.

The U.S. Bureau of Consular Affairs estimated that in 1999, close to four million Americans were living abroad and 95,000 of those people were in Spain. Clearly, the decision to live somewhere different—even if only for a while—has widespread appeal. Those numbers are not surprising if you consider that Americans are in a unique position. We come from a country that's the world's third largest in population and fourth largest

Churros and hot chocolate are a must at any open-air festival.

The Spanish Clock

Benjamin Franklin's old adage, "early to bed and early to rise makes a man healthy, wealthy, and wise," is not often repeated Spain—a country where there's an altogether different approach to time. The Spanish clock's face may in fact look like the American one, but the hour marks have entirely different meanings.

Unless you have to catch a train or be at the office, morning is leisurely in Spain. People can sleep until noon on a Sunday morning and when they finally rise, the day still stretches out before them. Afternoon kicks off around 4 P.M. or so and goes until about 8 P.M. when you've officially hit evening; it's perfectly appropriate to greet people with a *buenas tardes* (good afternoon) until then. Lunch is a late meal that's usually eaten around 2 P.M.

In the late afternoon or evening, it's time to head out for some tapas, and by about 9:30 P.M. you can begin considering your options for dinner. If you try to make it any earlier than 9:30 P.M., most restaurants will be so vacant that you might expect tumbleweeds to blow through the dining room. Dinner is typically served until about 11 P.M. and sometimes even later.

Should you want to head out after your meal, midnight is a good hour to meet up with friends, and you may find yourself returning home in the *madrugada* (early morning), just before the sun rises.

The siesta was once an occasion for a nap in Spain, but that's no longer the case. However, a form of the siesta is still alive and well. Stores generally close between 2 P.M. and 5 P.M. after which they reopen for another three hours. In the peak of summer when the sun is at its strongest, people spend midday indoors—usually biding their time over lunch.

It's also worth noting that the idea of punctuality is only sometimes taken seriously. For example, if your boss tells you to be at the office by 9 A.M. every morning, it's a good idea to be on time. Planes and trains also leave and arrive according to their schedules. However, if you make a plan to meet a Spanish friend for lunch and she arrives ten or fifteen minutes late, she's still on time by Spanish rules.

The process of adapting to the Spanish clock is a lot like overcoming jetlag—it's a rocky adjustment but once you're acclimated, you'll feel right in sync with the locals.

geographically. The United States is now the world's sole superpower, and a place where people speak English—one of the world's dominant languages and as many proclaim, the international language of business. It's easy to forget just how different things are off of U.S. shores, and it's common to want to step into another culture for a reminder.

What you seek in your move might be as simple as leisurely days, good wine, and proximity to a beautiful beach. Or you might want to expose your children to another language while they're young enough to soak it up with minimal effort and to open yourself to another set of customs. Those customs may surprise you at times—the transition isn't always smooth. But if you're patient and curious enough, you'll soon be comfortable slipping into your new community and acting just as the locals do. That means eating dinner after 9 P.M., joining in fiery debates, and adopting a whole new set of road rules in which you'll find yourself stomping on the gas, swearing with gusto, and beating on the horn more than you used to. Hey, when in Spain, do as the Spanish do. . . . You'll probably discover that a little distance can allow you to view your own culture from a wholly different vantage point and the value of that perspective is tremendous—you'll benefit from that new outlook for life.

However, if you don't approach Spain with an extra dose of patience and an openness to its differences, you can expect to be frustrated. Customer service is nearly nonexistent in the country, the clock moves at a slower pace, and unlike in the United States, business does not come first. Consider whether or not you can accept those cultural divergences before you put yourself in the position of confronting them on a daily basis.

Of course, Spain isn't the same everywhere you go. In order to enjoy what Spain has to offer you, you have to know what's out there. You'll find metropolitan centers in both Madrid and Barcelona—both cities topple the one million mark in population and are charged with a buzz of business and culture converging. Both of Spain's main cities have tremendous cultural gifts to offer, but neither will make you feel as if you've stepped back into a quieter, simpler time. Granada and Seville usually beckon the people who want a compromise between urban life and slow-paced days. Both have a few international restaurants and a choice of movie theaters, yet they're small enough that you'll regularly bump into your neighbors around town.

If small-town tranquility is what you're after, Basque Country has more than a hint of old-worldliness to it, especially in San Sebastián and its surroundings. Breathtaking scenery and the friendly, neighborly culture can also be found in Galicia and along the Costa Brava. Even Andalusia—built up though it is in some parts—has an oasis or two left to offer. Some southern towns are so small that you can know your neighbors by name, yet they're also places where you can have a DSL line installed at home.

The Lay of the Land

Spain takes up the bulk of Europe's Iberian Peninsula—five-sixths of the bulging landmass to be exact. Stated differently, that's 312,965 square miles of country. Spain is Europe's second largest nation and arguably the continent's most geographically varied country, too. Step away from the beaches in Andalusia, and you'll find pockets of cracked, sunscorched earth strikingly similar to the American Southwest. Whether you know it or not, you've likely seen those settings before—during the

1960s and 1970s, several Hollywood directors shot big-budget westerns in the parched landscape of Andalusia. However, the north couldn't be more different. The grassy hills of Basque Country gently roll west until the Pyrenees Mountains jut up dramatically with their snow-capped summits; Galicia which lies in the country's northwestern corner, is rainy, fertile, and chock full of salty coves and inlets that are wholly unlike the broad, sandy beaches in the south. In between Andalusia and the northern area is the *meseta* (tableland), a high and flat area that aside from Madrid, is sparsely populated with people but is packed with olive groves, wheat farms, and vineyards. The *meseta* takes up about 40 percent of the country, and in places exceeds 3,300 feet in altitude. Along the eastern coast, the climate is far more temperate than it is in the harsh center, and in the small, Mediterranean coastal towns the scent of the region's orange groves perfume the air.

In addition to the mainland, the Balearic Islands and the Canary Islands are also part of Spain, and the shores of the country are touched by the Atlantic Ocean in the north, northwest and southwest, while the Mediterranean Sea washes onto Spain's eastern shores. France borders Spain to the north, Portugal lies west of the country, and to the south

© Nikki Weinstein

Fresh strawberries for sale   Olives hanging from a tree

you'll find the Straits of Gibraltar—a mere nine-mile stretch of water separating Europe from Africa.

The River Ebro is Spain's largest in volume and also the country's best known—it starts in Cordillera Cantábrica and extends all the way to the southern side of the Pyrenees Mountains. Other important rivers include the Duero, the Guadiana, the Tajo, and the Guadalquivir. Spain's rivers snake across the country providing both water and electricity to different regions, and the bulk of them drain into the Atlantic Ocean.

It's notable that a country that features a good number of powerful rivers did not choose to put its capital city alongside any of them. Many people who visit Spain are struck by the fact that unlike most European capital cities, Madrid's river, the Manzanares, trickles alongside the city like a geographical afterthought. The capital was chosen for its strategic location—Madrid marks Spain's exact geographical center—and not for its waterway.

Although coal, copper, iron, ore, lead, mercury, potash, pyrite, uranium, and zinc, are all found in Spain in varying amounts, the country is not a particularly productive source of such natural resources. Spain's agricultural staples are far more important to the economy. Those crops include wheat, sugar beets, strawberries, barley, tomatoes, olives, citrus fruit, grapes, and cork. In fact, Spain is the world's largest producer of olive oil and prime vineyards are found in Rioja (the Ebro valley) and in Andalusia.

COUNTRY DIVISIONS

The 1978 constitution divided Spain into 17 *comunidades autónomas* (autonomous communities), thereby creating a decentralized form of government. Each of the separate communities has its own local government and the mayors and town councils that oversee matters such as education and the arts are elected by the people; the central government is based in Madrid and it handles issues of foreign policy and national affairs. As is the case in the United States, many issues demand overlap between the community governments and the national one.

Spain's regional communities are further broken down into 50 provinces which are usually named for their main city. Smaller units of division emerge from there—townships. Towns also have a say in government affairs via their administrations called *municipios* (town councils).

POPULATION DENSITY

Given its immense size, Spain is thinly populated with just 40.5 million inhabitants and that number is inching upwards at a slow pace. Why?

Spain's extremely low birth rate (that's an average of 1.23 children for every woman of childbearing age) doesn't do much to help population growth. Moreover, the numbers of immigrants who are moving to Spain have picked up in recent years, but those numbers are still low—too low to contribute significantly to population growth.

Of course, some places are more crowded than others. During the late 1950s through the 1960s—Spain's economic boom years—citizens living in rural locations packed up and moved to the cities where money could be made. Today, most people in Spain still congregate in the cities and as a result, Spain's population is dense in some areas and thin in others.

With a population of three million, Madrid is Spain's largest city. Barcelona is Spain's second most populated city with 1.5 million people. Every other town in Spain has a population that falls below the million mark, but Valencia is also large by Iberian standards—753,500 people live there, and Seville is the Spain's fourth most occupied destination with 702,500 people who call the city home.

WEATHER

Although Spain lies on the same latitude as southern New England, the climate is milder. However, that's not to say you'll find a temperate climate in Spain. Spanish summers produce at least a few days that are so hot, you might wonder if the scalding pavement will melt the soles of your flip-flops; winter days in some parts of Spain are chilly enough to require a hat and gloves. Away from the mountains, it rarely snows.

Spain's weather patterns vary depending on altitude and proximity to the ocean. The plateau that takes up the center of the country experiences soaring summer temperatures and cold, dry winters. On winter days, the temperature can occasionally hover just above freezing while on the rare summer day it climbs up to 100°F. However, on typical August days (and August is Spain's most brutal month), the mercury settles somewhere a little below the 90°F mark.

Summers are even hotter in Andalusia—average August temperatures are in the upper 90s although the winters there are milder than they are on the *meseta*—lows are in the 40s. The Mediterranean has cooler temperatures in the north and the region grows hotter towards the south but as a whole, the coast rarely sees blazing temperatures like those that occur in the center of the country—mid 80s is the average for summer days. Yet the area is more humid, especially in Barcelona. Except for the Pyrenees Mountains, winter isn't especially bitter on Spain's eastern coast—days are usually in the low 30s or above.

The coolest, wettest part of the country is in the north. Galicia is often compared to England's southwestern corner in both weather and scenery, and indeed the temperature fluctuations are less dramatic than they are elsewhere in Spain. Winter seldom brings days that are close to freezing; temperatures in the 40s are the norm. The summer months are also mild—average temperatures are in the 70s and low 80s.

Social Climate

While people from around the world have long sought out lives in Europe, immigration is still relatively new to Spain. Undoubtedly, the delay was partly due to Franco's rule, and also a result of Spain's formerly weak economy. Today Spain is both democratic and fiscally strong, and waves of immigrants have made their way to the country—often with the idea of carving out a better life. The majority of Spain's immigrants come from North Africa, South America, and increasing numbers of eastern Europeans are also moving to Spain. The numbers of foreigners living in Spain has tripled over the past eight years but the final tally is still small. By the end of 2003 there were 1.6 million legal residents living in Spain. Of course the number would be higher if it could include those without papers, but the increase wouldn't be tremendous.

That number—1.6 million—may seem paltry to an American, but Spain has historically been a homogeneous country and the mere fact that Spain is attracting newcomers is big news. While some applaud the development and argue that the new arrivals offer Spain a variety of benefits including a bolstering of the economy, others view the changes as a threat to Spain's traditions. Though a volatile issue, immigration has been a less explosive topic than it is in other western European countries, and that bodes well since it's certain that immigration will only continue to increase in Spain.

Spain is also a popular destination among people who are simply looking for a change and northern Europeans in particular have forged their own communities throughout Spain's coastal regions. In some cases people just buy a holiday home but for others the move is permanent. Americans have moved to Spain in smaller numbers than their northern European counterparts—too small to create distinctly American communities, but an estimated 95,000 Americans are living throughout Spain.

A stucco detail in the Alhambra, one of Spain's most emblematic landmarks

Although immigration is new to Spain, the country does have one ethnic minority that's been around for centuries. The Romas (previously called Gypsies or in Spanish, *Gitanos*) are Spain's most historic ethnic minority—they have been in the country since the 15th century and today they number between 500,000 and 600,000. The Romas have been forced to endure persecution throughout Europe and sadly, Spain is no exception to that. Standard prejudice usually takes the form of job and housing discrimination. Existing laws should prevent such occurrences and a number of Roma organizations have worked towards improvement, but the situation remains a tremendous concern.

SPAIN AND FOREIGNERS

On the whole, Spanish people are friendly. They'll quickly help you with directions, correcting language foibles, they'll compliment your Spanish, and they might even pepper you with questions on everything from where you come from to how you're enjoying Spanish culture. Socializing is big fun in Spain, a place where life is lived in the public sphere, not behind closed doors. It's not unheard of to begin an evening in a restaurant at a table adjacent to strangers, and to finish the night by sharing a drink with those people. Most people are pleased to chat with someone foreign. However, Spanish society is also very polite. People dress just a little more formally than they do in the United States, personal questions are reserved for good friends, and an invitation to someone's home is a breakthrough symbol of friendship—such invitations are not extended casually.

And are Spanish people so open with *everyone,* even Americans? You betcha, but you will find infinite complexities in Spain's relationship with the United States. Just about every Spanish marquee advertises a lineup that's loaded with Hollywood films, television programs such as *The Simpsons* are adored, Levis jeans spell cool, McDonalds and Burger Kings mark the streets of every city, and hits from American pop bands blare out of radios around the country. Given all that, it sure seems as if the Spanish have warm feelings towards the United States—or at least they like American stuff. There are occasional charges of cultural imperialism (yep, the very thing that brought Big Macs overseas), and these exports might cause a few benign misconceptions about what U.S. culture is *really* like, but nothing too serious.

The real anti-Americanism stems from U.S. global policy and its more conservative writers, and the frustration of the Spanish on that point can cause grumbling among the older generations and angry protests by the younger ones. The love/hate relationship with the United States is deeply complicated but ire towards the American government rarely bleeds into attitudes towards Americans themselves. Most everyone makes a distinction between a country's politics and its citizens, and in Spain anyone who makes an effort to learn the language and enjoy the surrounding culture will likely be warmly regarded.

Besame Mucho (Kiss Me a Lot)

The first time you meet a Spanish person you'll immediately notice a cultural difference. In Spain, people pucker up just to say hello. Whether two people meet for the very first time or they're old friends, in both social situations and work ones, Spanish people kiss twice—once on each cheek. (For the novices, go for the right cheek first.) This custom is the norm when two women are introduced and when women and men meet. The one exception is a greeting between two men—in those cases a handshake will suffice.

To many Americans, this custom can seem hilariously time-consuming, especially when large groups of people come together and twenty minutes later, every conceivable pair has exchanged a total of four pecks on the cheek. All practicality aside, the custom is a reflection of the country's warmth and it's for that reason that most foreigners appreciate the two-kiss routine. But whatever your opinion on it, it is considered polite behavior and it's a good idea to adopt it. Every introduction will be an awkward one if you thrust out your hand for a handshake just as someone leans in for a smooch.

©Jessica Chesler

History, Government, and Economy

The Spanish have a tangled family tree with various branches belonging to Africans, Greeks, Phoenicians, Celts, Romans, Visigoths, Jews, and Moors. Legendary heroes, visions of saints, horrifically bloody battles, and clashes among kings all punctuate the country's timeline. When Spanish monarchs famously sent explorers across unknown oceans to discover new worlds, those trips changed the earth's maps. One royal couple fueled by religious zeal began the Spanish Inquisition, and that same pair also united a previously divided country, thus defining Spain's current borders. The recent past brought a brutal civil war followed by the rise and fall of a corrosive dictatorship, and a fledgling democracy arrived in the wake of the tyrant's iron-fisted rule. The new, egalitarian form of government flourishes today. No doubt about it, Spain's history is a rich one and the country would never be what it is today without all of those milestones behind it. But despite that passionate story, the country's beginnings were relatively quiet ones.

15

History

THE EARLY DAYS

In 1879, the young daughter of a wealthy nobleman wandered into an empty cave near Bilbao where she stumbled upon some of the world's most outstanding prehistoric art. The Magdalenian people (Paleolithic hunter-gatherers) who lived in the area around 15,000 B.C. decorated the caves with stunning depictions of bison, horses, and wild boar. Although the famous Altamira cave boasts some of the country's most impressive prehistoric art, other Spanish caves also offer valuable glimpses into the culture of early people.

The New Stone Age brought a store of new developments such as agriculture, livestock, pottery, and textiles—and with those innovations came settled life. Between 1000 and 500 B.C., the Celts arrived from northern Europe and settled by the Ebro River. They mixed with the existing population, giving rise to a Celtic-Iberian people.

Around 1100 B.C., the Phoenicians arrived on Spain's Atlantic Coast and the traders (who came from what is Lebanon today) discovered that sweet riches existed in Iberia. Cádiz—once a Phoenician town called Gades—dates back to this period and is thought to be western Europe's oldest city. Under Phoenician rule, Gades was a prosperous port that laid claim to an impressive fishing fleet. Soon, Greek traders also arrived on the Iberian Peninsula, and by 600 B.C. they had fully settled in. Between them, the new arrivals brought vital advances including the pottery wheel, formal currency, and two of Spain's most famous staples— olive trees and grapes.

ROMAN RULE

The Iberians thrived for about a millennium until 218 B.C. when the Romans arrived. Rome ruled Spain for more than 500 years, and the legendary empire made a strong imprint on the nation in ways that are still evident today. Roads, amphitheaters, urban planning, aqueducts, baths, and the foundations of the nation's current legal system all came with Roman rule. Seville, León, and Pamplona were founded by Romans, and Córdoba, Tarragona, and Mérida developed as the capitals to the three Roman provinces in the country. The Romans also brought one of their most lasting legacies—Latin, which eventually evolved into Spanish.

Scores of Romans came to the country they called Hispania. The new arrivals settled in and imposed their culture onto the Iberians, but however mighty the empire, the transition was not an entirely smooth one. Insurgency regularly exploded and rebellion was fiercest in the north—par-

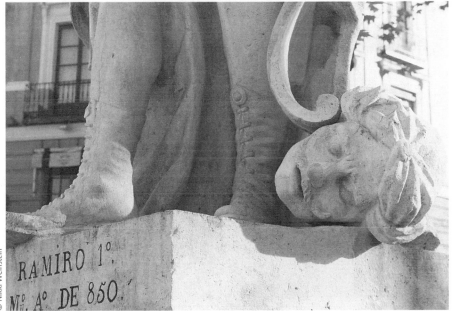

© Nikki Weinstein

The statues of the royals outside the palace in Madrid reveal both the best and the worst of Spanish history.

ticularly in the Basque region, a place that was eventually subdued but never completely romanized. Despite the bursts of revolt, the north remained firmly under the thumb of Rome during the period of Pax Romana—the Empire's run of great prosperity and unchecked leadership.

During the course of Roman rule, large numbers of Jews arrived to Hispania and settled in the Mediterranean area. Yet another religion arrived in the 3rd century A.D.—Christianity. The faith took root in Andalusia and conversion quickly followed. Things were beginning to change in Hispania. The glory of Pax Romana had ended and by the 3rd century A.D., the Roman Empire began showing crippling fissures.

VISIGOTHS AND THE CHURCH

As the Roman empire continued to crumble, marauding groups of people took advantage of the country's weak base of power and launched a series of invasions. The Germanic Visigoths took control around A.D. 410; Toledo became the capital and Visigoth rule endured for 300 years. The Visigoths have been immortalized in history as a particularly coarse and brutal crew.

Life deteriorated under Visigoth rule and the group's power was undermined by nasty infighting among the kings. The most important

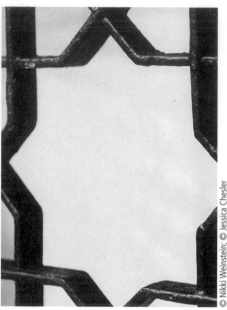

The Roman aqueduct in Segovia

Moorish flourishes like this one can be found throughout the south.

legacy left by the Visigoths in Spain was a spiritual one—in A.D. 587, King Reccared converted from the Aryan version of Christianity to Orthodox Christianity, and that incident helped shape Spain's future. Although the Visigoths adopted the Roman way of life in many ways, city life continued to decline, revolts continued, and the group's leadership was precarious at best. Unbeknownst to Spain, the Moors were preparing to invade from North Africa, and they chose to do so at a moment in which the country was deeply vulnerable.

THE MOORS

After the death of Mohammed in A.D. 632, Islam began to spread across the globe and the new religion soon reached North Africa where the locals were quick to embrace the laws of the Koran. News of al-Andalus (the Isle of Vandals) also reached North Africa, and the enticements of a land of riches just across the water must have been a powerful draw. In 711, Tariq ibn Ziyad—the governor of Tangier—led an army of about 10,000 Berbers across the Strait of Gibraltar and to the shores of Andalusia. The Moorish leader deftly took advantage of the feuds raging among the Visigoths, and in addition to his own men, the Moorish ruler also took along a group of Visigoths as allies. Ostensibly, the

Moors were merely providing soldiers to bolster one side of a power struggle in which they played no part. However, the Moors quickly turned their place in Spain to their advantage and by 714, they controlled most of Spain.

By the 9th century, the golden era of Muslim Spain had arrived; Andalusia functioned as the heart of the country with Córdoba as the capital. (The capital would later be moved to Seville and then to Granada.) In total, the Moors would occupy the country for nearly 800 years and despite constant battles and insurgency coming from the Christians in the north, the Muslims ushered in a time of unrivaled prosperity.

> Compared to the previous rule, the Moors were markedly just; the slaves of the former era had been liberated, and Jews and Christians were allowed to practice their religion freely.

A host of important new crops such as figs, oranges, dates, rice, saffron, and cotton were introduced; agriculture changed, irrigation methods arrived, and marketplaces, public baths, and universities were created. The cultured atmosphere encouraged scholarly pursuits such as philosophy, literature, and science, all of which thrived. Ultimately, the sophisticated society that developed in much of Spain (and especially in Córdoba) was unmatched by the rest of Europe. Compared to the previous rule, the Moors were markedly just; the slaves of the former era had been liberated, and Jews and Christians were allowed to practice their religion freely.

However, the superb civilization flourishing in Moorish Spain was undercut in two important ways. Power struggles among the Moors weakened the group's rule, and in the northern part of the country, Christian monarchies united and gathered strength due to their collective desire to rid Spain of the Moors. While the Moorish government weakened, the Christians continued to grow more powerful. Indeed, the Reconquest had begun. The Moors would remain in the country until the end of the 15th century, but the golden era of Moorish Spain had slowly slipped away.

THE RECONQUEST

The four Christian kingdoms of Spain—Castile, León, Navarra and Aragón were initially weak from infighting in the 11th century, but the four districts gradually established something akin to peace as they directed their forces towards their common goal: to rid the Iberian peninsula of the Moors.

In 1469, when Ferdinand (Fernando) of Aragón married Isabella (Isabel) of Castile, the kingdoms of Aragón, Castile, and León joined and

Saint James of . . . Spain?

During the Reconquest, the Christian effort to purge the country of the Moors was growing forceful and it became clear that the northern armies had more than military might—they also had God on their side. The Christians widely accepted that Santiago Apóstol (Saint James) aided them in their quest to establish a Christian country. Of course, it helped that the guy was buried in Spain.

But wait. . . . Didn't St. James die in Jerusalem? Okay, perhaps it's best to begin with a little background. Legend holds that after St. James died (yes, in Jerusalem), his remains were carted off to Galicia in a stone boat, and the apostle was finally laid to rest in Spain's northwestern corner. Exactly how the stone boat became buoyant is unclear. However, that's not the important part—this is: during the battle of Clavijo in 834, lore maintains that a vision of St. James astride a majestic white horse appeared and the apostle slew 70,000 Moors right then and there.

The Catholics won the battle and from that pivotal moment came the popular rallying cry, *¡Santiago, Matamoros!* (St.

James, Moor slayer!). St. James is Spain's patron saint and many maintain the long-held belief that his remains lie in the Catedral del Apóstol (Cathedral of the Apostle) at the end of the Camino de Santiago in Galicia.

The story is colorful, but it's also telling. National identity and religious pride are inexorably linked in Spain—a country where church attendance has been on the wane for years, but most Spaniards are still quick to proclaim themselves Catholic.

The saint's alleged grave also spawned a famous pilgrim's trail that's still used today—the Camino de Santiago. In 2001, 60,000 people traveled on foot or bike to the end of the 500-mile trail, where it's said the saint is buried. The path has been a Cultural Heritage Route since 1993, and although many of the trail's travelers today aren't there for religious reasons, the ancient route is broadly enjoyed and its modern pilgrims pass the romantic lore of St. James around. Many will concede that Santiago may or may not rest in Spain's soil, but he undoubtedly lies in Spain's heart.

together the territories formed a potent force. Moreover, almost the whole of modern-day Spain fell under King Ferdinand and Queen Isabella's reign. The Christians were growing ever stronger, and they were angling to take Spain as their own. The final, pivotal battle occurred in 1492 when the Christians won Granada—the last Moorish capital and kingdom. Backed by Ferdinand and Isabella, the Christians took over the Alhambra—the Moorish fortress built between 1248 and 1354. The Alhambra was one of the crown jewels of Islamic architecture and the loss of the magnificent structure proved to be a gutting defeat for the Muslims. After hundreds of bloody, volatile years, the Christians at last wrested control of Spain from the Moors.

THE GOLDEN AGE

The year 1492 marked a pivotal change for Spain. The Catholic monarchs not only established their rule at home but they also flexed muscle abroad; they began a powerful empire. King Ferdinand and Queen Isabella left their indelible stamps on the country—Ferdinand with his cunning and Isabella with her stern piety; together, they were an indomitable force.

The same year that the monarchs won Granada, the Italian-born Christopher Columbus (Cristóbal Colón) set sail in search of a new passage to Asia. Wealth was the primary enticement, but the idea of converting more people also motivated Ferdinand and Isabella to fund the voyage. (The two weren't known as "the Catholic Monarchs" for nothing.) Columbus famously lost his way to Asia, but his three voyages were not for naught. The explorer found the islands in the Caribbean Sea, the West Indies, and the coasts of South and Central America. During the reign of Ferdinand and Isabella, colonization truly began and its impact was tremendous.

Although Columbus was the first voyager sent by the Spanish to hit the Americas, he was not the only one—a long line of explorers followed in his wake. The conquistadors returned to Spain with hoards of gold and silver that helped build the immense wealth of the Spanish empire. Hernando Cortés claimed Mexico and Vasco Núñez de Balboa sailed into the eastern waters of the Pacific Ocean and began to conquer South America's western coast. Spain's naval power was exceptional.

> The conquistadors returned to Spain with hoards of gold and silver that helped build the immense wealth of the Spanish empire.

The Spanish brought their culture and religion to far-flung regions of the globe and the treasures reaped in South America helped Spain to grow even wealthier. The country's Golden Age was well underway. Meanwhile, back in Spain, the fanatically religious queen helped usher in strong measures that would forever cast a dark cloud over Spain's most prosperous time in history.

The Inquisition began in 1231 outside of Spain as a Roman Catholic Church–backed effort to root out heretics. But the Spanish Inquisition has gone down in history as the most horrific of all the Inquisitions, and Spain's Jews were the first victims to suffer its effects. Many of the country's Jews had previously converted to Catholicism in order to escape other forms of persecution and those individuals became known as *conversos* (converts). Isabella and others questioned the sincerity of the former Jews' new beliefs and thus began the practice of systematic torture with the purpose of uncovering the true spiritual leanings of these *conversos*. In 1492, the law was further stiffened—any Jew who refused baptism was forcibly expelled from the country. It's estimated that anywhere from 60,000 to 150,000 Spanish Jews left and many also remained in Spain as converts.

Under the menacing direction of Tomás de Torquemada—the king and queen's personal confessor and the overseer of the Inquisition—Muslims and suspect Christians were soon targets as well. The monarchs initially allowed Muslims to freely practice their religion, but they later reneged on their promise and the Moors were driven from the country. The Inquisition lasted for about 300 years and an estimated 12,000 people died. To make matters more appalling, the state benefited handsomely from the victims of the Inquisition in the form of confiscated land and property.

AN EMPIRE SLIPS INTO TURMOIL

In 1512, Ferdinand had succeeded in pulling the small kingdom of Navarra under Spanish rule, and with that coup he created an officially united country and bolstered the already tremendous Spanish empire. Moreover, Ferdinand and Isabella had insured their power in Europe by marrying their four children into important European monarchies including the Habsburg family of central Europe. After the Ferdinand and Isabella's death, Carlos I, the son of one of those auspicious pairings, came from Flanders in 1517 to succeed his grandparents' thrones.

Carlos I was initially unpopular among the locals in part because he neither spoke Castilian nor did he spend much time in the country (Carlos I lived in Spain for only 16 years of the 40 years he held power). However, the new king also expanded the empire and in that way he was good for Spain. When Philip II (Felipe II) took over the throne in 1556, Spain's rule covered the New World colonies, vast portions of Italy, Belgium, the Netherlands, and sections of Austria and Germany. In fact, Spain controlled a greater portion of Europe than any single power had since the 9th century.

It was during the rule of Philip II that the empire began to deteriorate. The king devoted himself to the Counter Reformation, and the fiercely Catholic monarch was especially set on battling Protestant England. In 1588, Philip II sent the celebrated Spanish Armada off to Britain, and when the English won that famous fight, the world saw that Spain's great empire was not in fact unbeatable; the empire had reached its zenith and with the defeat of the Armada, the world knew that Spain's glory days were over. By 1714, Spain had lost Flanders, its Italian possessions, and Gibraltar.

THE 19TH CENTURY

Spain continued to weaken throughout the 19th century, and although the economy strengthened and the country's infrastructure improved, the era was marred by its involvement in a series of small, international conflicts and the larger Peninsular war. During that monumental event, Napoleon took full advantage of the chinks in Spain's armor when the French emperor made his brother, Joseph Bonaparte, the king of Spain in 1808. The French occupation was swiftly ended by the people's revolt and a tentative constitution emerged in the wake of the turmoil. However, the changes proposed by the *liberales* (liberals)—the constitution's advocates—were not widely embraced.

By 1825, Spain's colonies had dwindled to just Cuba, Puerto Rico, the Philippines, Guam, and a few African settlements. Meanwhile, things were unruly in the country—conflicts between the liberals and the conservatives raged on. The First and Second Carlist Wars (1833–1839 and 1872–1876, respectively) were disputes over Spain's leadership and the country's future seemed wholly uncertain.

By 1876 Spain was a fledgling constitutional monarchy, yet that milestone was anything but a happy ending. The country was in the midst of chaos so virulent that it undermined every political step forward. Labor disputes were constant, the countryside's working class angrily objected to the rich landowners who controlled them, and Basque and Catalonian separatists were becoming alarmingly unruly. Everyone had an opinion, no one could agree, and the country was ripe for a revolution.

THE 20TH CENTURY TO THE PRESENT

Spain was floundering and its few remaining colonies took the opportunity to rebel. The United States backed Cuba's fight for independence and the conflict led to the Spanish-American War, which Spain lost in 1898. Utterly defeated, Spain also relinquished its remaining colonies save for some minor African outposts.

Meanwhile, things were still bleak at home and by 1923, the Parliament was dissolved and General Miguel Primo de Rivera headed a military revolt. With the king's support, Primo took over the government. His brief dictatorship ended unhappily just six years later when the general resigned and the king resumed his place on the throne. Yet disorder continued to plague the country.

Revolution came on April 14, 1931, when the liberal constitutionalists proclaimed Spain a republic and the King's family was forced into exile. The Republicans on the left drafted a new constitution, which granted women the right to vote, legalized divorce, and created a separation between religion and state. Conservatives, who supported both the monarchy and the Roman Catholic Church, staunchly opposed the radical changes. A 1933 election proved the conservatives the majority

The King of Hearts

In most cases, the reigning monarchs of democratic countries do little more than hit the resorts, throw a few good parties every year, and smile pretty for the ever-present paparazzi. King Juan Carlos Borbón y Borbón is an exception. Sure, these days he spends a lot of his time sailing and kicking back, but you have to give the guy credit—he's one of the key reasons that Spain is a democracy at all.

The king was born in exile and he first stepped onto Spanish soil when he was 10 years old. The then-prince was groomed to take General Franco's place and when the 82-year-old dictator was clinging to life, no one in Spain doubted that Juan Carlos would take the reins of the country upon Franco's death. And why should they

have thought so? Juan Carlos had always been obedient to Franco—he stood loyally by his side and he had even sworn an oath of loyalty to both the dictator and the conservative Movimiento Nacional.

Yet when the general died on November 20, 1975, Juan Carlos shocked the country by devising a transition to democracy rather than assuming Franco's position. Free elections took place in 1977 and by 1978 the country had a constitution in place. The 39-year-old king had proved his mettle at last. Thanks to his actions, Spain could officially close the chapter on the malignant Franco years.

Good news, right? Yet not everyone was pleased, least of all the military,

and consequently, a revolt against the government exploded in Barcelona; more than 1,000 people were killed before the uprising was suppressed.

It was obvious to everyone that the country was dangerously fractured and an election was called in 1936 with the idea of appeasing the people. The Popular Front represented the political left, and it beat the conservative Falange Española party (a party similar to the fascist parties then in Germany and Italy) by a hair. Supporters of the losing party immediately flew into a violent uprising. In July 1936, an army unit based in Morocco rebelled against the new government and that fueled the disarray. About half the country's military units joined in the coup against the government and the Popular Front fought back with everything it had. The Spanish Civil War had begun. With the backing of the Falange Española, General Francisco Franco was chosen as the leader on the Nationalist (or conservative) side. He came in from Morocco where he had been stationed to head his party in the war.

It's impossible to exaggerate the horror of the Spanish Civil War. Although it only lasted for three years, the fighting was ruthlessly brutal and the death toll reached catastrophic proportions. Both sides massacred civilians, and in total, more than 350,000 people died as a result of the tragedy. The battle for Spain caught the world's attention and in many ways the war acted as a precursor for the issues that would embroil Europe in World War II. Nazi Germany and Fascist Italy stood firmly behind

which had been favored by Franco during his rule. On February 23, 1981, a group of machine gun–toting Spanish Civil Guard soldiers burst into the 350-member Spanish Cortes while its members were in the midst of voting in a new prime minister. The rebels took the politicians hostage. Antonio Tejero Molina, the leader of the coup, announced that a military authority would henceforth lead Spain. Those who had orchestrated the plan to overthrow the government figured that Juan Carlos would support them; they assumed that the king wasn't serious about his commitment to democracy. But when the rebels called the palace and the king was told that Tejero planned to put a bullet in any member of the court who tried to stop his plans, Juan Carlos did not respond as the rebels had hoped. "In that case, they will have to put two bullets in me," replied the king.

Juan Carlos made anxious calls to wavering members of the military and within a matter of hours he had deftly stopped the coup. That night he made a television appearance with his son, the 13-year-old prince Felipe. The whole country tuned in to see Juan Carlos explain what had occurred, and he made a long, articulate defense of democracy. No one has forgotten what the king did for his people. Twice, he gave the country back to them, and Spanish democracy remains stronger than ever.

Franco, while the Communist Soviet Union assisted the Popular Front (or the Republicans). International brigades from around the world rushed to the Republicans' aid, including the American Lincoln Brigade. The fight also won the efforts of some notable figures including Ernest Hemingway, John Dos Passos, Martha Gellhorn, and George Orwell, all of whom rushed to Spain to fight the onslaught of fascism in Europe.

However, the Nationalists were the stronger of the two sides on March 28, 1939 Nationalist troops marched into the capital without confrontation. When the Republicans surrendered the next day, Spain was fully controlled by Franco.

The general's rule was tyrannical. His party—the Movimiento Nacional (National Movement) became the country's sole political party. Massacres of prominent Republicans continued long after the war ended and it's estimated that after the Republicans had surrendered, 100,000 people were either executed or died while incarcerated. Franco abolished the vote, reestablished the country's link to the Roman Catholic Church, and did away with regional autonomy. Divorce was made illegal, church weddings were obligatory, and the press was fully controlled by the government.

Just a few months after Franco rose to power, World War II began. The general avoided direct involvement in the war although he vaguely supported the Axis powers with which he was ideologically aligned. Franco's stance during the war alienated him from the world community and in 1945 and 1946, most countries broke off diplomatic relations with Spain; until 1955 Spain was not invited to participate in the United Nations.

The forced isolation hurt Spain's economy and led to the *años de hambre* (years of hunger) during the 1940s. However, things were on the upswing by 1953 when the United States (appeased by the general's intolerance for communism) created four military bases in Spain in exchange for a tremendous aid package.

As Franco aged, he softened his policies, but he undoubtedly intended for the Movimiento Nacional to carry on after his death. In 1969, prince Juan Carlos I, a grandson of King Alfonso XIII, took an oath of loyalty to the party and the young monarch was groomed to take the general's place as Spain's leader. When Franco died on November 20, 1975 the Spanish people fully expected Juan Carlos to pick up right where Franco had left off—but Spain was in for a surprise.

In 1976, Juan Carlos appointed Adolfo Suárez prime minister—a man who was well known to favor democracy. A new, two-party system was quickly established, the Movimiento Nacional was eradicated, and elections were held in 1977—the first Spanish election since 1936. The next year, a new constitution was approved in which assured civil rights and created an official division between the government and the Roman Catholic Church.

Adolfo Suárez's Unión del Centro Democrático won the majority of Parliament's seats, but not everyone was pleased. Franco had more supporters than is commonly thought and plenty of Spaniards wanted to see a return to his form of government. In 1981 a military coup took control of the parliament and demanded a return to Francoism. The king did not buckle, and in this event he really proved his mettle—the leaders of the coup were arrested and Spain remained a parliamentary monarchy.

In 1986, the Socialist Prime Minister Felipe González brought Spain into the European Community, and with that accomplished, the Franco era was truly a thing of the past—Spain was once again an active part of western Europe. In 1993 the European Community grew into the European Union, a group in which Spain plays a prominent role today.

In 1996, José María Aznar of the conservative Partido Popular (Popular Party or PP) was elected prime minister; the victory marked the first occasion in which a conservative leader had won an election since Franco's death. In 2000 Aznar was reelected, and under his leadership and with the help of European Union aid, Spain progressed rapidly—by 2000, the country's economy was the fastest growing in Europe and unemployment had dropped dramatically. The Prime Minister experienced some dips in popularity towards the end of his term, especially regarding his support in 2003 for the war in Iraq and his handling of the 2002 oil spill off of the coast of Galicia. Aznar did not seek reelection in the 2004 election—instead, Mariano Rajoy ran as the Partido Popular's candidate. During the campaign, most everyone agreed that Rajoy was destined to win, but a tragic bombing in a Madrid train station changed everything.

During morning rush hour on March 11, 2004, a series of explosions were set off on commuter trains in Madrid and left close to 200 people dead and about 1,800 wounded. In the hours after the bombings, Aznar publicly blamed ETA, the Basque separatist group, despite strong evidence that implicated others. When the news broke that Islamic fundamentalists and not ETA were responsible for the bombing, the Spanish people were outraged. They felt that Aznar had lied about the bombers' identity in order to protect his own party's reputation. (During his time in office, Aznar maintained rigid policies regarding ETA; he also supported the war in Iraq despite the fact that approximately 90 percent of the Spanish people opposed it.) The ensuing political scandal also stirred up old antiwar sentiment. Just two days after the bombing, the Spanish people went to the polls, and thanks to unusually high voter turnout and disgust for the week's events, José Luis Rodriguez Zapatero of the Spanish Socialist Workers' Party was elected prime minister.

Government

Back in the heyday of *Saturday Night Live,* Chevy Chase delivered a trademark, tongue-in-cheek news flash about General Francisco Franco *still* being dead. The joke, of course, was that the general's decease was hardly news. In fact, the general's death was big news in Spain and even 30 years later its repercussions are still felt. The country had suffered under the dictator's near-fascist rule for almost 40 years until he died in 1975. In the wake of Franco's passing came a brand new constitution and democracy—a form of government Spain hadn't seen since 1936. So not only is Franco dead, but his form of government isn't coming back.

Spain has been a parliamentary monarchy for more than 25 years—since 1978 to be exact. The prime minister is the single most important person in the government and the elected official who heads a cabinet much in the way the president does in the United States. In Spain, the leader of the political party that wins the majority of seats in the Cortes Generales (Parliament) steps into the role of prime minister. The Cortes Generales consists of two houses—the 350-member Congreso de los

Diputados (lower house) and the 208-member Senado (Senate, or upper house). Members are elected for four years, although early dissolution can occur. Anyone 18 years old and older can vote.

The Popular Party (PP) and the Socialist Workers' Party (PSOE) are the largest political parties in Spain, and the two groups constantly vie for the upper hand. From 1982 until 1996, the PSOE had that advantage with Felipe González as Prime Minister. However, González's run of success came to a scandalous end in 1996, in which both the prime minister and his close colleagues were accused of corruption on several counts. The right-of-center PP took majority control in the 1996 general election, and it held its power until the election of March 2004, which the left-of-center PSOE won.

Just as the term parliamentary monarchy assures, Spain does have a king. However, he plays a minimal part in the government. The king's current role is nothing like what it once was when the appointed monarch ruled the country; his modern role is mainly advisory and diplomatic. Many applaud the monarchy simply due to tradition of the royal institution—the royal family has been a pillar of Spanish society since before the official formation of Spain itself. Other Spaniards want to abolish the monarchy, and that group argues that such an institution plays an inconsequential role in today's society. Despite the debate, it's unlikely that the monarchy will be dismantled any time soon.

Economy

During the course of the 20th century, Spain moved from financial hardship to a strong economic position, and one that is still strengthening today. Following the end of the Spanish Civil War in 1939, Spain was nearly destitute from the war, and because Franco was at odds with the world community, no foreign aid was coming in. As a result, the country entered *los años de hambre* (the years of hunger). Things picked up in the 1950s when the United States gave a tremendous sum of money to Spain in exchange for the use of four military bases. Following that assistance, Spain's "economic miracle" began.

In 1959 the peseta (Spain's former currency) was devalued in order to check inflation and suddenly Spanish industry thrived. Tourism developed and it was as if all at once, the world discovered that Spain was the ideal place for a vacation. Resorts sprung up along the Costa del Sol in Andalusia and along the Costa Brava in Catalonia. Spaniards from rural locales throughout the country moved to cities and tourist resorts in order to find work. The number of foreign visitors skyrocketed from three million in 1959 to more than 34 million in 1979, and the country was utterly transformed.

The 1982 oil crisis devastated Spain and caused profound setbacks, but the economy was partly lifted from its crippling slump in 1986 when Spain joined the European Community—now the European Union (EU). Spain has benefited handsomely from European aid. In 2002 the country discarded the peseta in favor of the euro—the new European currency currently used by 12 countries. Spain was one of the biggest advocates of the new money and people are largely pleased with the result.

It can be presumed that much of success enjoyed by the former prime minister, José María Aznar, was due to his economic reforms. Aznar advocated both privatization and the deregulation of the economy, and the benefits have paid off. The prognosis today is good but not perfect. Spain is growing at a rate faster than most EU countries and while that *is* promising, Spain also began with far more room to grow than countries such as France and Germany. Agriculture measures 4.5 percent of Spain's gross domestic product—that's more than most EU countries, and tourism is still the vital part of the Spanish economy that it's been since the 1960s. More than 50 million tourists visit Spain every year, and tourists spent an estimated €26 billion ($33 billion) in Spain in 2001.

Some experts worry that Spain depends too heavily on foreign visitors, and one recent event has proved that such reliance is risky. Spain has long been a popular destination for German tourists and when the German economy recently took a nosedive, many potential tourists had less money with which to travel. The effect of German's economic woes has been sorely felt in scores of Spanish resorts, and there's now intense pressure on Spain to diversify its economy. Unemployment is another thorn in the side of the Spanish economy—at 11 percent, it remains very high. In most cases the unemployment rate dips in cities and Barcelona has the country's lowest rate of unemployment at 7 percent. As was the case in the mid-20th century, Spanish people tend to congregate in urban areas for the better work opportunities.

People and Culture

eople in Spain are quick to declare that they work to live rather than live
to work and it does truly seem that careers, though important, take a
distant second place to personal lives. Americans often say that while
the general standard of living is lower in Spain than it is in the United
States, the quality of life is much higher. Of course, the Spanish are as varied
a group as any and the serene days of a tiny Andalusian town are nothing like
the more frenzied activity that makes up daily life in Madrid. Still, even in the
Spanish capital people obey the infamous, Spanish *mañana* (tomorrow)
and if they can, they'll put aside business to enjoy the day. The afternoon siesta
still dominates business hours and some honor the tradition over a long,
boozy lunch. The differences don't end there. Spaniards also have more vacation days than people in the United States and people will make time for
an evening *paseo* (walk), to linger over dinner, and to take part in the ubiquitous fiestas that draw crowds into bacchanalian, all-night revelries. This is
unquestionably a country that knows how to have a good time.

Regionalism and Nationalism

Is it any surprise that a country that borders both the Atlantic Ocean and Mediterranean Sea and is one of Europe's most mountainous nations is also regionally diverse? There's no underestimating the profound differences born from Spanish geography.

The fact that Spain is home to four separate languages is just one small indication of the cultural mixture within Spanish society. More often than not the differences between people simply take the form of local pride. That means that people from Andalusia maintain ties to their agrarian roots and to flamenco. Those from Asturias might brag about the superior food back home or talk wistfully about the area's verdant landscape. Likewise, if you speak to someone from Galicia you can expect to hear proud descriptions of the region's profitable fishing industry—the result of the locals' hard labor off the wild Atlantic coast.

Americans often say that while the general standard of living is lower in Spain than it is in the United States, the quality of life is much higher.

Yet regional pride has also been taken to the political arena. Catalonia remains deeply tied to its local identity and has placed increased emphasis on the use of Catalan in recent years (though Castilian is known and spoken by all who live there). Moreover, the region seems to be in perpetual battle with Madrid for more autonomy and Catalonian politicians have even recently repeated their request to be officially referred to as a separate nation.

The Catalans are not the only ones bickering with the capital. Basque Country harbors a strong separatist movement and the terrorist group Euskadi Ta Askatasuna (ETA) relies on violent tactics to make its point; ETA has killed more than 800 people in the name of autonomy. While the group's campaign of violence is executed against the wishes of the majority of Basques, many from the region also support a separation from Spain. For evidence of that, you don't have to look any further than the success the nonviolent but independently minded Basque Nationalist Party enjoys in local elections.

Ethnicity and Class

Although modern Spaniards came from a mix of people including Celts, Romans, Moors, and Jews, the country has remained remarkably homogeneous and almost entirely Catholic since the Reconquest in the Middle Ages. Yet there is one ethnic minority that has lived in Spain for about six centuries—the Romas (once called Gypsies or in Spanish, *Gitanos*). The first record of Romas in Iberia dates back to the 15th century when they arrived after a journey that began in India and today they number approximately 10 million across the European continent while between 500,000 and 600,000 Romas call Spain home. Although Romas were once nomadic, they now live relatively settled lives when compared to their ancestors. Today, Andalusia is home to more than half of Spain's population of Romas.

Despite a strong presence in Spain and a record of significant cultural contributions such as bringing the origins of flamenco to Spain, Romas continue to endure persecution throughout Europe and in Spain. The discrimination can take many forms including prejudice in schools and restricted access to housing. A large piece of the invisible wall separating the Romas from the Spanish is undoubtedly the long-held, presiding view of the minority group as outsiders. Of course plenty of Romas are university students or professionals and they live in a way that appears indistinguishable from the broader Spanish way of life. But many Roma-rights organizations refer to such people as the invisible Romas—they don't fit into the established stereotype and thus are not seen as representative.

While the Romas are Spain's first ethnic minority, they are not the country's only one. For decades, economic hardship made Spain a less appealing refuge for many immigrants than more prosperous European countries—but that's quickly changing. Today, democracy flourishes, the economy has improved and the numbers of foreigners in the country reflect those developments. Officially, only 250,000 foreigners held residency visas in 1986 but by 2000 that number grew to 895,720; combine that with a figure from 2002 showing that 74,467 illegal immigrants were deported and it's clear that Spain is now seeing a wave of immigration it hadn't previously known.

So what does that mean exactly? The answer is a complex one. A huge percentage of those who seek a better life here take jobs that Spain (which has a diminishing working-age population) will not be able to fill in the near future. Thus many agree the new immigration works well—both for the Spanish and for the immigrants. But others, including some prominent politicians in the center-right Partido Popular (PP) party, blame immigration for the current unemployment problem. The issue isn't purely economic either. Many of Spain's immigrants arrive from North and sub-Saharan Africa, South America, and Asia. This growing presence of minorities in a formerly homogeneous country has led to a

Spain's Kitchen

If you come to Spain for just a brief visit, you'll have a good time traveling food-first. If you make the country home you'll discover that all your days can leave you well-fed on the local, culinary bounty. Yet you'll find that Spaniards are just a little defensive about their cuisine and their reaction is justified. Italy's reputation for olive oil and cured ham, and France's exalted sheep's and goat's cheese and fine wines have eclipsed some of Spain's greatest treasures. People here are quick to let you know that those same delicacies are all here, too, and in many cases they're just as good if not better. What's more, those items only begin the country's long list of edible riches.

You can't spend an hour in Spain without noticing the bulging legs of *jamón* (ham) hanging in windows, in bars, and in restaurants. There's no question about it, *jamón* is *the* national cuisine. It's an adored staple that appears in sandwiches, with vegetables, accompanying seafood, and if the cut merits showcasing, served alone on a plate. The logic there is obvious—why garnish perfection?

Today, Spain still boasts the largest fishing fleet in Europe and you'll find succulent piles of various *mariscos* (shellfish) spilling off plates, broiled, baked, and added to bisques. You won't have to stick to the coast to find those dishes either; seafood is an important part of the Spanish diet as far inland as Madrid.

Despite the fact that Spain's culinary tradition is an assorted one, there are a few people who struggle and vegetarians top the list. Just a few years ago it was next to impossible to eat meat-free in Spain. Now . . . well, it's merely difficult. Big cities are the best place to drop the word *vegetariano* (vegetarian) to the waiter and even some urban Spaniards are cutting meat out of their diets. However, in a rural area, if you try explaining that you're vegetarian, you might receive a plate of vegetables sprinkled with chunks of ham. It is possible to get your point across but it's certain that your diet will be a blander one than it would be in the United States.

Some Americans also struggle with the relative lack of diversity in the restaurants but that too is beginning to change. As immigration has hit Spain, restaurants featuring food from around the world have begun popping up across the country. Granted, the sushi might not measure up to the quality you're used to from home but if you're in Madrid or Barcelona you'll have a few international options from which to pick. Better still, Asian sauces, Mexican tortillas, and other international staples have begun to appear on supermarket shelves, too, so if you're not happy with the restaurants' creations, you can go home and cook up most of your old favorites.

Churros and hot chocolate ready to be served

rise in xenophobia. In 2000, a violent, two-day riot flared up in El Ejido, an Andalusian town where at the time about 11,000 North Africans lived. Although that degree of violence is not the norm it does show that the tension surrounding immigration mirrors the rate with which immigration is growing.

As hot as the current debate about immigration has become, Spanish people are relatively temperate on the issue when compared to people in neighboring France, Germany, and even England, where racially motivated violence has grown more common in recent years. Undoubtedly the difference is partly due to the fact that in Spain, the big numbers haven't changed all that much yet—approximately 2 percent of the overall population is made up of immigrants and the country is still more than 90 percent Catholic.

Fair or not, the raging immigration controversy does not generally target those who arrive from other parts of western Europe or the United States. American and European executives who spend a few years in their office's Madrid branch, students enjoying a semester in Salamanca, and retiree couples who move into an old ranch in the Navarra wine region are all considered *extranjeros* (foreigners), but not necessarily immigrants. This might seem like semantics but the distinction means that relatively well-off émigrés from northern Europe and the United States are viewed differently by the Spanish than people who are in more critical economic situations.

In some ways, the issue of immigration has changed Spain's view of class, too. For centuries, Europeans born into poverty often were resigned to a life of poverty and that was certainly true in Spain. Today, every Spaniard has access to a state-provided higher education and thus people all enter the work force on a level playing field—at least in theory. The fact is, some people come from wealthy, well-connected families and that advantage can grease the wheels for young people looking for jobs. Fair? Not exactly, but it's not an issue limited to Spain, it's worldwide.

Immigrants are the least likely to have familial advantages, most especially because many foreigners left untenable situations elsewhere and they often start off with very little in Spain. The result of that is clear. It's often immigrants who take Spain's least desirable jobs such as street cleaners and agricultural workers, simply because those are the jobs most available to them. As a result, a new class divide is forming down ethnic lines. Presumably, things will become more equitable with each passing generation, but in order for that to happen the government will have to work towards that end.

Customs and Etiquette

Spanish people are loud, boisterous, and openly friendly. You can easily spend 20 minutes wrapped up in a conversation with the guy you buy cheese from every week. As a foreigner you will find that it's easy to rely on the kindness of strangers for everything from directions to ordering the best meal off a menu. Yet, despite the gregarious warmth of Spanish society, the culture is also ruled by a distinct formality. In the United States, everyday exchanges might begin with a casual "hello," while Spanish people begin conversations with more traditional greetings like *buenos días* (good day) or *buenas tardes* (good afternoon). This is especially true in work situations and with strangers.

> *As a foreigner you will find that it's easy to rely on the kindness of strangers for everything from directions to ordering the best meal off a menu.*

You might also detect a sense of tradition in the natural evolution of friendships. You'll likely know a Spanish person for much longer than you would someone in the United States before exchanging the personal details of your lives. That is likely due to the fact that this is a far less transient society, people often live in the family home long into adulthood and people have close-knit circles of friends made up largely of those they've known since childhood. Of course it's possible to form close and lasting relationships with Spanish people but it's not done quickly. Questions that an American might ask easily of a new friend can come off as pushy or probing in Spain. Although patience is required, the payoff is that the notion of friendship in Spain runs deep and is usually something that lasts for years or even a lifetime.

Similarly, it may be a long time before you're invited to someone's home, but when you are it's a meaningful gesture and people typically do not show up for the meal empty-handed. A small token of food or wine is an expected offering from dinner guests.

Gender Roles

In the early 1980s, Pedro Almodóvar began releasing his movies into a society still smarting from General Franco's conservative rule and just taking its first bold democratic steps. At that time, the films' depictions of sexually liberated women and daringly gay characters did more to assault Spain than to reflect its cultural norms. But today, those same themes—ones that once depicted a nearly invisible subculture—now mirror some

Do Spaniards Really Love Bullfighting or Is That a Lot of Bull?

Ernest Hemingway wrote about it in *The Sun Also Rises*, a museum in Seville showcases the sport, and prime seats to the *corrida de toros* (bullfight) in Madrid and Seville are as hard to get as Knicks tickets when the team is in the playoffs. The Spanish sure love bullfights. Right?

In fact, many people do adore the sport. It's consistently shown on television. El Juli, a young, successful *torero* (bullfighter) is worshiped like a demigod. And aficionados make pilgrimages to the grave of Joselito El Gallo, one of history's greatest *toreros* and a man who died in the bullring in 1920 at the tender age of 25. However, a huge portion of the population objects to the sport.

While masses crowd into the bullring in their finest duds, you'll also find scores of people walking around town with signs decrying the sport as murder. So is it artistry or slaughter? Perhaps it's best left to the Spanish to decide. Unfortunately, they can't seem to agree amongst themselves. Here are some of the stats.

One 2003 poll revealed that 63 percent of the people in Barcelona wanted the city to outlaw bullfighting and while there were multiple bullrings in the city just a century ago, now there's only one in use. Yet bullfights are big business, too. They're most adored in Madrid and Seville but the revenue pulled in by the sport is significant all around the country. Pamplona makes a ton of cash thanks to the Fiesta de San Fermín and approximately 170,000 people across the country receive some sort of work due to bullfighting. Some supporters don't care about the culture of the tradition but they want it to carry on anyway for the financial benefits.

The debate is growing hotter, and it burned at least one prominent politician. When Ángel Requena, the mayor of San Sebastián de los Reyes and a key figure of the Green coalition came out in support of bullfighting, members from his own party pushed for him to resign.

Yet while the anti-bullfighting movement has picked up steam in the past few years, a resurgence of affection for the sport has taken place and new bullrings have sprung up in some parts of the country. Despite the protests, bullfighting isn't going to disappear anytime soon. In Spain, *toreros* epitomize masculinity. When they're good, they're heroes and even when they're mediocre the crowds all come out to see them anyway—even if a few in the group are standing outside the arena waving banners of protest.

A picador poised in the bullring

very real traits within a shifting society that is at once completely modern and equally bound to a strong sense of tradition. In the past three decades, Spain has changed dramatically and so too have women's roles within the country.

Mainstream feminism reached Spain egregiously late when compared to the United States and other countries in western Europe, and that postponement is largely due to Franco's nearly 40 years of dictatorship. Although the General eventually loosened his control over women, his regime was known for Draconian restrictions that included laws prohibiting divorce and contraception, and another edict that prevented women from opening bank accounts without their husbands' or fathers' permission. Furthermore, Franco's strong ties to the Church enforced an archconservative morality that all but officially restricted women to the home and kept their presence in the workforce to a minimum.

Today, contraception is both legal and readily available, women make up about 40 percent of the workforce, they're entitled to generous maternity leave, and female politicians are hardly an anomaly. But Spain's society is not a utopian one. Men still enjoy higher salaries on average and plenty of women criticize a glass ceiling that prevents them from reaching higher positions in the office—two complaints that are also voiced in the United States today. Moreover, while Spain is much closer to being an equal society than it was a few decades back, it also staunchly maintains traditional gender stereotypes.

While women have been making remarkable strides in their careers, things have remained largely the same at home. It's the wife and mother who shoulders the burden of running the house, from caring for the children and elderly relatives to cooking and cleaning—although that injustice is beginning to change, albeit slowly. Some point to the glaring inequity as one of a few probable reasons for Spain's conspicuously low birthrate. With an average of just 1.23 children for every woman of childbearing age, Spain has one of the lowest birthrates in the world. The speculation is that working women choose to have smaller families specifically because women in Spain do most of the work in raising their children—men still take a passive role in child rearing.

Moreover, problems in the home don't end with the woman's role of almost single-handedly running it. An old Spanish saying advises *la mujer en casa con una pata rota* (the woman in the home with a broken leg). Sadly, some men have taken that suggestion to heart. Unsettling statistics show an alarmingly high rate of domestic abuse and the number of such reports has been on the rise. Ironically, the spike in reported violence against women probably indicates a change for the better—there's now enough support from families, friends, and women's organizations for victims of abuse to go public about tragedies that would have been suffered in secrecy a few years ago. The national crisis is a worry consistently addressed by even the most conservative newspapers; undoubtedly the situation is in urgent need of remedy, but thankfully things are moving in that direction.

Religion

Officially, Spain is a secular country; its constitution assures freedom of religion and also states that there is no single official religion. But the country has undeniably strong ties to the Roman Catholic Church   it's impossible to visit Spain and miss the important place that the Church holds in the country's history. Spain was once a collection of warring kingdoms that were eventually unified in the Church's name. Cathedrals make up a high number of Spain's landmarks, many holidays are religious in origin, and the vast majority of Spanish citizens are baptized and married in churches. On the other hand, it's estimated that less than half of the Spanish population regularly attends mass and church attendance continues its steady course of decline. So just how religious is Spain?

To answer, more than 90 percent of the country is at least nominally Catholic and many people, even atheists, describe themselves as Catholic. But while the majority of Spaniards once proudly proclaimed their religious beliefs, polls reveal that far fewer people will describe themselves as religious today. One 2002 survey revealed that only 19 percent of Spaniards attend mass regularly. Religion classes are mandatory in public schools but for those who don't want to take the class on Catholicism, a secular class on world religions is also offered. Holidays are in many cases linked to Catholic events but the modern celebrations often don't reflect the religious roots. Spain has about 23,000 churches but far fewer priests—too few to fill the churches. Ultimately Catholicism plays a strong role in the Spanish identity, but religious practice is on the wane.

Catholicism isn't the only religion in the country. About 350,000 Protestants also live in Spain—mainly expatriates from northern Europe and North America. Islam has an increasingly strong presence in the country, too, with the vast majority of Spain's Muslims coming from North Africa. In 2002, it was estimated that 500,000 Muslims had by then settled in Spain and that number is still rising. In fact, a new mosque was built in Granada in 2003. That might not sound so newsworthy, but the relatively small structure made headlines around the world. The mosque was the first to be built for Spanish Muslims since the Moors lost control of Spain in the 15th century and were subsequently expelled from the country. Spain's Jewish population was once thriving but the Jews, like the Muslims, were expelled during the Spanish Inquisition. (Those who remained were forced to convert.) In 1982, Spain issued an official invitation of return to Sephardic Jews (of Spanish and North African origin), and some do now live in Spain, but not many. The country's Jewish population numbers about 15,000 today.

The Arts

Spain's beauty isn't limited to the natural world, it's all around in other forms, too. Magnificent cathedrals show the vision of artisans from centuries back, museums house paintings that range from the medieval to the ultramodern, and celebrated odes of love and tales of heroes line bookshelves throughout the country. For as long as Iberia has existed, its people have been writing, painting, sculpting, and building. Today, the country has a fine collection of artistry to brag about.

LITERATURE

If your Castilian is fluent enough to read Spanish literature in the original language or even if you're relying on good translations, you'll discover that Spain's wealth of exceptional prose has made great contributions to world literature. Yet it's not merely the quality of the writing that makes the country's collection of literary trophies so valuable; Spanish literature vividly tells the intricate story of Spain itself from ancient, bloody wars fought over land and power to modern-day satires of popular, urban culture.

Academics have squabbled over establishing a starting point to Spain's literary timeline, and in order to settle the debate people have looked to the beginning of Spanish—the very language itself. It's largely thanks to the efforts of Alfonso X, the king of Castile and León (1252–1284), that Castilian emerged as the dominant tongue of Spain. The King—also known as *El Sabio* (The Wise)—advocated the use of Castilian as a written language for fiction, philosophy, and history. So while Spanish literary tradition harkens back to the era before Spanish took root, Castilian poems first appeared in the 13th century.

Among the important works that emerged during and in the wake of Alfonso X's reign, *El Cantar del Mío Cid* is the most famous. The poem tells the story of Rodrigo Díaz de Vivar, a national Spanish hero who ef-

© Nikki Weinstein

Modern architecture appears throughout the country, even at small seaside museums like this one in Galicia.

fectively acted as a soldier-for-hire after falling out of favor with a certain king. The hero later went on to capture Valencia for the Christians. While the epic poem first appeared in 1140, it is a version from 1307 and written in troubadour verse that remains best known.

Of all the various periods in Spanish literature, Spain's Golden Age has won perhaps the most acclaim—and justly so. The era began with the end of the Reconquest in 1492 and carried on until the mid-17th century. The Golden Age saw the flowering of drama, the picaresque novel, mystic poetry, and prose—and all while tremendous upheaval wrought by the Inquisition unfolded throughout the country. Although it might seem unlikely that some of the country's greatest works were created in the midst one of history's darkest periods, some say that the country's mayhem fed the artistic movement.

Two especially well known schools of Spanish poetry emerged during the Golden Age: The Castilian school of Salamanca and the Andalusian school of Seville. Both were influenced by the Italian Renaissance and prominent in their own right. Additionally, mystic poetry reached new heights in popularity during the 16th century, especially the poems of Santa Teresa de Ávila and San Juan de la Cruz. However, the era's poet who is best remembered came a little later; Luis de Góngora, who focused less on morals or spiritual values than on art for art's sake, won enough acclaim to spawn a poetic movement in his name.

During the 17th century, several theaters opened and fostered a flurry of playwrights eager to fill the freshly built stages with their works. Many plays of the age earned lasting critical praise—especially those by Lope de Vega who also worked as a poet, Lope de Rueda, and Tirso de Molina, whose play *El Burlador de Sevilla* is the origin of Don Juan, literature's most notorious playboy.

Miguel de Cervantes (1547–1616) is so famous that his name is almost synonymous with Spain itself. The author is best remembered for his opus *Don Quixote,* a masterpiece that centers on the adventures the landowner Don Quixote of La Mancha and his squire, Sancho Panza. But the author was markedly prolific and wrote both novels and plays well up until his death on April 23, 1616—the same day that Shakespeare died.

The Generation of 1898 emerged as Spain was in a period of upheaval, and this notorious group is exalted not just for the inherent value of its work but also for its determination to define the Spanish identity while the country was in the midst of a profound upheaval. During the chaotic time, Spain lost its colonial power, the economy slumped, and rebellion began to brew. Yet while Spain was turning into a political hotbed, literature shifted its focus from the external world to the exploration of the mind. Miguel de Unamuno's works such as *Tres Novelas Ejemplares* typifies early Spanish existentialism, while poets such as Antonio Machado, explored the metaphysical realm.

The Generation of '27 further contributed to Spain's changing literary tradition. This literary movement is usually associated with its most celebrated author—Federico García Lorca, who was eventually executed by a firing squad during the Civil War. Like his colleagues, Vicente Aleixandre—who won the Nobel Prize for Literature in 1977—mixed the country's traditional forms with more avant-garde themes.

It's impossible to emphasize how drastically literature changed after Franco's death in 1975. Suddenly, insufferable restraints were lifted and Spanish writers were free to express themselves however they chose. Among the notable authors who have produced works since then, are Juan Goytisolo, José Luis Sampedro, Josefina Aldecoa, and Rosa Montero—a journalist and novelist.

ART

Spain's artistic tradition began when prehistoric people gorgeously rendered wild bison and boar with crude paint on cave walls. The practice of fashioning stunning images of Spanish life has continued through the

centuries. El Greco, Diego de Velázquez, and Pablo Picasso are all prominent figures marking Spain's fine-arts timeline, and new work is still
being created today.

During the Middle Ages, Spanish artists created beautiful frescoes,
some of which can be viewed in churches and museums throughout
the country. Few of the period's great artists are known by name, but the
14th-century painter Ferrer Bassá is a notable exception. He has been
credited with establishing the Italo-Gothic style that became so popular
at the time. Soon, the dark realism of the Flemish school also influenced the country's paintings.

Spain's most applauded Renaissance artist, El Greco (The Greek),
began his work in the 16th century. Born Domenikos Theotokopoulos
in Crete, the painter studied under Titian in Italy and he later moved to
Toledo where he spent most of his working life. Tintoretto's use of color
can be spotted in his work but the mystical, religious imagery that he
chose is entirely Spanish in nature and the somber, elongated figures that
so distinguish his work are uniquely his own. El Greco's most awe-inspir-
ing painting, *El Entierro del Conde de Orgaz* (The Burial of the Count of
Orgaz) is displayed in Toledo's Iglesia de Santo Tomé.

The end of the 16th century marked the beginning of Spain's Golden
Era—arguably the richest time for Spanish art. The Inquisition was
erupting around the country and just as you might expect, the era's art re-
flected passionate religious themes. Two of the period's greatest painters,
Jusepe de Ribera and Francisco de Zurbarán, both painted for the
Roman Catholic Church but in notably different manners. Ribera had
studied in Italy and Caravaggio's influence was strongly exhibited in
his work; he played with shadows and light by bathing a figure in a
bright, white halo dramatically set against a dark backdrop. Thematically,
he favored the epic struggles of martyrs while Zurbarán (who also
showed touches of Caravaggio's realistic style) favored more mystical
imagery and painted a more muted sort of candlelight.

If there was ever an artist who represented Spain itself, it was Diego
de Velázquez—another master who hailed from the country's Golden
Era. Born with undreamed of talent, Velázquez became Philip IV's
court painter in 1623 when the artist was 24 and he held the position
until his death. His portraits included kings, queens, and servants, as
well as jesters and dwarfs. Velázquez enhanced his work's realism by
presenting his subjects engaged in some activity or seemingly dis-
tracted by some unseen influence. *Las Meninas* is by far his most famous work although *La Rendición de Breda* (The Surrender of Breda)
is a close second.

Francisco Goya was Spain's most applauded 18th-century painter and rightly so. Truth be told, the time produced little art of note—except for Goya's. He began his career as a cartoonist in the royal tapestry factory and based on his work's obvious superiority, he was soon plucked from the workshop for greater things. By 1799, Goya was instated as a court painter for Carlos IV, but his most celebrated works encompass a wide variety of subject matter, not just court life. *La Maja Vestida* and *La Maja Desnuda* are nearly identical paintings featuring a woman reclining; in one version she's dressed and in the second work she's nude. Goya also created a now famous series of scathing etchings of the royals and of the clergy. His cynicism (or perhaps realism) also showed up in a series of paintings illustrating the viciousness of the French occupation. From that collection, *El Tres de Mayo* (May Third)—a painting that boldly highlights the victims of war rather than the victors—is the most famous.

Goya also created a series of bucolic scenes featuring happy peasants in light colors, and those stand in sharp contrast to his other works, loaded with biting satire and obvious political statements. Yet Goya is notable for more than his range in subject matter. His use of bright colors and loose brushwork foreshadowed the impressionists, and his inquiry into the depths of human emotion arguably heralded the modernists that were soon to come.

By the early 20th century, Spain was in turmoil and disorder. Revolutionary movements were emerging throughout the country but revolutionary spirit was especially strong in Barcelona. It's not coincidental that bold surrealists and cubists hailed from the city. Although Modernism truly took root in Paris, the movement was partly ushered in by Pablo Picasso, a Catalonian artist who spent years living in Paris. Picasso painted in a more traditional style when he was young, but he soon began playing with perspective by showing three-dimensional objects from a range of angles on a two-dimensional surface. By pushing form beyond its limits, he sought to transcend his works' physical limitations and in an odd way, he succeeded. The use of perspective has subtle, political tones but Picasso took an even bolder political step in his most famous work—*Guernica,* an enormous canvas of black, white, and gray images showing the aftermath of a 1937 German bombing raid on the Basque town Guernica in 1937. Juan Gris was another Spanish cubist who lived in Paris. He remained dedicated to the cubist form and his work is set apart by its vivid colors.

Salvador Dalí and Juan Miró also came from Catalonia and each established his own surrealistic style. Dalí played on Freud's theories in his famous dreamscapes—finely rendered portraits of the mind complete with melting clocks, nude women, horses, and other gorgeous and nightmarish images strangely intermingled. Miró is most strongly associated with his last series of paintings in which lines, shapes, dots, blank space, and bright colors fill the canvases. However, the apparent simplicity of the work belies a world of complexity; like his colleagues, Miró was using simple forms to tackle the intricacy of the psyche.

Few contemporary artists can measure up to the standard set during the earlier part of the 20th century, but a couple are worth noting. Antoni Tàpies, an abstract surrealist, was part of the 1950s, Catalonian movement Dau el Set. Esteban Vicente initially enjoyed more fame in the United States than he did in Spain. He painted colorful, abstract works as part of the Spanish New York school, and his work is now celebrated in Spain as well.

ARCHITECTURE

It's tempting to dub the Alhambra the Taj Mahal of Spain. Some people travel all the way to Granada just to stand on a certain hill at sunset and watch when the medieval, Moorish fortress turns a dusky, ruby hue as the sun dips lower towards the horizon. When the spectacle is over, no one on the hill leaves disappointed. During the days, tourists pack into the Alhambra's rooms to marvel over each fountain, every stucco detail in the walls, and the finely rendered, colored tiles.

Yet the Alhambra can't be dubbed Spain's finest building—that would do a disservice to the rest of the country's architectural marvels. Toledo's cathedral—a colossal structure that took hundreds of years to build—incorporates styles from different eras and it's one of the Spain's most stunning buildings. The aqueduct in Segovia, while not necessarily beautiful, is a fascinating testament to the ingenuity of the Romans. Not only did the aqueduct work as it was meant to when it was built, but it's also still standing more than 2,000 years later. Gaudí's whimsical flourishes and sand-dripping designs enchant Barcelona's visitors and his unusual masterpieces broke new ground in design. Truth be told, even the simple, baked-clay, whitewashed homes with Spanish-tile roofs in the south of Spain have a rustic prettiness to them. The oversized eaves deflecting the rain from the stone homes in the north are minor architectural feats. Both those styles are designed for their climates, and they perfectly meld with their surroundings.

The dominant styles throughout the country are Moorish (hailing from North Africa), Romanesque and Gothic (French imports), and Renaissance and baroque (thank you, Italy). The styles have intermingled to create something that's uniquely Spanish, and in fact the rendering of each individual form is also distinct to Spain. Exactly where you'll find each style hints at Spain's history. For example, churches in a Romanesque (8th-century–13th-century) style—with angular lines but rounded apses—are mainly clustered around Catalonia (where you can find about 2000 buildings in this style) and along the Camino de Santiago near the border of France. However, the Romanesque style can be found in other parts of the country, too.

You'll see the Moors' vision in Andalusian buildings with geometric designs, vividly colored tiles, rounded archways, and fine calligraphy in stucco walls. Moorish architecture dates from the 8th century to the 15th century. It crops up throughout much of Spain, but without question, Andalusia has the greatest collection of it. Although the Alhambra is the quintessential example, the Córdoba Mezquita is another masterpiece in the genre.

In the late 12th century, the Gothic style made its appearance in Spain and you'll know it when you see external buttresses, pointed arches, and—in its later incarnation—carved decorations. The Burgos cathedral displays just about every element in the genre. However, Gothic wasn't always strictly rendered—the Mudejares (Muslims in Christian Spain) created a hybrid between the Moorish style and the Gothic one. With brick and plaster, they created distinctly Moorish flourishes. Aragón has some lovely examples of Mudejares style, especially the tower of the Teruel Cathedral.

Italian craftsman and Spanish architects who had studied in Italy brought the Renaissance (16th century) to Spain. This style nods to ancient Greece and Rome with its use of symmetry and touches such as Doric, Ionic, and Corinthian columns. If you see a building with medallions pushed into its facade, it's likely a Renaissance structure. Granada's cathedral was built in this style.

When the baroque style arrived in the 17th century, buildings began to show extreme ornamentation and a dramatic flair. Think of wedding cakes and you've got the idea. The brothers Alberto and José Churriguera were the leaders of the pack when it came to this extravagant style. The style can work well or it can be overdone. Alberto designed Salamanca's Plaza Mayor, which happens to be one of the most gorgeous spots in Spain, yet the exterior of the Museo Municipal in Madrid seems gaudy and flamboyant.

In the 19th century, Modernism burst forth in Catalonia. The new trend was a Spanish one, but it was similar to Art Nouveau in France and Lo Stile Liberty in Italy. The most famous of all the modern architects (and rightly so) is Antoni Gaudí. Like his colleagues, he experimented with form and ornament, always placing a curve where a straight line would normally have appeared. Spiraled chimneys jutted up, organic shapes evolved, and in the process, architecture's rules were rewritten. Interestingly, the style never really took root elsewhere in Spain, and in Madrid and a few other places, you'll see much more Art Deco when you catch sight of 20th-century architecture.

New buildings still pop up all the time. Barcelona is producing innovate designs and the 1992 Olympics gave the city an opportunity to flex some creative muscle and show off. Frank Gehry's Museo Guggenheim in Bilbao—an outstanding silver structure of interlocking shapes—was a feather in Spain's cap when it was opened its doors in 1997. Granted, Frank Gehry is from the United States, but that his masterpiece is in Spain demonstrates the country's ongoing commitment to innovative design.

© Nikki Weinstein

Planning Your Fact-Finding Trip

I f you're only considering a move to Spain but you haven't yet decided to make it home, perhaps it's time to take a trip to the country so you can learn more about it. Your vacation certainly won't be like living in Spain but it's the closest thing to that aside from actually moving there. First-hand experience is your opportunity to fill in your impressions of Spain with empirical knowledge, and that's no small thing. From a distance, it might seem that Spain is nothing but bullfights, beaches, and flamenco shows. If you want to add nuance to that picture, you'll have to see the country through your own eyes and there's just one way to do that—go there.

Once you get to know Spain, you'll find layers of complexity that no one could have told you about. You'll sample the delicacies off various menus, tour the museums, and wander through a labyrinth of streets filled with sights, smells, and sounds that are entirely new. You'll speak to people you meet over the course of your trip—maybe a waiter who wants to practice English or a friendly bartender, or perhaps someone you sit next to on the train. Inevitably, you'll make a lot of those conversations and at the end of your vacation you'll have your own sense of the country. So there it is: your excuse to head off to Spain for a little while. And anyway, who wouldn't want to?

Preparing to Leave

Spain is an awfully big country and chances are you won't be able to cover all 312,965 square miles of it on your trip. Consider the time you have and with that in mind, work out an itinerary. Start looking through guidebooks to get a sense of what areas interest you. Read the travel pages of the newspaper, too—Spain is often featured in them. If you want to make it to a major festival such as Las Fallas de San José or the Fiesta de San Fermín (a.k.a. the running of the bulls), plan your trip around those dates, after all, those parties only happen once a year.

WHAT TO TAKE

As soon as you you've determined when you'll leave and exactly where you'll be going, you can buy an airline ticket. The good news is that you don't need a visa to enter Spain. As long as you have a U.S. passport that's valid for at least another six months, you can roam the country for up to 90 days. The only things you'll need to worry about are travel insurance, packing your suitcase, and making it to the airport on time.

Most U.S. medical policies cover emergencies in another country but don't assume that yours does—call to confirm that. You also might receive limited coverage if you pay for your airline ticket with a credit card but again, check that. Even if you are covered for medical problems by either your credit card or your health policy, travel insurance can be a big help, not only with health issues but with lost luggage, delayed or canceled flights, and theft or loss. Numerous companies offer policies, and a travel agent can make a specific recommendation. However, be sure to read the fine print before you sign on the dotted line. Some companies leave you on your own when it comes to "dangerous activities," some of which are surprisingly run-of-the-mill. (Hiking and scuba diving are two examples.) Also be sure that your policy covers ambulances and emergency flights home. Lastly, some companies expect you to pay for doctors' bills and they'll reimburse you later. You can avoid an unneeded headache by seeking out a policy that pays doctors directly.

© Nikki Weinstein

Spain provides plenty of opportunities to enjoy sun, sand, and surf.

You can't possibly pick the wrong month to visit Spain—it's beautiful year-round. However, you won't be referring to the country as the land of the sun if you visit in the winter. The southern coast stays temperate throughout the year, but even there, you'll probably need a sweater and you should take a jacket, too. In the mountains and on the *meseta* (tableland), the weather fluctuates dramatically. Temperatures in the winter can plunge below the teens and the mercury will hit the high 90s on some summer days. Whatever your destination, you'll want to pack a few T-shirts and flip-flops if you're traveling in July or August. Before you pack your bags, check the forecast in the paper or online (www.weather.com) so you'll know what to wear.

Take at least one nice outfit for dinners and the like, but unless you're headed to a cocktail hour at the royal palace, you can leave the gowns and tuxes behind. True, Spanish people tend to dress up more than Americans do, but you'll want to pack light enough to move around and be comfortable. If you plan to pound the pavement in search of the sights, pack a comfortable pair of shoes. Chances are you'll view at least a couple cathedrals and for that you should dress modestly. What's a historical monument to you is someone else's place of worship and it's considered thoughtless to wander through the chapel in a tank top and itty-bitty shorts. You don't have to dress like a monk, just make sure that your out-fit has sleeves and doesn't reveal too much leg.

Temperature aside, you'll want to add a few things to your carry-on bag before you head off to the airport. Make a photocopy of your pass-port's picture-page. Hopefully you won't ever need it, but if your passport is lost or stolen, it's extremely helpful to have a copy in order to speed up the process of replacing the original at the U.S. embassy. Also make a copy of your airline ticket, your driver's license, and your credit cards along with the company contact numbers for cancellation in the event of loss or theft. If you have travel insurance or traveler's checks, photocopy those as well. The last item you need is a list of emergency phone num-bers that you should carry in your wallet and while you're at it, go ahead and make a photocopy of that, too.

Currency

When you reach Spain, you'll have to find a way to turn your dollars into euros and you have two choices for that: traveler's checks or your ATM card. It used to be that nearly all vacationers used traveler's checks—that's no longer the case although the method does have certain benefits. As long as you hang onto the receipt and the individual check numbers, you're protected from theft or loss. However you can't use the checks as cash, they need to be exchanged and that requires paying a commission fee. (Amounts vary depending on the vendor and on the day's exchange rate.) To lower the amount that you spend on exchange fees, make sure you get checks in high increments—say $100 or so—and that way you'll receive more cash for each transaction.

Relying on your bank card is much easier than any other method. You'll find no shortage of ATM machines throughout the country and you can take out cash at all hours of the day, every day. Moreover, the ex-change rate usually works in your favor more than it does if you're trad-ing in traveler's checks for euros. Unfortunately, you'll almost certainly pay a fee. Most U.S. banks charge a commission for the use of another bank's ATM machine and although rates vary, they're almost always a lit-tle higher than they are in the United States. Before deciding that this is the method for you, speak to someone at your bank to find out what the charge is per transaction and also ask what your daily withdrawal limit is. If you rely on your cash card, be sure to have a back-up method (such as traveler's checks) in the event that your card is lost or stolen. Moreover, if you are somehow parted with your card, call your bank right away to report the incident.

Security

Once you put cash in your wallet, guard it closely. Unfortunately, petty theft is common throughout Spain and people have found creative ways of lifting foreigners' money. Be especially vigilant at ATM machines, women shouldn't toss their wallets into bags without zipped closures, and men shouldn't keep their wallets in their back pockets. Some people use money belts and that's a good solution if it makes you feel more secure—just make sure the belt is kept under clothing so it's not visible.

Tipping

Service charges are added onto menus but it's polite to leave a little extra. Unlike in the United States, wait staff in restaurants earn decent salaries so they don't rely on tips for their income—leaving a little extra is truly just a way to thank someone for good service. Between 5 and 10 percent is standard. Hotel porters expect about €1 ($1.25) for assistance with luggage.

WHEN TO GO

You can enjoy Spain at any time of year but each season has its advantages. Summer is the hottest time of year and if you're a beach lover, this is the time of year when the sun is strongest. Scores of Spaniards take vacation for the whole of August and en masse, they'll head for the mountains or the ocean. If you visit Spain in the summer, the more famous resorts will be heaving with people so you should probably stick to the lesser-known beaches where you can enjoy a festive atmosphere, sun, and sea but you won't have to face a nonstop crush of vacationers. Although cities will be crawling with tourists, thousands of the local residents will have vacated the urban areas and as a result, restaurants and stores will conform to strange hours. Some places even close for the entire month of August. You won't struggle to find what you need but your options will be more limited than usual.

> *You can't possibly pick the wrong month to visit Spain—it's beautiful year round. However, you won't be referring to the country as the land of the sun if you visit in the winter.*

Fall and spring are Spain's most pleasant seasons, especially May, June, and September. During those months you can enjoy balmy weather and you'll beat the throngs of foreign vacationers by a couple of months. If you come the week before Easter you'll be able to take in the spectacle of Semana Santa (Holy Week). This wholly Spanish tradition is best enjoyed in Seville but wherever you go, it will be quite a sight.

Party Through the Year

If you think people are exaggerating when they say that Spaniards really know how to party, just check out the country's calendar—it's more loaded with events than the king's Palm Pilot. Whichever month you choose to visit Spain, you'll be able to catch some sort of festival and you should take advantage of those occasions—to see Spain in the midst of a public event is to see the country in its prime. Whether the festivities are religious, centered on the arts, or just an excuse to eat, drink, and take it to the streets, you'll find a riotous good time. Here's one kick-up for every month of the year.

January: Who says that San Sebastián is stately? There's nothing mild-mannered about the Basque city when January 20 rolls around and it's time for the **Fiesta San Sebastián.** The patron saint of the city is honored as any religious figure might be—with frenzied fun complete with drum beating and a whole lot of booze.

February: The 10-day *carnaval* that rocks Cádiz with equal amounts of pageantry and debauchery every February is lauded as Spain's best. Music is the focus of the gala, and various *murgas* (bands) show off their skills before a panel of judges and plenty of townsfolk. However, you'd be forgiven if you mistook the festival for a drinking competition.

March: There's just one place to be between March 15–19—Valencia for **Las Fallas.** Although the towering puppets that were artfully created over the course of the year take center stage, the crowds are equally enamored with the fireworks, bulls, bottomless plates of paella, and dancing in the street. If you can make it for just one day, make it the last one—that's when the puppets are set on fire in a monumental display that attracts hundreds.

April: After Seville finishes with Semana Santa, the holy week processions, it's time to break out the tents and let loose. **Feria de Abril** is a weeklong celebration that takes place during the second half of the month. *Casetas* (canvas tents) are set up, traditional costumes are donned, flamenco fills the air, people drink heartily, and everyone returns home for a power nap around 7 A.M. or later. By afternoon, everyone is back on the streets to keep the party going.

May: Córdoba is renowned for its pretty Roman and Islamic patios, and the city isn't shy about strutting its stuff. During the first half of May, all the flowers are in full bloom and those who have kept their patios behind closed doors through the year swing open the wrought-iron gates and let people gaze at their goods. General appreciation is welcome, but the real goal for the patio-owners is winning a prize in the **Concurso de Patios Cordobéses.**

June: Alicante may be a small city, but there's nothing petite about the bash it throws every summer. Much like Valencia's Las Fallas, Alicante's **Hogueras de San Juan** calls for gigantic, papier-mâché puppets, fireworks, open-air bars, music, dancing in the streets, and round-the-clock partying. Come morning, everyone flops on the beach for some rays and a snooze until it's time to dress up and begin all over again.

July: Ernest Hemingway wrote about it in *The Sun Also Rises* and it's splashed across international papers every July. Naturally, I'm talking about the **Fiesta de San Fermín** in Pamplona or, as it's commonly called, the running of the bulls. From July 7–14, the small city is transformed into a mutinous street party in which Spain's famous fighting bulls are central. Bands wake the townspeople up before 7 A.M., people begin tippling at breakfast, and the truly fearless (or arguably, moronic) run with the bulls to the bullring.

August: For most of the year, Buñol doesn't have much going on, but come the last weekend in August (or the penultimate one), about 30,000 visitors descend on the tiny town for **La Tomatina.** The gala really gets going when truckloads of ripe, juicy tomatoes arrive, and everyone in the area lobs the pulpy fruit at each other in a massive food fight. About an hour later, the fire department drenches everyone with hoses, capping the party.

September: Barcelona stops at nothing when it comes to the **Festes de la Mercè,** a four-day party that kicks off on September 24. You'll see *castellers* (human castle builders) who pile onto each other until they form a towering, jiggling structure; traditional folk dancing; swimming contests; and endless costumes and pageantry. Don't skip the

corretoc, a surprisingly beautiful race in which masses run before fire-breathing demons.

October: An old saying advises us to eat, drink, and be merry, but the small Galician town, O Grove has amended that to just eat—piles and piles of food. The **Fiesta de Exaltación del Marisco** (celebration of shellfish) pulls in more than 200,000 people with hearty appetites who sample from piles of seafood, watch dramatic cooking contests, and chase all those vittles from the sea with fine, Galician wine. You can begin to gorge yourself on October 3 and keep on eating for the next nine days of festivities.

November: The dates for **Festival Internacional de Jazz** in Barcelona *sometimes* hit October or December, but they almost always fall in November. The musical event pulls in some of the best international jazz musicians from around the world, and both posh venues and tiny bars fill with live acts strumming on bass, blowing into saxophones, and singing scat—the lingua franca of melody.

December: During **Christmas week,** Madrid stages one of the most delightfully weird celebrations of the baby Jesus. The city's famous Plaza Mayor fills with vendors hawking wigs, rubber noses, and fake vomit. It's no surprise that kids flock there, but even elderly ladies and distinguished gentlemen don enormous wigs and walk the streets in their silly gear.

The brotherhoods of various churches—some carrying statues of the virgin, others of Christ—congregate into packed processions that wind slowly through the city streets. You'll immediately note that everyone in the procession is dressed just like members of the Ku Klux Klan. But don't worry; although the resemblance is uncanny, it's also coincidental.

Valencia has long been known as a town that can throw a mean party and nothing proves that point better than Las Fallas de San José. The festival runs from March 12–19 and locals will keep the drinking, music, and dancing going through the night. You'll also have plenty of opportunities to fill up on paella, check out some bullfights, and take in elaborate firework displays. The party is named for the more than 350 gigantic, papier-mâché puppets created by local artists. The dolls are so stunningly rendered that it's almost a shame to see them set ablaze to a chorus of fireworks at the end of the event. *Almost.* They're not lit in effigy, they're burned for the sheer spectacle of it all and it really is something memorable.

It's hard to hit Spain at a time of year when there's no festival happening in one corner of the country or another, but perhaps you'll ignore the revelry because you've come in search of a quieter vacation. Winter is ideal if you want to avoid the masses of tourists and better still, if you can ski—yes, in Spain. The Spanish resorts don't rival the Swiss Alps but they get the job done. If you head to Sierra Nevada just south of Granada, you can hit the slopes on one day and tour in the Alhambra the next. The skiing in the Pyrenees Mountains is a notch higher in quality and the rustic, mountain ambience makes for an ideal, country vacation. If you want to head to Madrid or Barcelona you can expect a chill but nothing severe. As a winter traveler, you'll have a distinct advantage over summer's day-trippers, too. You'll dodge the crowds, have the run of the museums, and you'll dine alongside locals wherever you go. That perk might sound like nothing much but it can really change a vacation for the better. In general, Spaniards are easy-going and quick to banter with foreigners, but they're more apt to strike up a conversation with a vacationer if that person isn't one in a sea of hundreds.

Arriving in Spain

When you arrive in Spain you'll have to go through customs and in most cases, that simply means that an official flips through your passport and stamps it. Once you've collected your bags and entered the main terminal, you can convert money or take some out of an ATM machine. At that point, you'll be on your way.

CUSTOMS AND IMMIGRATION

Chances are you won't have to open your suitcases when you go through customs but it is of course a possibility—the officials have the right to stop anyone and they seem to choose at random. Keep in mind that you're allowed to travel with restricted amounts of duty-free goods. You can't take in enough to open your own liquor store but you are allowed either two liters (or 0.52 gallons) of wine or one liter (0.26 gallons) of wine and one liter of liquor. You can also take 200 cigarettes or 50 cigars, and you'll have a good time smoking those in Spain where tobacco isn't as taboo as it is on U.S. shores.

PUBLIC TRANSPORTATION

Most of the country's airports are connected to the metro system, bus lines or trains that run to the city center. If there's a metro station connected to the airport as is the case with Madrid, just follow the signs and once you reach the station you can buy a ticket from the booth and refer to the subway map hanging on the wall. Barcelona has a train departing the airport every half-hour and anyone working the airport information booth will be able to provide directions to the platform. The information booths are clearly marked. In airports with buses you'll likely have to ask people at the information desks for help as the directional signs are not always intuitive, but the good news is you'll probably speak to someone bilingual so you can get directions in English. Taxis to and from the airport tend to ratchet up the highest fares but after a long international flight, you might prefer that mode of transportation despite the cost. Outside every airport you'll see a clearly marked taxi stand where you can find a ride. Don't expect your driver to speak English, so if you don't speak Spanish, have your address prepared in written form so the driver can read it.

Accommodations

Hotels span a wildly broad spectrum in Spain. You can live luxuriously in a place where mints appear on plumped pillows every night or you can travel on the cheap by sharing a spartan room filled with bunk beds occupied by backpackers. Not surprisingly, prices are equally disparate. High-end accommodations will run you between €150–450 ($188–563) a night. Mid-range means that you can find a double room for €50–100 ($63–125), and a budget prices begin as low as €20 ($25) and move up from there.

Even within each price range, the variance of the country's accommodations is tremendous. In Madrid, you can live it up in old-world style at the Ritz—the hotel has been a city fixture since it opened its doors in 1910. Even if you miss out on the rooms, stopping by for tea is a must because the experience is as close to time-travel as you can get. It's not at all unusual to wonder in and find a group of fur-clad ladies sipping tea and smoking perfumed cigarettes. Their very presence evokes the elegance of a bygone era—one that's felt throughout the hotel. For a similarly exorbitant price, you can instead stay in modern luxury. Barcelona's Hotel Arts is one example of what that can mean. The monolithic beachside structure offers opulence with a view. Bang & Olufsen gadgets complement soft-hued rooms with modern finishes. If you want to upgrade to the duplex apartment you can even have your own butler.

Mid-range also runs the gamut from clean and simple to charming and rustic. Spain's paradors are a secret that's been guarded far too well, and it's high time more travelers learned about them. Here's how they work: the country has a network of 87 government-sponsored hotels in remote

Seeing Spain with a Guided Eye

Before you begin contacting hotels to make reservations, have you considered a guided tour? If you're conjuring up an image of a throng of name-tagged folks descending from a bus to take a quick snapshot of an ancient monument, erase that picture from your mind. Some travel companies cater to special interests, and as a result, tours have grown a whole lot more interesting than they once were. Here are a few recommendations. (See Resources for contact information.)

• Pack your appetite and hit the road with a gastronomy tour. You can explore the Rioja vineyards, taste the best of Basque Country or make the most of La Boqueria—Barcelona's famous market. You'll have several choices, lots of meals, plenty of wine, and a few cooking lessons as well. (Don't forget to take your Tums.) Gastronomy tour operators include Food & Wine Trails and Culinary Adventures.

• If you want to travel around Spain on two wheels, you can sign up for a bike tour. Some groups roll through the olive groves of Andalusia, others whiz by the hikers on El Camino de Santiago, and some pedal through wine country. A few companies that have won big points with cyclists are Easy Rider Tours, Bike Riders, and Euro-Bike & Walking Tours.

• For a little explanation with your cubism, join in on an art-history tour of the country with Icscis Inc. You'll view the collections in vast museums such as the Prado and more intimate ones such as the Dalí Museum in Figueres. In addition to the lectures and guided viewings, you'll also have some time to explore your surroundings independently.

• You can saddle up with Euro Adventures and trot through Galicia on a horse-riding tour of medieval towns, Celtic ruins, gentle hills, and cool rivers. At the end of each day you can hobble into a rural hotel or manor house and rest your weary bones for the next day of riding.

places. The first one was founded in 1928 and more have been added to the list every year. You'll get more bang for your buck in the paradors, which can take the form of cozy ski chalets, out-of-the way stone houses with country charm, or sprawling villas. No two paradors are the same—in one you might find a lavish dining room where game dominates the winter menu, and in another perhaps you'll be able to settle down with a book in an orange-scented Andalusian courtyard. To find a parador in or near your destination, look online (www.parador.es).

Similarly, *casa rurales* (rural homes) appear throughout the country and they have much of the charm of a New England inn, only Spanish style. You'll find warmth, comfort, and breakfast in most such places and they're usually located a little outside of cities. Mid-range hotels in city centers can be cozy and welcoming or merely efficient but unremarkable. As a general rule, refer to a guidebook if you can't go by the recommendation of someone you know.

Hostels offer the cheapest beds in Spain and they're usually taken by backpackers or college students traveling through Europe. Some have private rooms with attached bathrooms and others offer dorm-style accommodation with shared bathrooms. Naturally, the cleaner the place and the more privacy offered, the higher the price.

Food

Traditionally, Spanish food didn't rely on fancy sauces and overly elaborate cooking methods. The ingredients were always fresh and simple and the outcome was an understated art in its own right. Jamón has long been a beloved staple, and the variety of hams in Spain is worthy of its own book. Beef, lamb, stews, cod, hake, tomatoes, olives, and loads of olive oil are all featured heavily in old-word Spanish fare. You can still find those time-honored dishes but you're also just as likely to find Spanish cuisine with modern twists.

It should come as little surprise that Barcelona is becoming a foodie hot spot. After all, it was there that Gaudí broke new ground in the field of architecture and Picasso received the artistic education that inspired him to go on to shake up the art world with cubism. Today, the city's new restaurants are making waves with innovative dishes that have attracted gourmands from around the world. You'll still find ample amounts of ham, beans, and the other hallmarks of Spanish cuisine, but visionary chefs are amending old recipes with light sauces and fusion cooking.

The overhaul isn't limited to Barcelona either—new restaurants with international flavors have popped up throughout the country. Of course, if you're looking for hearty Spanish fare you can find it everywhere. You can sample the menu at numerous tapas bars in just one night, tasting everything from bacon-wrapped figs to *tortilla española* (Spanish omelette) cut into a pie-shaped wedge and served at room temperature. Madrid is well known for its *cocido* (stew), a succulent mix of beans, meat, and vegetables.

> Dinner is served around 9 p.m. or even later. By the time you top off your meal with arroz con leche *(rice with milk)*, flan, or ice cream you'll be coming up on midnight.

It's a virtually uncontested fact that Valencia has the best paella in the country, and if you want a good gazpacho (a cold, tomato-based soup), head to Andalusia in the summertime when the dish is most enjoyed.

Both lunch and dinner are not taken lightly in Spain—they're elaborate affairs to be relished. However, breakfast is usually small, just a pastry or toast accompanied by a cup of coffee. Restaurants usually open for lunch after 1 P.M. and the meal is served until about 4 P.M. In the early evening, people convene for tapas and drinks, and dinner is served around 9 P.M. or even later. By the time you top off your meal with *arroz con leche* (rice with milk), flan, or ice cream you'll be coming up on midnight. Spain's late dinner hour is unquestionably an adjustment, but don't go in search of a restaurant serving food any earlier than 9 P.M.—if you find one, you can bet that it's catering to foreigners. Instead of caving, just nibble on another round of tapas and hold out just a little longer. If you do that, you're just about guaranteed a better meal at a restaurant serving local clientele. Within a few days, you'll be used to the schedule.

Sample Itineraries

A few locales are particularly high on most visitors' lists. Those places include Madrid, Barcelona, Seville, and Granada. All of those destinations are well worth a visit but if you have more time in Spain, you can pick a few places from the usual circuit and mix in a few off-the-beaten-path destinations as well.

ONE WEEK

If you have just one week, it's best to limit your trip to a few places rather than spending your time in transit. You can fly into Madrid and spend two days taking in the sights including the "Golden Triangle" of art museums: the Museo del Prado, the Thyssen-Bornemisza, and the Reina Sofia. The elegant streets by the museums are perfect for strolling, but don't bypass the old part of the city, especially the stunning Plaza Mayor where bullfights and executions used to occur. Today, you'll see old cafés lining the plaza. On the third day you can take a day-trip to nearby Toledo. The tiny city is one of Spain's true gems. During the Middle Ages, Islam, Judaism, and Christianity coexisted peacefully within the town. You can see relics of the past, visit the breathtaking cathedral and the old synagogues (no longer in use but fully intact), and still make it back to Madrid in time for dinner.

The next day you can fly or take the train to Barcelona in order to get a taste of Catalonia. Spend a couple days in the city and be sure to work your way through the tangle of streets in the old city. In the same part of town, the history museum offers a phenomenal introduction to Barcelona's past. Stop by La Boqueria on the Rambla, the age-old food market where meat, fish, and vegetables are sold in individual stands and hordes of people come by daily in search of dinner's ingredients. Don't skip Gaudí's landmark buildings; between July and September, you can even climb your way to the roof terrace capping La Pedrera to take in the view of the city while sipping a glass of *cava* (a drink similar to champagne). The beach is packed with bars and hot, new restaurants—all well worth a visit. The day before you leave, you can take a day-trip to Sitges just outside the city. The town draws in travelers for its intense party atmosphere, artistic air, the 18th-century mansions along the coast, and of course the beaches, too. You can return to Madrid by plane or train for you flight back to the United States.

TWO WEEKS

A two-week trip allows you more mobility and you can wind your way from Barcelona to Andalusia at a leisurely pace. After enjoying Barcelona for a few days, you can take the train or fly to Madrid—the capital and the center of the country. Spend at least three days taking in the sights and be sure to take part in Madrid's intoxicating nightlife. Restaurants are open past midnight, the bars pick up from there, and the clubs take over until dawn.

After spending a week between the country's two largest cities, you can catch the high-speed train to Seville. The city is rich with historic monuments and you can easily pack two to three days of sightseeing in. Moreover, the city is one of Spain's most enchanting places for long strolls. Orange trees line the streets, gorgeous plazas are plentiful, and don't miss the opportunity to climb the Giralda tower—it's a long trek up but you'll be rewarded with a panoramic view of the city. (One word of caution: Don't eat the oranges on the trees unless you also like sucking lemons—believe me, I learned the hard way.)

Too many people skip over Córdoba on their way to Granada, but you'll have enough time to spend a few hours in the town. Córdoba was once the biggest city in western Europe and the Moorish capital—at its height, the city was home to Jewish, Christian, and Arab scholars. The Mezquita will immediately be recognizable to you when you see its often-photographed red-and-white-striped arches and domes, but reproductions pale in comparison to the stucco details and workmanship of the original. The city is worth a visit for this historical building alone. The Jewish quarter and archaeological museum are also interesting enough for a brief visit.

Next stop: Granada. The Alhambra, a 9th-century Moorish fortress, is the city's crown jewel and it's a place so legendary that some people come to the city just to see it. Give yourself at least half a day to wander through the grounds and view the pillars, archways, and gorgeously precise details of each room. (Only 2,000 tickets are sold at the public entrance each day, so it's a good idea to buy a ticket in advance, especially during holidays and peak season; if you decide to just show up and hope for the best, try to make it early in the morning.) Also be sure to walk through the Albayzín—the old Arab quarter. Two days is a good amount of time to spend in Granada if you're planning to pack your days with touring. Three days is enough time to see the city's treats at a more leisurely pace. From Granada you can return to Barcelona on an overnight train or by plane for your return flight to the United States.

ONE MONTH

A month is a good, long time to spend in Spain and you'll be able to see a few regions in that time. In addition to visiting Barcelona, Madrid, Seville, and Granada, you'll have plenty of time for side trips. Fly into Barcelona and after spending four days there, hop a southbound train to the city of Valencia. Two or three days in the city will give you a strong sense of the place. Be sure to hit the port, where you'll find the town's best paella restaurants, and don't skip over the historic Mercado Central.

When you return to Barcelona, take the train to San Sebastián in Basque Country. The city is a bayside city known for its sophistication and for its exceptional food. Stop by the tapas bars in Parte Vieja where you can pile your plate full of the goodies heaped onto platters lining the bar tops. After spending a couple of days in town, take the bus south to Larraitz, a tiny town where you'll have an opportunity for a day-hike and a picnic. Return to San Sebastián and the next morning, head to Bilbao by train. When you reach the city you should visit the Museo Guggenheim, an architectural marvel designed by Frank Gehry. You won't need more than two days in Bilbao. Next, move on to Madrid by train.

By the time you've reached Madrid you'll have hit the midway mark in your trip. Spend a few days in the capital taking in the sights and make a special day-trip out to Toledo. Then move on to the south by high-speed train to Seville where you can enjoy strolling the city and visiting the many monuments. After three days in Seville, take a day-trip to Córdoba before reaching Granada—a city worth visiting for a couple of days. From Granada, return to Barcelona on an overnight train or by plane.

Practicalities

Once you reach your destination, you'll need a place to sleep and naturally you'll want to eat, too. Restaurants and hotels in Spain can be positively bare-bones establishments, decadently plush, and everything in between—you'll find a little bit of everything in most spots along on the tourist path. Still, some places come particularly recommended—here are some of them.

MADRID
Madrid is a perfect place to take a gamble with your meals and come out ahead. The city is loaded with eateries and if you stumble into some hole-in-the-wall joint that you haven't read about in any guidebook, you just might be rewarded with the best plate of tapas you'll eat in Spain. However, your course of adventure might lead you to a few duds as well and so it's best to arrive prepared with at least a few recommendations. Hotels? Well, they're a different story. You really should book a room in advance, especially if you're traveling during the summer or are looking for something nicer than budget digs.

Accommodations
Hotel Santander
Calle Echegaray, 1; tel. 91 429 95 51; fax 91 369 10 78

Hotel París
Calle Alcalá, 2; tel. 91 521 64 91; fax 91 531 01 88

Hotel Villa de la Reina
Gran Vía, 22; tel. 91 523 91 01; fax 91 521 75 22

Hotel Alcalá
Calle Alcalá, 66; tel. 91 435 10 60; fax 91 435 11 05

Food
La Cruzada
Calle Amnistía, 8; tel. 91 548 01 31

Albur
Calle Manuela Malasaña, 15; tel. 91 594 27 33

La Musa
Calle Manuela Malasaña, 18; tel. 91 448 75 58

Paradis Casa de América
Paseo de Recoletos, 2; tel. 91 575 45 40
Alternative location: Calle Marqués de Cubas, 14; tel. 91 429 73 03

La Bola
Calle de la Bola, 5; tel. 91 547 69 30

BARCELONA
Barcelona lends little to Spain's reputation for superb tapas, yet it has some of country's best food—especially when it comes to nouveau Spanish cuisine. That's not to say that you can't find delectable morsels on a small plate—you certainly can do that—but restaurant dining is the local tradition and you'll eat best if you play along and make reservations for multi-course meals. And when it comes to hotels, the Catalonian city is much like Madrid—rooms book up fast during the summer months so plan ahead. You'll fare better with late planning during the off-season, but even then, you should book in advance if you want posh accommodations.

Accommodations
Banys Oriental
Calle Argenteria, 37; tel. 93 268 84 60; fax 93 268 84 61; www.hotel banysorientals.com

Hotel Oriente
La Rambla, 45; tel. 93 302 25 58; fax 93 412 38 19

Hotel Gran Vía
Gran Vía de les Corts Catalanes, 642; tel. 93 318 19 00; fax 93 318 99 97

© N kki Weinstein

Gran Hotel La Florída
Vallvidrera, 83-93; tel. 93 259 30 00; fax 93 259 30 01; www.hotel-laflorida.com

Hotel Arts
Calle Marina, 19-20; tel. 93 221 10 00; fax 93 221 10 70; www.ritzcarlton.com

Food
Mastroqué
Calle Codols, 29; tel. 93 301 79 42

Brasserie Flo
Calle Jonqueres, 10; tel. 93 319 31 02

Pla de Garsa
Calle Assaonadors, 13; tel. 93 315 24 13

Jean Luc Figueras
Carrer Santa Teresa, 10; tel. 93 415 28 77

El Bestial
Carrer de Ramón Trias Fargas, 2-4; tel. 93 224 04 07

VALENCIA

Know one thing: this is paella town, and it would be a crying shame to visit Valencia and miss out on the city's staple dish. Naturally, some restaurants are better than others but as a general rule, you're bound to have good luck with the places serving up saffron-infused rice by the port. Valencia is a popular city (and not a huge one either) and hotel quality is hit or miss, so planning ahead is a smart idea. Arrive in town with a reservation.

Accommodations

Hotel Continental
Calle Correos, 8; tel. 96 53 52 82; fax 96 353 11 13; www.contitel.es

Hotel Ad Hoc
Calle Boix, 4; tel. 96 391 91 40; fax 96 391 36 67

Hotel Astoria Palace
Plaza Rodrigo Botet, 5; tel. 96 398 10 00; fax 96 398 10 10; www.hotel -astoria-palace.com

Food

La Enoteca
Plaza Vincente Iborra, 3; tel. 96 315 20 72

Ca Sento
Menéndez Nuñez, 27; tel. 96 330 17 75

Albacar
Calle Sorni, 35; tel. 96 395 10 05

ANDALUSIA

Olives and hams will be doled out in abundance wherever you go in Andalusia, and you'll find both items served up in an endless array of styles. You can dine on the cheap in Granada, where free plates of tapas arrive with each round of beer, but both there and elsewhere in Andalusia, small amounts of cash can buy big flavor in tapas bars and restaurants. Andalusia is one of the most popular stops for tourists, so book your hotel room ahead of time, especially if you're hoping to stay somewhere picturesque and memorable.

Accommodations
Hotel Amadeus (Seville)
Calle Farnesio, 6; tel. 95 450 14 43; www.hotelamadeussevilla.com

Hotel Alfonso XIII (Seville)
Calle San Fernando, 2; tel. 95 491 70 00

Hostería del Laurel (Seville)
Plaza de los Venerables, 5; tel. 95 422 02 95

Hotel Reina Cristina (Granada)
Calle Tablas, 4; tel. 958 25 32 11; www.hotelreinacristina.com

Parador de Granada (Granada)
Calle Real de la Alhambra; tel. 958 22 14 40

Food
Restaurante La Albahaca (Seville)
Plaza de Santa Cruz, 12; tel. 95 422 07 14

Enrique Becerra (Seville)
Calle Gamazo, 2; tel. 95 421 30 49

El Ladrillo II (Granada)
Calle Panadcros, 35; tel. 958 29 26 51

Casa Cristóbal (Granada)
Campo del Príncipe, 19; tel. 958 22 30 53

SAN SEBASTIÁN
If you're a foodie, you'll find that you've hit the jackpot in San Sebastián. Sample the edibles sold off bar-tops in Parte Vieja and you might just be satisfied enough to return for every meal. However, if you're looking for a more formal experience you won't be disappointed—a few restaurants in town are among the very best in Spain. Hotels can be pricey or cheap and both sorts of rooms sell out realy fast during the summer season when the city is transformed into a popular resort town, so make your plans before you arrive.

Accommodations
Hostal La Concha
Calle de San Martín, 51; tel. 943 45 03 89

Hotel de Londres e Inglaterra
Calle de Zubieta, 2; tel. 943 44 07 70; fax 943 44 04 94

Hotel Europa
Calle de San Martín, 52; tel. 943 47 08 80; fax 943 47 17 30

Food
Restaurante Portaletas
Calle del Puerto, 8; tel. 943 42 42 72

Aloña Berri
Bermingham Kalea, 24; tel. 943 29 08 18

Arzak
Alto de Miracruz, 21; tel. 943 28 55 93

BILBAO
When you get a taste of Bilbao's food, you'll know that the city's reputation as a mere industrial hub is deeply unfair. The opening of the Guggenheim museum helped spawn an overall revitalization, and that's evident in a few choice restaurants. Hotels don't book up as quickly as they do elsewhere, but it's still not a bad idea to do a little research and make a reservation so you know you're getting just what you want.

Accommodations
Pensión Iturrienea Ostatua
Calle Santa María, 14; tel. 94 416 15 00; fax 94 415 89 29

Hostal Begoña
Calle de la Amistad, 2; tel. 94 423 01 34; fax 94 423 01 33

Food
Amboto
Calle de Jardines, 2; tel. 94 415 61 48

Gaminiz
Areatza Kalea, 38; tel. 94 677 30 93

Daily Life

© Jessica Chesler

© Nikki Weinstein

Making the Move

So you've visited Spain and fallen head over heels for the place—now you're ready to move over there and make it official. The question is how do you do that? How do you transport all your stuff across the Atlantic since renting a moving van is out of the question and you're probably not coming by steam ship. Oh, and then there's the issue of visas . . . the only kind that you have right now is a credit card. Exactly what sort of a visa do you need to live in Spain? And should you take your alarm clock—the one that's been with you since freshman year of college? Not to worry. With a little planning, your move to Spain shouldn't be too difficult. Your biggest obstacle will be the process of obtaining a visa and even that is manageable.

Red Tape

A move to a new country will mean facing a lot of bureaucracy and Spain is no exception to that. You'll have to deal with official stamps, official documents, official translations, and stern-looking officials—face-to-face. Just remember that if you've paid your taxes and dealt with the IRS in the United States, you can certainly handle *this*. And when you're finished, you'll be rewarded with access to Spain and that really is a rich prize.

VISAS AND IMMIGRATION

Applying for your residency visa will likely be your biggest bureaucratic challenge, but most people have to bite the bullet and go through the necessary steps. Residency doesn't only allow you to work, it permits you to simply live in Spain for more than 182 days of the calendar year. The range of visas vary tremendously—some are only valid for the duration of a work contract while others are good for as long as five years; you're likely to score a more liberal visa if your work contract exceeds one year.

Keeping It Together

There's a lot to keep track of when applying for a visa—passports, forms, the official application, and don't forget a good dose of patience. Each type of visa has slightly different requirements, but here's a checklist to cover the basics of what you'll need.

- the application itself
- your passport—be sure that it's valid for at least the next six months
- a letter of good conduct from the police department of your city, accompanied by an official translation
- a letter from your doctor typed on official stationery and confirming that you do not have yellow fever, cholera or the plague, accompanied by an official translation
- the original deed to your home in Spain (if applicable) and an accompanying photocopy

If you want your visa to cover your spouse and children, include the following in your application:

- an application on behalf of each member of your family
- your family's passports, all valid for at least six months
- your marriage certificate and children's birth certificates
- letters from your family doctor and the local police department confirming good health and good conduct

Lastly, make sure that everything is submitted within 90 days of issue, and keep photocopies for your own records.

So can you skip all that residency stuff and go right for the gold—citizenship? Sure you can—as long as one of your parents is Spanish or if you were born in Spain and your parents happen to have no nationality or one that you can't share. Barring those two reasons, you'll have to wait in line. Most foreigners who become citizens have held residency status for about 10 years.

If paperwork gives you a headache and you decide to live in Spain for more than six months out of each year but you ignored the need for a visa, you run the risk of being fined about €300 ($375) and being barred entry to Spain for three years. (As you might suspect, the enforcement of that edict *is* lax, but don't take that news as your cue to break the law.)

Tourist Visas

Tourists have it easy. U.S. citizens with a passport valid for the next six months need not concern themselves with visas at all, they can just go through border control at the airport, collect their baggage, step onto the street, and hail a cab. If that's you, you're in luck—the stamp in your passport is effectively your tourist visa and there's no red tape to worry about.

However, there is one key thing to keep in mind. Rules have changed since the formation of the European Union (EU), and borders are not what they once were. Your tourist visa no longer applies to Spain alone, it applies to all the Schengen countries. (The Schengen countries are as follows: Austria, Belgium, Denmark, Finland, France, Germany, Greece, Iceland, Italy, Luxembourg, Netherlands, Norway, Portugal, Spain, and Sweden.) With just the stamp in your passport, you can travel throughout the Schengen countries for three consecutive months, but when your visa is on the brink of expiration you may no longer stay in any of the Schengen countries—not just Spain.

Student Visas

Every year, thousands of Americans study in Spain. In many cases they enroll in undergraduate programs for a year or semester, other times they come as graduate students, and many people also come specifically to learn Castilian in a language institute. If you want to study in Spain for longer than three months, you'll need a student visa. You can't get one in Spain nor can it be mailed to a Spanish address, so you have to apply while you're still in the United States. Because Spain is such a popular study-abroad locale, the processing time for the applications can take longer than a month so submit all your paperwork well in advance.

The rules vary slightly at each of the separate Spanish consulates in the United States, but in most cases applications should be submitted in person. That rule is more ironclad in some consulates than others—the laxer ones allow the parents of a student to apply on the student's behalf. To find out the specifics at the consulate appropriate for you, call in advance. (See Resources for a list of consulates.)

The first thing you'll need is the application itself, and that can be downloaded from some of the consulates' websites including New York's (www.spainconsul-ny.org). As soon as you've filled that form out, you'll have to add a few more things to your list before you're ready to apply.

Include your passport (which must be valid for at least the next six months) with your application. Also add four current passport-size photos with white backgrounds to the pile. Additionally, you'll also be asked to submit the original letter that verifies your enrollment as a full-time student at a university or school, and that should have a section assuring that you have paid tuition. Have your doctor write a letter assuring the Spanish government that you do not have yellow fever, cholera, or the plague, and also stating that you do not suffer from any drug addictions or mental illnesses; the letter must be translated into

Spanish. If your stay in Spain will be longer than six months, you'll also have to add a letter of good conduct from the police department of any city that you've lived in for as long as six months during the past five years, and that also must be translated into Spanish.

You're almost done, but there's still one more document to toss in. The Spanish government will want to know that you have enough money to live on while you're in Spain, and you'll have to show them that you do. That can be done in several ways. You can present $350 worth of traveler's checks for every month that you'll be in Spain. Alternatively, the consulate will accept proof (usually in the form of a letter) that you have received financial aid or a scholarship that covers tuition, room, board, and personal expenses amounting to not less than $350 for every month of your stay. Another option is to present a notarized letter from your parents in which they promise to assume financial responsibility for you while you're abroad, and they must specify that they'll give you at least $350 dollars a month. (If you've been waiting for an excuse to hit your parents up for money, there's your chance.) If you have a Spanish bank account, you can show evidence that you have sufficient funds for your time in Spain—of course, "sufficient" means at least (you guessed it) $350 for every month of your stay. Your final option is to include a letter from your academic program that guarantees complete coverage for your tuition, room, and board. However, that last choice is only available to students earning credit towards a bachelor's degree or an associate's degree. If that applies to you, the letter must mention that you will be receiving such credit.

Once you've compiled the paperwork you should make two photocopies of everything—one set is for the application and the other is for you. Add a stamped and addressed, Express Mail envelope and a money order for $100 to cover the processing fee, and you'll be ready to go to the consulate and apply. Once you receive your visa, you'll be all set to head across the ocean and begin your studies. If your program is for six months or less, your visa process is entirely complete but if your stay in Spain will be longer than that, you'll have one more step to take. As soon as you arrive at your destination in Spain you'll have to register with the police department to receive a student card.

Residency Visas and Work Permits

Some people complain that applying for a Spanish residence visa is as fruitless as trying to ride a bicycle to the moon. But try to tune that buzz out—those rumors are worse than the reality. Getting your hands

© Nikki Weinstein

You'll have to face a little bureaucracy in order to unlock the door to Spain.

on a visa is a big effort but it is possible, and as long as you're eligible for a Spanish visa, it will likely be granted to you. However, the government will not make the process of actually getting the visa easy for you. Spain's bureaucracy is infamous and your first brush with it will likely come in the United States when you apply for a residence visa. Applications must be submitted through one of the Spanish consulates and exactly which Spanish consulate is the right one for you depends on where in the United States you live. (See Resources for a list of consulates.) You should call the consulate as soon as you've decided to apply for a visa in order to find out how far in advance your application must be submitted—each consulate sets its own rules, but in some cases applications can take longer than six months to be processed. Most of the consulates will only accept applications that have been delivered in person, and some suggest arriving early in the morning to improve the chances of your application merely being received—some consulates enforce daily limits.

Before you begin, there's one important thing to know: While you can't just move to Spain and begin working without the proper papers, you don't need a work visa exactly—permission to earn money in Spain is built into specific visas. That means that independent business owners must apply for one kind of residence visa that grants *permiso de trabajo* (permission to work), while those who will be employed by a company should apply for a different visa. Depending on your job offer (for example, permanent or temporary), your visa might have any number of time and geographical restrictions.

The Ministry of Labor ultimately grants foreigners the right to work in Spain (your visa won't be approved without the department's permission), but it's worth knowing that some jobs *don't* require the official go-ahead. Civil and military personnel employed by the Spanish government need not worry about getting permission to work in Spain, nor should accredited members of the foreign press, foreign teachers who have been offered positions at Spanish universities, and foreign technical employees invited to work for the Spanish government. Ultimately, your career and specific job matter a lot so peruse the various kinds of visas with special care and make sure that you apply for the correct one so you can earn a living when you reach Spanish shores.

The next step is figuring out exactly which residence visa to apply for—you have six options. The residence visa to work in Spain as an employee is for anyone with a job offer from a Spanish company. The residence visa to reunite a family does exactly what its name suggests; that's the visa of choice for U.S. spouses of Spanish citizens, but it can also work for the parents of children who are either Spanish citizens or legal residents. The same visa works for people under 18 who are financially dependent on a Spanish citizen or resident. The residence visa to retire in Spain is straightforward—it's for retirees. If you want to open a business independently, such as running an inn or restaurant, you should apply for the visa for investors or the self-employed. Another option is specifically for non-lucrative purposes and is only good for people who will live off money earned outside of Spain. (You must already have a large sum of cash in your name if you want that particular visa.) Finally, the residence visa exempt from requesting a work permit (a.k.a. the visa with the most unwieldy name) applies to those who will be in Spain for a religious, scientific, or cultural activity that is not applicable to work visas; that often translates into grant-related work, but not always.

Once you've found the visa that fits, you'll need to put the application together. Not all of the individual consulates have websites, but the New York one does and you can download the application itself from that page (www.spainconsul-ny.org). Once you've filled it out, there will be a few more things to add.

Wish List

You can plod through every step of your move with great care, judiciously selecting what to take and what to leave behind, and you'll still get it just a little bit wrong, especially when it comes to creature comforts. Don't worry—that's an impossible step to nail in any move. Undoubtedly, the things you'll occasionally pine for will take you by surprise and even if you can anticipate your cravings, you simply can't do anything about them.

Me? When I first arrived in Spain, I longed for takeout Chinese food from a restaurant on Houston Street in New York—a place that serves salt-and-pepper shrimp that's to-die-for good. I occasionally wished that I could spend a couple of hours watching bad American televi-sion, and I really wanted the *New York Times* on Sundays. Don't get me wrong—I adore living in Spain—it's just that I still craved certain luxuries from home.

The instant I moved to Madrid, friends and family began planning their Spanish vacations and I was thrilled to have visitors come—not only for the opportunity to see people I missed, but also because each one of their visits gave me an opportunity to stock up on American goods. They'd each arrive carting strange packages full of Skippy peanut butter (creamy not chunky, please), my favorite body lotion (a brand that I'd been using for years and just couldn't find in Madrid), and Band-Aids, which I swear stick better than the

Each of the six visas demands a slightly different list of goods, but in all cases you should include the same list of goods that's required for student visas: your passport (valid for six months), photos, your doctor's letters, and the letter from your local police department. Remember that both letters require official translations. Additionally, if you own property in Spain, you should include the original deed as well as a photocopy of the same. To have your application cover your spouse or children, include separate applications for them, medical certificates of good health, your original marriage certificate, and for your children, add their birth certificates.

That takes care of the areas in which the various residence visas overlap, but each specific visa requires a little more information. If you're applying for the work-specific visa, be sure to have your doctor add to the letter stating that you don't exhibit any health conditions that would prevent you from working at your proposed job. You must also include a written job offer from the Spanish company where you intend to work, and that offer should also have already been filed with the Ministry of Labor in Spain. That's mandatory for Spanish branches of American companies, too. The good news is that in most cases, your employer will take care of that detail.

If you're applying on the family reunion visa, your family member in Spain should have already filed a formal petition with the local police de-

Spanish kind, although no one else seems to have noticed.

With each visitor my list grew increasingly shorter until friends and family anticipating their Spanish vacation would ask me if they could bring me anything. Much to my surprise, I began replying that I couldn't think of anything offhand but thanks all the same. The fact is, settling into a new country is a process, and it's not one that happens instantly. You *will* miss things that you're used to, and after a while you'll miss them less. Give it several months and you'll have new creature comforts that are exclusively Spanish, and that's when you'll know that Spain is home.

I knew that I was truly Spain's adopted daughter when I began hitting the same wine bar on Sunday nights for its incredible fried mushrooms with aioli (garlic and mayonnaise), and stockpiling duty-free chorizo and bottles of Rioja for my trips back to the United States. Sure, when I'm stateside I still run for the *Times* on Sundays but when I read it, I always wonder how *El País* is covering the same stories. If I can work it into my visit, I'll head out to my favorite Chinese place for dinner, too, but I'd be lying if I said I didn't miss those fried mushrooms back in Madrid. However, I don't waste my time stocking up at the drugstore or looking for that lotion that I used to use. You see, I discovered a new Spanish lotion that's great, and you just can't find it in New York.

partment in Spain, and you must include a stamped and registered copy of that. If you're the parent of a foreign resident in Spain, include your child's birth certificate. Also be sure to submit the passport of your family member living in Spain, whether they're a Spanish citizen or a foreign resident. If that person is not accompanying you to the consulate, a notarized photocopy will do just fine. Lastly, the Spanish government will want to know that you have a place to live in Spain, so submit that address in the form of a *certificado de empadronamiento* (certificate of residence)—a form that should have already been processed with the local police authority in Spain. If that form doesn't apply to you, a work certificate or official change of your Spanish family member's residence will do the trick.

If you're a retiree applying on the related visa, you'll have to add an official form certifying that you receive social security and stating its monthly amount. Additionally, add proof of any other source of income that you might have—and that includes all properties in Spain. Also submit an official document from the company that provides your medical insurance guaranteeing continual coverage while you're in Spain.

Those applying as investors or as the self-employed must also have their doctors add to the letters that they are healthy enough to do the work proposed. A copy of the *solicitud de permiso de trabajo* (work authorization application) should have been filed previously with the Ministry of

Labor in Spain—both an original and a copy of that should be included. The last form should document proof of the medical coverage to be received while in Spain.

If the residence visa that you're after is for non-lucrative purposes, you'll have to offer proof that you have enough money to live on while in Spain. More specifically, you must submit bank account statements, investment certificates, and any other proof of funds that amounts to no less than $75,000 annually. If you own stock or partnerships in any companies, the Spanish government requires assurance that you do not make money from direct labor in those companies.

The application for the visa exempt from requesting a work permit also calls for a letter or invitation from the organization in which you'll be involved while in Spain. The Spanish government will want assurance that your financial needs will be taken care of, so be sure that the letter includes that information as well as some detail on the activities that you'll be performing. Also submit forms proving that your Spanish organization is accredited with the appropriate government authority. (If you're not sure which public office to contact for that confirmation, speak to someone at the Spanish organization you'll have contact with in Spain in order to find out.) Finally, by the time you apply for a visa, a *solicitud de exención de permiso de trabajo* (application of exemption from permission to work) should have been filed with the Ministry of Labor in Spain. (Presumably that was done by the Spanish organization you'll be affiliated with.) Be sure to add the original form with your application.

Once you've completed the list you must make two photocopies of all the documents and include those in the packet, but it's not a bad idea to make an additional photocopy for your own purposes, too. Finally, you have to add a money order of $100 to cover the processing fee along with your application. Now just sit back and wait for your reply. However, you should spend that time in the United States because once your visa has been processed, you'll have to pick it up in person at the Spanish consulate.

Now you have your visa, but you're not done quite yet. The visa itself is only valid for 90 days and it offers you just one entry into Spain. As soon as you arrive at your Spanish destination you'll have to go to the local police department to get your residence card. That residence card can be renewed from within Spain for the duration of your visa, but as soon as your visa expires (and they're all valid for varying lengths of time), you'll have to apply for a new visa. That can only be done by repeating the same process from the beginning.

Moving with Children

Believe it or not, moving your pet to Spain requires more work than moving your children does—at least when it comes to paperwork. As long as you include your children's individual applications, medical certificates of good health, and their birth certificates in your visa application, they'll also have visas. However, once you arrive in Spain things get a little trickier.

Young children adapt to new cultures with mind-boggling ease and they pick up new languages at breakneck speed. Yet adolescents and teenagers tend to struggle a little bit. At the risk of sounding like Oprah, I'll point out a few things that might make the transition easier. First, think back to the time when you were a teenager. Do you remember adults telling you that those years would be the best of your life and blah, blah, blah? What a bill of goods. Anyone who's made the volatile transition from childhood to adulthood remembers that it's anything but easy, and an upheaval like a move into another culture will have its rocky moments—initially, anyway.

Rather than trying to amp up your children's enthusiasm for Spain by asking them to build shoe-box dioramas of the country's great historical

Plazas provide a pleasant retreat for families on summer days.

moments and dragging them through one museum after another, pursue things that they'll actually enjoy. Once they're having fun and meeting people, their excitement about the move will build naturally.

Extracurricular activities are well provided for in the international schools. After the school day ends, students usually have a range of activities available such as sports, music, dance, and various interest-based clubs. If you're looking for classes outside of school, you'll also find schools offering dance, martial arts, and the like. The municipal civic centers are also a good place to begin looking for activities, and they usually have a few classes that cater to kids.

Give them time to hang out online and just instant message with their friends. And doing something as simple as buying a soccer ball may lead your kid to take it into a plaza, begin kicking it around, and come home with a few new friends.

Moving with Pets

You won't have trouble taking your pet to Spain. Most standard household animals are allowed in the country without being quarantined—even ferrets get the green light so long as their papers are in order. The laws on pets are currently in flux, but this much is known: as of October 2004, all pets must be identified with either a tattoo or microchip; a special certificate must be completed by vets regarding vaccinations and you'll also need a written description of your pet and its origin. You can get your

> *Believe it or not, moving your pet to Spain requires more work than moving your children does— at least when it comes to paperwork.*

paws on all the details you need through the Spanish embassy's office of Agriculture, Fisheries, and Food (www.mapausa.org).

In the case of dogs and cats—the most common pets—a veterinarian will have to provide certain stamps and your pooch or kitty will need to have had a rabies vaccination within the past year, but at least one month prior to your travel date.

Once you arrive you'll have to register your dog with the government and you should attach contact information on your pet's collar tags. Any dog older than three months will also require a health card in its name. If you've been to Spain before, then you've undoubtedly weaved your way along public streets dodging piles of poop; you'll be shocked to discover that Spain does in fact have pooper-scooper laws but they are broadly ignored. (However, you should feel free to buck the system and pick up after your dog.) Each municipality has its own rules regarding where dogs are permitted to run free, but all dogs must be leashed in public areas.

If you are the owner of what the government deems to be a potentially dangerous dog, your pet will need a microchip inserted under its skin with identifying information. (That sounds like a far more painful procedure than it actually is.) You'll also require a license from your municipality as an owner. Potentially dangerous dogs are pit bull terriers, Staffordshire bull terriers, American Staffordshire terriers, rottweilers, Dogo Argentinos, Fila Brasileiros, Tosa Inus, and Akita Inus. If you own one of those breeds and want to know if you qualify for a license to be in Spain, more information is posted on the consulate website.

On the whole, life is good for Spanish pets. Animals are adored and dog owners out on walks with their pooch will discover that their dog is a great conversation starter. Everyone seems to have a question for the owner and plenty of strangers are happy to scratch behind the ears of any dog that looks good-natured. Vets are easy to find and in the case of an urgent health scare you'll be pleased to know that the country has plenty of 24-hour emergency clinics for animals. However, you should take particular caution if you live in a rural area. Spanish hunters and some farmers are known to leave pieces of poisoned meat strewn about in an effort to kill foxes and other animals viewed as pests. If your dog were to eat that meat instead, it could be fatal. Additionally, you should speak to your Spanish vet about any health hazards that might be endemic to your area of Spain.

What to Take

Once you've received your visa you'll have taken care of the hard part, but you still have to make the actual move. Relocating to Spain has little in common with packing up your stuff and carting it to a new house on the other side of town; in this case you'll have an ocean to cross. The catch is that everything you take will also have to make it across the ocean, too. It's generally agreed upon by expatriates that the best approach is to first figure out what you can leave behind, and that assessment is more personal than practical. Anything that you need and most of what you want can be found in Spain. Of course, getting rid of your worldly goods is easier said than done. You've undoubtedly spent years collecting the objects that fill your home. From the books that line your shelves to your salt-and-pepper shakers, everything has a history.

Movies to Get You in the Mood

While packing up your home for the big move, you might want to leave your DVD player and TV plugged into your U.S. outlet until the last possible second. After all, you might want a celluloid reminder that all those hours spent sorting through dusty old junk, taping up boxes, and packing enormous suitcases are for good reason—soon, you'll be living in Spain. You'll likely need to get you through the frustration of your move, and you can pick through a long list of flicks that will put you in a Spanish state of mind. Some of the movies are good and a few . . . well, are not. Yet all of them are worthy of a viewing for one reason or another, and it will be nice to see that you're not the first foreigner to go to Spain. Chalk it up to education, call them mood movies, or justify it however you'd like, but you can go ahead and plop down on the floor to enjoy a dose of cinematic Spain.

You should kick off your session with *L'Auberge Espagnole,* a 2002 French movie directed by Cédric Klapisch and set in Barcelona. In French patois, the name means "free-for-all," and that's exactly what the movie is about. When a 25-year-old Parisian student lands in Barcelona, convenience throws him into an apartment with a cluster of young Europeans. Sex and comedy feature prominently, but the film's real star is the gorgeous, Catalan city itself. Barcelona shows off its glamorous, bohemian side and proves that the town is indeed ready for its close-up.

Offset that vision of the city with Whit Stillman's 1994 movie, *Barcelona*—a film that wryly shows two Americans being smacked with a post-Franco Spain (and both love and drama, too, of course). The movie was adored by some and loathed by others. What will you think? It's safe to say that if you loved *Metropolitan,* Stillman's satiric ode to New York, you'll like *Barcelona.*

You can't talk about Americans in Spain without getting around to old Ernest, the quintessential expat who helped make bumming around the cafés of Europe the trendy thing to do. *The Sun Also Rises* and *For Whom the Bell Tolls* usually take the number one and two spots on people's "All About Spain" reading lists, but you can enjoy the cinematic Cliffs Notes instead. Henry King directed the 1957 version of *The Sun Also Rises,* starring Tyrone Power as the American journalist Jake Barnes and Ava Gardner as Brett Ashley, Barnes's ex-fiancée.

You can catch up on your history, feel literary, and gaze at Gary Cooper's chiseled mug all at once with a viewing of *For Whom the Bell Tolls,* a film adaption of Hemingway's Spanish Civil War drama, directed by Sam Wood. Cooper plays Robert Jordan, an American who fled to Spain to fight the good fight and help fend off the fascist forces.

Save the best one for last—*Wheels on Meals* (1984), a sorely underrated Jackie Chan vehicle directed by Sammo Hung Kam-Bo. Chan plays Thomas, a blundering restaurant owner who, together with his cousin Moby and a private detective, sets off to save an eye-catching pickpocket named Sylvia. The movie takes place in Barcelona and it actually delivers the goods promised in its goofy tagline, "Not since Don Quixote has Spain had so much fun!"

Still, you should probably leave the baby grand behind unless you're a concert pianist. Large items are the most expensive to move internationally, and all of those same things can be replaced. Leaving cherished belongings behind really smarts, but it might help to know that Spain offers a wealth of opportunities to buy beautiful home furnishings that span the spectrum of design. Barcelona is a veritable workshop of one-of-a-kind fixtures envisioned by internationally applauded designers, and samplings of those showpieces are stocked in stores throughout the country. Hand-carved, older pieces also abound. If you're looking for things that are reasonably attractive and cheap, you'll be relieved to know that Ikea—the Swedish supermarket of home furnishings—has locations in Spain, too. In fact, you'll probably run across the superstore's catalog every other time you open your mailbox.

You're probably wondering if you should take your electronics and the answer to that is a resounding maybe. Here are the basics. Spain's uses a 220-volt electrical system, like the rest of continental Europe. You don't have to know what that means, you just have to know that the North American system is different (it uses 60Hz) and the bottom line is that you can't plug the hairdryer that you bought at Wal-Mart into a Spanish outlet—the plug itself won't even fit. Yet in the case of your hairdryer you can use an adapter because they work best for small, low-draw items with no significant motors in them. Battery chargers and small CD players should also fare well with transformers. However, lugging your refrigerator to Spain and expecting an adapter to do the trick will be a colossal error.

Computers are more expensive in Spain than they are in the United States so you might want to hang on to the one you have if you can. Some U.S. desktops have a switch that transfers the rate of power and allows the computer to function in Europe with an adapter, and most laptops have extension cords that can be entirely detached and replaced with ones that fit Spanish outlets.

However, there are a couple of drawbacks. As soon as you leave U.S. soil, the warranty that came with your computer is meaningless—you can't make good on it in a Spanish store that sells the same item and most companies won't ship replacement pieces abroad. Likewise, you'll have to dial internationally if you ever want to reach the help line associated with your American computer. While you're sitting on hold for 30 minutes listening to Muzak and waiting to talk to a tech-savvy trouble-shooter, you'll be mentally calculating what you're paying for each minute on the phone. The keyboard is one more detail to consider. In Spain, keyboards have accents and different keys and even the layout isn't the same. Those extra keys are vital tools that allow you to type correct Spanish sentences, so if you'll be writing in Spanish that's a worthwhile feature to have. However if you use your computer to surf the web, keep in touch with people on the other side of the Atlantic via email, and to write in English, a U.S. keyboard will serve you better.

The last note on electronics is only for people with Macs. You will be a rare (but growing) breed in Spain. Until recently, Spain priced Macs far higher than PCs and the discrepancy resulted in fewer Mac users. The prices have begun to drop down but most people still use PCs and you'll have to look a little harder to find service and parts for your Apple. When I had a DSL line installed on my iBook, the technician spent three hours struggling with a job that usually takes about 20 minutes. Halfway through the ordeal he confessed that he had never even touched a Mac before and he was relying on a lot of guesswork. Although you can find what you need here, it's not always easy.

SHIPPING OPTIONS

You don't absolutely have to see the contents of your house sold off in a tag sale or on eBay—you can ship just about anything to Spain, but the cost for that service adds up fast. One couple on the verge of relocating hoped to ship 1,500 pounds of beloved possessions from Los Angeles to Barcelona. When an international moving company gave them a quote of $2,700 for the service, they shopped around for a better price but they didn't find much improvement. Ultimately, the couple arrived in Spain with a lighter load. Many people take one look at the quadruple-digit price tag that's typically attached to shipping the entire contents of a home and quickly come to the conclusion that sentimental value is overrated.

But for some people, especially for families with young children, sending some items separately is unavoidable. The Yellow Pages is full of listings for international shipping companies that will be able to pack up your home for you, deliver your cargo to your Spanish doorstep, and take care of every detail in between. As is usually the case, the better the service the higher the price. You can knock down the cost by boxing your things yourself and collecting them from the port or drop-off center in Spain. A few weeks later, you'll have to pay a customs tax for your personal effects and those prices are steep.

Plenty of people manage to take just about everything on the flight. Most airlines allow you to check a hefty amount of baggage so why not take advantage of every pound that's offered? Typically you're allowed a maximum of two checked suitcases that can total about 70 pounds each, plus one carry-on bag. Perhaps you won't be able to bring everything you want with you when you move, but you'll have the essentials. The next time you visit the United States will be an opportunity to return back to Spain with one more load of your things. Slowly, your house will come together.

© Nikki Weinstein

Language and Education

A brief trip to Spain requires no more Spanish than that found in a pocket-sized phrasebook. But if you're interested in anything more than a train ticket or a cup of *café con leche* (coffee with milk), you'd be wise to dust off your high-school textbook and brush up on your vocabulary and verb conjugations. Of course you can find some fluent English-speakers living in towns from the Pyrenees Mountains to Seville, but the bulk of those folks are not Spanish—if you want to step into an expansive community and mix with the locals, the simple fact is you'll need to speak their language.

From popular television shows to political discussions to the humorous banter erupting at tapas bars throughout the country, almost every utterance one hears is in Castilian (a.k.a. Spanish). If you can't join the group, the mere sound of discourse can feel like an unintentional affront and without the ability to join in the conversations around you, you'll be resigned to a smaller cluster of foreigners and forced to remain on the fringes of your community. Just as language limitations can dictate foreigners' social groups in the United States, so too do they restrict people's lives in Spain. Language proficiency is the single most important step in being able to mingle with the Spanish.

Once you begin to speak and understand Spanish you'll find that the country and its language are profoundly intertwined. First you'll begin to catch onto the slang that people so casually toss around and before too long you'll even be able hear the wildly varied accents found throughout Spain—each one distinguishing the speaker as part of an equally distinct region. Ultimately, speaking Spanish offers a way of tapping into the surrounding culture—the language fuels word play and culturally specific jokes. By merely speaking and comprehending Spanish you'll be one step closer to understanding the country itself.

Learning the Language

Can you even manage in Spain if you don't speak Spanish? It's difficult but yes, you can get by. With the help of a decent phrasebook and an hour's worth of memorization, you'll likely be able to navigate a menu,

> *Once you begin to speak and understand Spanish you'll find that the country and its language are profoundly intertwined. By merely speaking and comprehending Spanish you'll be one step closer to understanding the country itself.*

buy a newspaper, ask for the bathroom, rent a car, and book a room in a pension; in other words, you can master the traveler's essentials. Even everyday tasks such as shopping for groceries or household goods can be managed with a minimal amount of conversing. Inevitably you'll hit a few situations that demand verbal communication and for some of them, pointing and pantomime can get the job done. However, be warned—that tactic requires pretty thick skin. Shortly after one American guy arrived in Madrid, he caught a stomach bug. After a day he managed to leave his bathroom for just long enough to make it to the nearest pharmacy and using just a handful of words and a lot of vivid gestures, he made his needs known. By the time he left he was flushed crimson but you have to give him a lot credit—he communicated his point and left with the medication that he required. Should you need to rely on interpretive dramatizations of your needs, anyone who's ever visited a country where they didn't speak the language will understand your predicament.

However, if you expect to use English with Spanish folks that you meet while out and about, you should probably rethink that plan. Most Spaniards who speak English at all have mastered just the basics. Of course plenty can justly claim fluency and some Spaniards take the opportunity to practice by joining English-language conversations that they overhear—but that is not the norm.

The simple fact is Spain cannot boast the same numbers of English-speakers as many of the country's European neighbors. Why the difference? It wasn't until after the death of General Francisco Franco in 1975 that schools began to emphasize second languages—long after the study of English was entrenched in the schools of many western European countries. Today Spanish schools require that students study a foreign language—usually English or French. In fact, these languages might be introduced to kids when they're as young as six years old. Initially, the quality of Spain's English instruction fell far short of similar programs elsewhere but the improvement of the classes has steadily increased over the years and it's still getting better. That said, the changes are not yet so entrenched that you can reasonably expect people to know English—more often than not, they won't.

The good news is that making an earnest endeavor to learn Castilian—albeit no easy task—not only allows you to communicate more easily while in the country. The effort also endears foreigners to the locals. Even broken sentences and botched grammar are generally rewarded with warmth and encouragement rather than disdain. There's really no need to feel shy about struggling with the language.

> *Everyone approaches learning differently, but you should figure out a tactic—the idea that adults can soak up an entirely new language from merely being around it is a myth.*

Everyone approaches learning differently, but you should figure out a tactic—the idea that adults can soak up an entirely new language from merely being around it is a myth. Many of the people who move to Spain live with a spouse or roommate who shares their first language, and that becomes the language of the home. Even Americans with the best of intentions usually speak English with others who speak it—that is particularly true when making important decisions such as those involving housing, finance, and jobs.

Talking with Spanish friends of course helps immensely, but typically your friends and acquaintances won't stop mid-conversation to correct your every error. Most people will let you slide by with mistakes because they won't want to make you feel bad when they know that you're making such an effort. In a way, their self-control is a good thing—the strain of constant instruction in social situations wears on both the teacher and the student. So while immersion alone works enviably well with young children who manage to become bilingual in what seems like the course of just one school recess, adults who want to learn Castilian should seek out formal instruction.

SPANISH INSTRUCTION IN THE UNITED STATES

If you're only considering a move to Spain but have yet to put your plans in motion, taking a few Spanish lessons while you're still stateside is a wise start to your preparations. Your options are numerous. If you're just starting out, you can take a course that teaches basic vocabulary and verb conjugation, or if your level is more advanced you'll find courses specializing in conversational skills. Some schools also add on an introduction to the culture of Spain to classes of all levels. The list of Spanish courses in the United States is both long and varied.

While the following gives a brief overview of the general sort of classes you can expect to find, more information on the classes in your town can be found by simply asking friends and family for recommendations or just looking online. The vast majority of institutions with language instruction have websites that give detailed information including schedules, teachers, instructors, and prices.

People commonly opt for adult-education courses offered by their local university or community college; those programs usually deliver exactly what official language academies sell but for a whole lot less money. A once-a-week class that provides an introduction to grammar, vocabulary, and conversation can cost as little as $100 at a community college. Most universities charge $300–500 for a semester-long class that includes conversation. If you prefer to study with Berlitz (the Bentley of commercial, foreign-language schools), the price will run you about $350 for a six-week class that meets twice a week. Every one of those options makes sense depending on your needs and wants.

College and university classes are ideal for a class that meets one to two times a week and can also fit neatly into your work schedule. Teachers might be native speakers or Americans fluent in Spanish. If you're intent on studying with someone who grew up speaking Spanish, call and ask about the teacher before enrolling. Those looking for a more specialized alternative such as programs for children, business Spanish, or an intensive class that provides several hours of instruction every week, a commercial language school will likely be a better choice. Many people turn to Berlitz and although it has long enjoyed its golden reputation, it is only one of many such options.

Several other specialized institutes throughout the United States also offer intensive classes, lectures, and group activities. The Spanish Institute in New York City (www.spanishinstitute.org) requires students to pay a $50 membership fee before signing up for a class—a chunk of change buys a year's access to a host of lectures, conversation groups, films, lectures, and other cultural activities. Similarly, the Spain-based Instituto Cervantes (www.cervantes.es) has centers throughout the world including schools in Chicago, New York, and Albuquerque; each of the locations offers an array of programs, many of which are intensive. Like Manhattan's Spanish Institute, lectures, films and other cultural events are also offered—in this case without a membership fee. If you don't live near one of the three locations or if you just cannot work the time for a class into your weekly schedule, Instituto Cervantes also has online options. The downloadable program for the three-month class costs $80 if you choose to tackle the curriculum autonomously, and if you want a virtual tutor and classmates the price jumps up to $150. For those who can't find the time to fit in classes or simply prefer one-on-one instruction, a private instructor is will be the best option and the classified ads will likely turn up an abundance of choices.

SPANISH INSTRUCTION IN SPAIN

Some Americans move to Spain specifically to learn the language while others go for a job, an interest in the culture, a spouse, or any number of other reasons outside of the language itself. But whatever your motivation for going to Spain, you can certainly find a way to learn Spanish. Teaching Spanish as a second language is big business in Spain; all the major cities have a long list of schools from which to choose and many smaller towns have quite a few, too.

Institutes offering intensive classes, options to live and eat meals with a Spanish family, and excursions to local sights are a popular choice for new arrivals to Spain. Those schools usually charge by the week but the longer the enrollment period, the bigger the discount; similarly, the fewer the perks (such as organized accommodation and cultural activities), the lower the price. If you choose to study Spanish in such an institute, it will usually offer preparation for the Diploma de Español como Lengua Extranjera (D.E.L.E.) exam. The Spanish Ministry of Education, Culture, and Sports officially recognizes the D.E.L.E., and the certificate awards competence in Spanish as a foreign language. Instituto Cervantes offers the exam on behalf of the government at three levels: *inicial* (beginner), *intermedio* (intermediate), and *superior* (advanced), and each level of the examination is given just a few times every year.

Along with Cervantes, Don Quijote (www.donquijote.org) is one of the most highly regarded among these specialized schools and it has branches in Barcelona, Granada, Madrid, Salamanca, Seville, Tenerife, Valencia, and Málaga. (See Resources for contact information.) A month-long intensive class plus home-stay with Don Quijote will run you about €920 ($1,150). True, that's pricey but it's not that much higher than the average for a package deal.

Some people prefer to take recommendations from language institutes they know and trust in the United States, and if you ask you might find that a school that you studied at back in the United States has an established relationship with a Spanish school. However most people simply look online and pick based on the information found on the websites. One such American in Madrid said he chose his intensive classes based on price alone, and he talked up the quality of both his 20-hours-a-week of classes and his accommodation with a family—a €800 ($1,000) package deal for one month.

Not everyone has the 20-plus hours a week to spare for an intensive class and if you prefer to learn privately, a tutor will be even easier to find than one is in the United States—after all, just about everyone in Spain is a Spanish speaker. However, a few people make the point that tutors tend to fall short with conversational practice—not surprisingly, a one-on-one session typically lacks the eruptive banter that schools can offer. The most common approaches to finding tutors are through *anuncios por palabras* (classified ads) and by word-of-mouth. If you know other foreigners, ask around, and chances are good that someone will be able to recommend a teacher. However, if neither of these methods turns up satisfactory results you can always subtly inquire among the instructors at one of the local Spanish-language schools in town. Plenty of those teachers will be looking for additional work.

Many Americans note that that Spanish classes in Spain cost more than language classes cost in South American countries and while that is true, there are valuable opportunities that can help chip away at the price. Every year, the Rotary Foundation offers hundreds Ambassadorial Scholarships to applicants pursuing language study abroad. The grant is awarded to further understanding and relations between people of different countries but most people merely view it as a chance to go abroad for little cash down. Students and professionals seeking a vocational education abroad are eligible to receive the grant but before applying, know that candidates must be flexible regarding the academic institution to which they might be assigned. The International Education

Finance Corporation also offers financial assistance to those seeking study abroad though only students are qualified.

Business Spanish

If you want something more specialized such as a class in Spanish-for-business, you can find that, too. Don Quijote offers Spanish for professionals. So does Elemadrid (www.elemadrid.com), a school located in Madrid just as its name promises. International House Spain (www.ih-spain.com) also offers a number of classes including Business Spanish. International House branches are located in Barcelona, Madrid, San Sebastián, and Seville. (See Resources for more information.)

A WORD ABOUT ACCENTS

Don't be surprised when you're told that you have an accent. Even Americans who have spent years in Spain and speak Castilian as naturally as they speak English reveal traces of their origin in their speech. If you didn't grow up speaking Spanish you will not sound Spanish, and if

Speaking in Tongues

Castilian is Spain's first language, but there's a three-way tie for second place. Spain's complex history of passionate culture wars gave rise to three minor languages, and each one has been doggedly maintained over the centuries.

Catalan is spoken throughout Catalonia, Valencia, the Balearic Islands, and parts of southern France. Like Spanish, it is a Romance language but one that sounds more French than anything else; it even employs some French accents that don't appear in Spanish. The language varies from one region to another. For example, in Valencia people speak Valenciano—a dialect of Catalan. It's similar to the version spoken in Barcelona but you can find some distinct discrepancies in both pronunciation and spelling.

Galician—the language of Galicia—sounds a lot like Portuguese and the two languages even overlap on some vocabulary. Take the word "sister," for example. In Spanish it's *hermana;* in Por-

tuguese it's *irmã;* in Galician it's *irmá*—just one squiggly mark away from the Portuguese version.

Unlike the other two languages, Basque (or Euskara)—the language of Spanish and French Basque Country—stands entirely on its own. It didn't develop from Latin or any other identifiable language for that matter; it remains a linguistic mystery with no known origins or sibling languages. Basque's romantically murky past has spawned a number of outlandish theories. To prove that point just see the website put up by Larry Trask, one of the language's most eminent scholars. On his home page, Trask wearily requests that no one contact him suggesting that Basque is somehow connected to the Egyptian *Book of the Dead,* the prophesies of Nostradamus, or the language spoken on the lost island of Atlantis. Evidently, he's heard it all. What's known for sure is that today, more than 660,000 people speak Basque and the vast majority of them live in Spain.

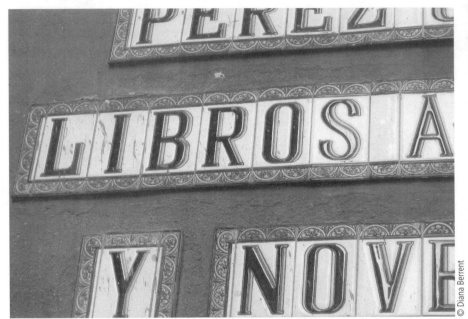

Plenty of Spain's bookstores sell Spanish-as-a-second-language study guides for beginners.

you're just learning the language your accent will probably be especially thick. You'll sometimes have to repeat a word multiple times until you can make yourself understood. Don't be too concerned about it. The Spanish talk about Spain's various accents as much as they do foreign ones. While a heavy accent can very occasionally hinder communication, people are forgiving of anyone who can speak Spanish at all and most humor about accents is good-natured.

But your own accent isn't the only one that will surprise you. If you're familiar with the Spanish spoken in South America, you'll find an obvious difference in Spain where many of the Cs and Zs in words have a "th" sound, so *gracias* (thank you) sounds like "grathias" and *cerveza* (beer) becomes "thervetha." Sound complicated? It's actually not. Lots of people find that without even trying, they naturally begin to absorb the Spanish lisp and those who don't are still understood without it.

REGIONAL LANGUAGES

The official language of Spain is Castilian, but it is not the country's only language. Catalan is also spoken in Catalonia, and although Catalan shares its Latin roots with Spanish, it sounds more French. The language's phonetic similarities to French come as little surprise; a variation of Catalan is also spoken in parts of southern France. In addition to Castilian, people in Basque Country also speak Basque (Euskara). You won't find any similarities to Spanish in Basque—the language's roots have perplexed linguists for centuries because it has no known relatives. Galicia is also a bilingual region where people speak Galician—a language similar to Spanish but also related to Portuguese—the country adjacent to the region.

Should you learn Catalan, Basque, or Galician if you live in an area where those minor languages are spoken? Yes. No. *Maaaybe.* You can learn any one of those languages—courses are offered; but it will only be worth the mammoth effort if you plan to spend years in the regions of those languages. So if you're only planning to spend a year or two in Spain, stick to polishing your Spanish skills. Everyone speaks Spanish throughout the country and so with Spanish, you'll be able to communicate. Moreover, you'll have mastered one of the world's most broadly spoken languages, and that's pretty useful. However, if your move is a permanent one you should try to learn your region's minor language. If it's what your friends are speaking in homes and at parties, you'll want to speak their language.

Education

It won't shock you to discover that you can learn a lot besides Spanish while you're in Spain. The country has 75 universities and foreign students cross the ocean to study in many of them on both undergraduate and graduate levels. Even if you're not planning on enrolling in classes yourself, you'll still want to know a little bit about Spain's education system, especially if you're a parent looking to place your child in a school.

Schooling is free from nursery school through the university level. About one third of students, however, attend Catholic schools, which are private but in many cases state subsidized. Nondenominational private schools are also widely available, but they're a less utilized option than religious schools.

Most college students take advantage of the public university system. Those who are not accepted to public university can attend a private one, but private universities in Spain are less prestigious than their public counterparts. Of Spain's 75 universities and vocational schools, 48 are state run and the rest are private.

Spain's public education is well regarded, and although the country can't boast of a Cambridge or a Sorbonne, the universities are some of Europe's best overall. However, the country's public education is not

Should You Send Your Children to Public School?

Deciding how to educate your child is entirely personal, but making your choice might be a little easier if you have a few facts first. If you opt to enroll your children in a Spanish public school, you won't be alone—plenty of other American parents have done the same and often with good results. Children younger than 10 years old pick up language skills much faster than adults and, not surprisingly, young children adapt best to Spain's public education system. Another perk to public education is that your child will have school friends in the neighborhood, whereas the kids in private schools usually live in homes scattered throughout the area. Expatriate parents commonly choose public primary schools for their child and later switch to private secondary schools.

If you prefer that your children be taught in English for part or all of the day, you'll have to enroll them in a bilingual private school because the curriculum in Spain's public schools is taught in either Spanish or the region's language. Furthermore, if your stay in Spain is temporary or if you want your children to attend a university in the United States, a private, international high school, will better prepare them for that college application process. Spain's international schools have their perks, too. The quality of the education is excellent and they almost always have diverse student bodies with children from around the world. Still, it's good to note that Spanish kids also attend international schools; in fact, they usually make up a large portion of the student body so your child would not be isolated from Spanish culture during the school day. There is no shortage of international schools in Spain, especially in Madrid and Barcelona. If you're sure that you want to send your children to private schools but you don't know which, you should do your research in advance and talk to school officials and other parents; for the latter, school administrations will usually provide you with names and numbers. Also know that in some cases there are waiting lists so you might not be able to send your child to your first-choice school.

without its flaws. The most common complaint voiced about primary and high schools is that the system relies too heavily on a traditional style of rote learning. At the university level, people grumble that the classrooms are too overcrowded for individual attention.

PRIMARY SCHOOL

In order to really understand the system, it's probably easiest to start at the beginning—primary school. The law mandates that anyone between the ages of six and 16 attend school, although the vast majority of children go to nursery school beforehand. Elementary schools teach students aged 6–12. Like the U.S. system, the government places a child in a given school based on geography—except for rare cases in rural locations, children attend a school close to home.

SECONDARY SCHOOL

Students reach secondary school at 12 years old and their academic performance during the next six years will determine a lot. At 16 they graduate and the students who did sufficiently well go on to the next level of secondary school where they will begin preparation for the university entrance exam. Students with lower grades will instead go on to a public vocational school where they will receive job training. In some key ways the curriculums vary from those in the United States. Classes such as drama and art are optional if they're offered at all, and the idea of extracurricular activities is practically unheard of. Special activities are usually sought out privately if at all.

UNIVERSITIES

More than 1.5 million students now attend university in a given year. They typically live at home while studying at their local university. Foreigners make up just 3 percent of university students, and the majority of that group comes from other parts of Europe.

Spain has a long tradition of university education. The Moors began a system of higher learning long before anything like it appeared in the rest of Europe, and Spain's oldest university still in operation, the University of Salamanca, was founded in 1218. The University of Salamanca has long been considered prestigious and that is still true today; it ranks among the country's top schools along with Complutense University in Madrid and Central University in Barcelona. Most Americans who pursue undergraduate studies in Spain go to Salamanca, Madrid, Seville, or Granada.

If you want to study in Spain and you're talking about more than just your junior year abroad, you'll have to go through the Spanish consulate in the United States to validate your credits and to take the exam required to enter a university. However, plenty of people come to Spain to study business, and if that's you, you can make your life a whole lot easier by enrolling in an international university within Spain. The admissions requirements vary from one school to another, but they're usually no more involved than gaining admission to a university in the United States. A few particularly popular schools are Barcelona Business School, European University in Barcelona, and Schiller International University in Madrid. (See Resources for contact information.)

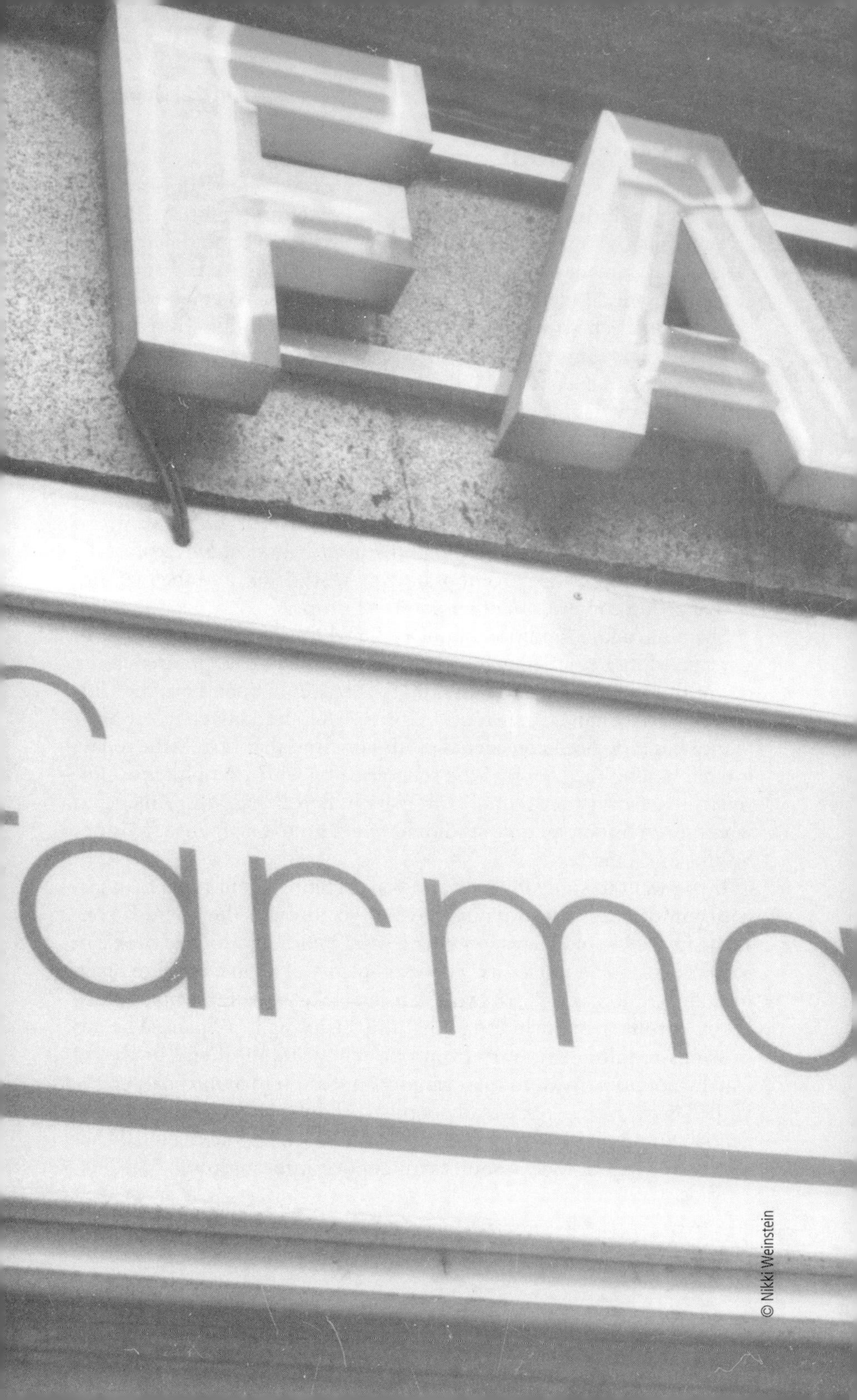

© Nikki Weinstein

© Jessica Chesler

Health

O h, those lucky Spaniards. As citizens, they have access to health care that's either dirt cheap or free. That's right, I said free—and theirs is a darn good system, too. As an American in Spain, you may have access to that same care. If you don't have that privilege, you can buy private health insurance that provides excellent treatment at low prices.

You won't face any more health hazards while in Spain than you would in the United States, although you might face slightly different ones. For example, stress is far less acute in Spain than it is in the United States, and the national rate of heart attacks reflects that difference. On the other hand, far more people per capita smoke cigarettes, and it's not at all unusual to find a bar or restaurant choked with secondhand smoke. Despite the slight differences, health can be easily managed in Spain. For more serious issues you can count on a solid medical system, and for minor complaints you can take your woe to any pharmacy and likely find relief. You won't have to go far for that either—Spanish pharmacies are ubiquitous.

Types of Insurance

You'll have no reason to go without health insurance while you're in Spain. You might be eligible for the public health care system, Instituto Nacional de la Salud (INSALUD), and if you're not, you can find excellent private insurance at solidly affordable prices. Both systems are good although private care is slightly better. Most Americans opt for private insurance, even if they can use the public system. Language is one reason for that. No matter how solid your ability in Spanish, it's only natural that you'd prefer to handle an issue as vital as health in your first language, and private insurance typically offers more bilingual doctors than public insurance does. If you use private insurance you'll also have faster access to nonemergency services. Public care has historically been beleaguered with long waiting lists, although that is beginning to improve.

PUBLIC CARE

In 1986, a health-care law that had long been in the making was passed. That moment marked the definitive move to a national medical plan that would be open and affordable to everyone. Today's public health care system—INSALUD—is a direct result of that law, and the system is a solid one that covers more than 90 percent of the Spanish population.

If you pay social security contributions, you and your family can take advantage of the services offered by INSALUD. Just what can you expect from the health scheme? A good amount but not everything. Here's how it works. You'll need to have a social security card (available via the social security agency), and once that's taken care of, you'll receive a booklet of vouchers, a list of local doctors, as well as information on hospitals, services, and fees where costs apply. Doctors used to be assigned to patients but that's changed. You can now select the *médico cabecera* (general practitioner) of your choice. In most cases, appointments with general practitioners and specialists cost a grand total of nothing. The same also goes for emergency room visits and hospital stays. In addition to seeing doctors, you can have lab tests, buy discounted drugs (you'll pay about 40 percent of the cost), and you'll receive basic dental care, maternity care, and ambulance rides.

You're waiting for the catch, right? Here it comes. INSALUD is overburdened and waiting lists for procedures deemed nonemergency can be insufferably long. Many gripe about the length of the waiting list for hospital beds, too. Depending on the area and the hospital, the wait can be as long as six months for an in-demand procedure or a bed for a nonemergency.

The last common complaint voiced is about the extras. Alternative medicine, thorough postoperative care, geriatric assistance, and psychiatric treatment are not as readily available as they are on private plans.

Ultimately, the system might seem strange to Americans who come from a place where health care is a paradox. While the United States offers some of the best medical treatment in the world, care is not accessible to everyone. Spain's health care is in some cases a slight step down in caliber. However, the public plan is a far more egalitarian one and the compromise on quality is slight.

PRIVATE CARE

Most Americans living in Spain choose private health coverage. Some go that route because paid plans offer more perks and shorter waits than IN-SALUD. Others are willing to pay for coverage because as nonresidents they have no other choice available. But deciding to go private is only half the issue—the other half is finding a plan.

> Deciding to go private is only half the issue—the other half is finding a plan.

You'll have a decent selection of medical plans from which to choose. Some of the companies cover people all over the world, others are only valid within Europe, and still others only protect those in Spain. Within each company you can opt for the deluxe package or the low-cost version depending on your needs.

Individual Coverage

More than six million Spaniards rely on private health insurance and a good number of foreigners do, too. Companies usually cover 90 percent of your bills, and you'll pay the remaining 10 percent. Care is top-quality and you'll be able to get appointments quickly. One of the most popular companies among foreigners in Spain is Sanitas, a company owned by the British company BUPA. Adeslas and Asisa are also widely used. (See Resources for contact information.) Each network has more bilingual doctors, and that alone is a huge help. The companies sell various plans. The monthly prices can range from about €40 ($50) for a spry young thing looking for basic coverage to more than €100 ($125) for someone older than 60 on a deluxe plan that includes extras such as dental coverage. Women might have to pay significantly more for their coverage.

Most people are pleased with the value they get from this plan. A typical story comes from one American in Madrid who spent several days in bed after suffering from a bout of food poisoning. Thanks to her private coverage, the entire episode cost her less than €50 ($63). Even better, her doctor made a house call when she was too ill to go to his office.

Some companies offer a range of plans and others have just one. In most cases, the plans work much like HMOs—you'll be given a list of doctors within network and you can choose among them. Some companies even run their own individual clinics. Check to make sure that all services such as dental care and alternative medicine are included in your plan of choice—those items are not necessarily provided. Read the contract carefully before signing. A few plans squish a little clause into the fine print about dropping people once they reach 65 years old or booting them should they come down with an expensive medical condition. (Yes, that's heartless—but it's also not the norm.)

Your U.S. Plan

If you already have U.S. insurance such as HIP or Oxford Health Plans, don't assume that your plan will give you the same coverage in Spain. Once you step off U.S. soil, you'll face a whole new set of rules with your insurance company. Before you shell out hundreds of bucks each month for an individual plan, be sure that's the most prudent thing to do. In fact, you'll likely find that remaining with your U.S. insurer is not the best move.

Granted, not all plans are the same and only a select few U.S. insurers will help you out with your medical needs abroad, but most companies only provide coverage in the case of emergencies. In other words, if you have the flu, you have to pay for your doctor's appointment, related tests, and medicine, but if you end up in the emergency room, your bills will be covered. However, you'll likely have to pay that hefty bill upfront and file the forms for a reimbursement that will come to you sometime down the road. It's imperative that you speak with your U.S. insurance agency about coverage abroad to learn exactly what sending in a fat check every month will actually buy you when you're out of the United States.

So should you leave your U.S. plan for a Spanish one? Probably. That is, unless you're moving to a Spanish branch of your U.S. company. If that's the case, your employer presumably sees to your health care, and you might be able to remain on the same plan while abroad. Insurance companies apply entirely different rules to individuals than they do to corporations. Take the American who moved from Chicago to Barcelona to continue working for his consulting agency—a U.S. corporation. That guy kept his company health plan through Aetna, as did his U.S. colleagues who also came to Spain, and the whole group received excellent coverage. To find out how your corporate plan measures up in Spain, speak to both your boss and your insurance company directly.

International Insurance

If your time in Spain is temporary but you'll be spending more time elsewhere in Europe, you can opt for international insurance and stick with the same coverage throughout the course of your moves. Although the specifics change from company to company, private insurers usually employ a similar coded language. Here's a rough key: basic coverage typically offers coverage with primary physicians, specialists, and diagnostic tests so long as all of those are within the network. Normal coverage will likely buy you both outpatient and hospital coverage with a little more flexibility on network regarding non-network doctors, but expect limits on the amounts that you can claim. Naturally, it's the priciest plan that buys the most. Comprehensive coverage will cover everything including psychiatric care and alternative medicine, but you'll pay for those perks in your higher monthly premiums.

HOSPITALS AND CLINICS

Every Spanish town—even the tiny ones—have at least one hospital or clinic. In most cases you'll find that they're stocked with top-of-the-line equipment and well trained doctors. However, the quality of hospital care in a few rural locations is inferior to the average.

The most important thing to know about Spanish hospitals and clinics is that they don't all offer the same services, and not all of them have emergency rooms. *Hospitales de la seguridad social* are entirely public while *hospitales privados* serve patients with private insurance. Public or private, all the bigger hospitals have an outpatient department and an emergency room. Emergency rooms are usually swamped with both urgent and nonurgent cases; people commonly try to jump the waiting list for care by seeking it at the ER.

Although about 40 percent of Spanish hospitals treat only private patients, the majority of them specialize in a particular field, such as surgery and they're not full service. While a bed is free under the public health scheme, it costs about €150 ($188) a day under private care.

Pharmacies and Prescriptions

If you're shy about sharing your health afflictions with a bunch of strangers, you'll find yourself blushing crimson when trying to adapt to the culture in Spanish *farmacias* (pharmacies). In Spain, the pharmacist will do a whole lot more than hand you the pills prescribed by your doctor. Pharmacists can suggest a shampoo for particularly dry hair, they can give you a hemorrhoid ointment and explain how to apply it, and they'll ring up your choice of nail polish once it's selected from the display case. The only catch (and it's a big one) is that you must explain what it is that you want. Yes, that means that you must say it aloud and quite possibly to the amusement of the customers standing in line behind you.

It takes true grit to shrug off the embarrassment that comes from describing exactly where that rash is or how long it's been since your last lengthy trip to the bathroom. However, such conversations are the norm in Spanish pharmacies and the upshot is that the person in the lab coat will almost certainly be able to help you out.

Of course, pharmacists also fill prescriptions. If you only know the brand name of a particular medicine that you habitually take, find out the generic name since that's probably the one the pharmacist will know. Pensioners and disabled people need not pay for medication under the public health-care system, but everyone else pays 40 percent of the cost. With private insurance, the cash you put down for medicine might be reimbursed entirely. Even if you're paying part of the cost on your pre-

Women, Sex, and the Law

You know that old saying about pregnancy, right? You either are or you're not, but you can't be just a little bit pregnant. Not all laws that govern sex are so simple. It seems that in Spain, abortion is just a little bit legal. While the law could be more permissive, the issue of sex isn't always handled conservatively. Contraceptives are both allowed and birth control pills can even be purchased in pharmacies without prescriptions. The morning-after pill (the one that prevents conception if taken within 72 hours of intercourse) is also legal. Surprised? Don't be. It's not by just crossing their legs that the Spanish have maintained one of Europe's lowest birthrates—the government has also pitched in with a few progressive laws.

But let's go back to the issue of abortion. It's an issue with a little bit of history in Spain. During his reign of power, Franco's strong ties to the Catholic Church had a tremendous impact on Spain's laws, and nowhere was that more evident than in the governance of birth control and abortion—both were strictly forbidden. With Franco's death in 1975, a public debate erupted about birth control, laws began to change, and a more progres-

scriptions, that won't total a lot—Spain has some of the cheapest pre-scription drugs in the EU. However, non-prescription medicines such as aspirin, decongestants, and cough syrup are costly, and that's partly because they're almost exclusively sold in pharmacies. There's no Spanish equiv-alent to Rite Aid where you can pluck those same items off the shelves.

Pharmacies are marked by a green cross—sometimes painted, sometime neon—and they're easy to find, even in small towns. Hours vary, but the standard schedule is 9:30 A.M.–1:30 P.M. at which point the usual siesta break begins. Business starts up again at 4:30 P.M. and runs until 8 P.M., Monday–Saturday. Sunday hours are unpredictable and some pharmacies don't open at all. However, no need to worry—every town has at least one pharmacy that remains open 24 hours. Yep, that means Sundays, too. Those special pharmacies are indicated by a red and green sign and often have a doorbell that is used at nights. Should you stop by late one evening, press the buzzer and the pharmacist will shuffle over to the door. You'll probably speak from a gate, a hatch, or through bulletproof glass, but the bottom line is you'll have your needs met, even if it's 3 A.M.

Preventive Measures

VACCINATIONS

The World Health Organization (WHO) doesn't recommend any shots be-fore a trip to Spain. The Centers for Disease Control (CDC) recommends

sive social climate emerged from the na-tional disputes. In 1983, contraceptives were decriminalized and two years later abortion was also made somewhat ac-cessible. That especially marked a pro-found change from the past.

So abortion is legal, right? Well, not exactly. Depending on how you view it, abortion is either legal with strict limita-tions or it is illegal except for three cir-cumstances: in cases of rape, severe fetal abnormality, and in instances of a preg-nancy that poses a risk to the mother's physical or mental health. Take note of that mental health clause in particular.

For doctors who unequivocally believe in a woman's right to choose, that section of the law allows a little wiggle room that's sometimes used to assist mentally sound women who have chosen to ter-minate an unwanted pregnancy. Not sur-prisingly, the passing of a more liberal abortion law was not without contro-versy. Some doctors bow out of per-forming abortions because they find direct involvement too divisive. Other doc-tors morally oppose abortions. Ultimately though, women who have decided to terminate an unwanted pregnancy are usually able to do so in Spain.

just two: immunizations for hepatitis A and B. Both vaccinations should be administered four to six weeks before leaving. Your risk of contracting hepatitis A is no higher than it is in the United States. However, hepatitis B appears in slightly greater numbers in Spain than it does in the United States, so inoculations are a good idea. That goes double for anyone who expects to be sexually active or health-care workers who might be exposed to blood while abroad. The CDC also suggests tetanus-diphtheria booster shots, and hepatitis B immunizations for kids who need to complete the inoculation series.

DISEASES

You should be as careful in Spain as you would be in the United States, but rest assured that you won't be any more at risk for any new diseases than you would at home. The Centers For Disease Control (www.cdc.gov) addresses key medical concerns in countries all around the world. To learn more about what the U.S. organization has to say about health hazards in western Europe, check the website—it has a wealth of information. Still, there are a few things to note.

It's no coincidence that a Spanish city—Barcelona—hosted the World AIDS Conference in 2002. After all, Spain has one of the highest AIDS rates in Europe. Although heterosexual sex is now the leading cause of transmission, AIDS hit the Spanish population especially hard in the early 1980s when scores of heroin addicts shared needles and the government did woefully little to inform the public about the disease. Today, the government is far more active in addressing the problem and some pharmacists choose to participate in a free needle exchange program that has met with some success. The rate of transmission has fallen but the numbers still look ominous. In 2002, Spain had 130,000 known cases of HIV or AIDS. It's important to be aware of the facts and to use caution. Most importantly, use latex condoms if you're sexually active. Despite the fact that the heterosexual population is now Spain's most vulnerable to AIDS, many Spaniards in that category are dangerously unaware of the risks posed to their own demographic.

AIDS is just one concern. All of the same sexually transmitted diseases that can be contracted in the United States are also passed along in Spain. That list includes chlamydia, genital warts, gonorrhea, hepatitis B, herpes, and syphilis. Only some of those are preventable with latex condoms. Others can be shared from relatively casual contact. For more information speak to a doctor about safe-sex practices.

HEAT EXHAUSTION AND SUNBURN

You should be careful on those gorgeous summer days in Spain—the sun can cause a few problems. People are frequently hit with heat exhaustion, heatstroke, and plain old sunburn, but all those afflictions are avoidable, too. In most cases heat exhaustion is not serious but it can occasionally turn into heatstroke, which is more dangerous and can even be fatal. If you are with someone suffering from the condition, remove the victim from the sun immediately and cool the person off with wet towels or the like and provide fluids. It is also very important to go to the hospital rather than attempting to handle heatstroke on your own—only a doctor can assess the severity of the situation.

> *You should be careful on those gorgeous summer days in Spain—the sun can cause a few problems.*

Sunburn seems to afflict many in Spain, and the victims are not difficult to spot—they tend to congregate around beaches and pools and they look bright enough to glow in the dark. Unfortunately, the biggest concern with sunburn isn't a bad burn. A serious scalding is painful in the short term and might cause skin cancer in the future. If you spend a long day outside in which you're exposed to steady sun, do take breaks in the shade or indoors, and be sure to drink plenty of water. Also use SPF protection (even on overcast days) and wear a hat when you spend time outdoors in the summer.

Environmental Factors

WATER QUALITY

The drinking water is perfectly healthy in Spain. That's true of Madrid and Barcelona, as well as most small towns. However, when traveling around the country a lot of people err on the side of caution and drink bottled water in case the water isn't potable. Another reason some people opt for bottled water is merely taste. The water in Madrid, for example, is so chlorinated that even a shower can smell vaguely like a swimming pool. Naturally that addition affects the taste of the water. Lastly, water from any dubious source—even a seemingly fresh stream—should not be drunk unless it has been treated.

AIR QUALITY

Spain is very much a part of the industrial age, and that means that the country's environment is less than pristine. However, pollution isn't the problem that it is in some other parts of the world. When Spain signed the Kyoto agreement, it had lower emissions than some other member countries but it wasn't the lowest of the bunch. In 2001, Spain produced 383 million tons of greenhouse gases. To put that in perspective, Ireland—another country that made radical economic changes during the 1990s and also has plenty of industry—only produced 70 million tons. In other words, there's a lot of room for improvement.

The government has taken steps to rectify the problem and adheres to the rules of various international environmental treaties, so things are already moving in the right direction. In 2003, Spain's emissions decreased by 1 percent compared with its figures for 2000. That improvement came as a result of more hydropower and less burning of fossil fuels. However, not everything is rosy. The air in Madrid and Barcelona—both confined areas full of cars—is visibly dirtier than the air in rural areas.

SMOKING

As soon as you step off the airplane and reach baggage claim, you'll inevitably notice the number of people who whip out cigarettes and light up while waiting for their suitcase. Naturally, that phenomenon isn't limited to the airport. People smoke in movie theater lobbies, restaurants, bars, cafés, and on the street. While the smoke is unappealing to many people, tolerance towards the habit is part of Spanish culture and you won't make any friends by loudly coughing and dramatically waving the smoke away from your face. So what can you do? More and more, restaurants are creating smoking and nonsmoking sections and taking advantage of that will secure you a spot that's far from the nicotine haze. Also, exercise a little patience. While you will be faced with more secondhand smoke in Spain than you're accustomed to in the United States, the EU has taken strong anti-smoking measures and you can expect to see results from that campaign soon. In the meantime, you'll probably grow accustomed to the smoke sooner than you might think—most people do.

Safety

Generally speaking Spain is very safe, but it isn't a crime-free utopia. Violent crimes have not reached epidemic proportions, and the biggest concern you'll face is petty theft. Guard your bag closely when you're in public, do not leave your belongings unattended, and don't leave anything of value in parked cars. Thieves are far more likely to steal wallets covertly than to mug people. However, should someone confront you with a demand for your belongings, don't argue—simply hand your wallet and jewelry over. Yes, you'll be outraged, but dealing with the hassle beats a face-off with someone who might have a knife.

In Spain, you should exercise the same caution that you would elsewhere. Avoid vacant streets and parks at night—you're always safer in a crowd and that goes double for women. If you live in an apartment building, never hold the vestibule door open to allow a stranger into the lobby. It might feel rude to close a door in someone's face, but being safe is preferable to being polite. Lastly, hitchhiking is illegal on *autivías* (highways) and it's not safe anywhere. Still, some people do it with fine results. The most important thing to note is that while hitchhiking is unwise for anyone, it's riskiest for women alone.

See Resources for emergency phone numbers.

Employment

Washington Irving had it good. He first came to Spain as an American diplomat, and after four years, he decided to settle in Granada and write a book. Once there, he found office space that just can't be beat—the Alhambra. Granted, he didn't have access to a kitchenette with vending machines, but he was both living and working in one of the world's most breathtaking buildings, so it seems like a decent trade-off. Of course, that was back in 1829 and things have changed since then, especially for Americans.

With roughly 95,000 U.S. citizens living in Spain today, you have to assume that most of them are earning livings. That's a good sign. It suggests that you might also find employment in Spain, but it's not as easy as it once was. Plenty of foreigners assume that if they pound the pavement and flash a winning smile, they'll land at best their dream job, and at worst a job teaching English—not a bad fallback. However, securing employment is a little trickier than that. For one thing, if

you're assuming that your English skills will open doors, think again. People from the United States are runners-up for jobs that require English—those who speak the Queen's English usually take the prize. That's not discrimination; it's just good sense. Because of European Union laws, English people don't require working papers but Americans still do. It's plainly easier for an employer to pass over the American by when there's a simpler option. The relatively high unemployment rate adds another complication. The rate is currently at 11 percent. That means a lot of Spanish people are looking for work, too. Naturally, they're in a better position to find jobs than foreigners are; they have connections from friends, family, and school that most Americans lack.

There's no need to spend sleepless nights over this issue. The news isn't all bleak. While finding work isn't easy, it's far from impossible. Some people find work with U.S. companies and they arrive in the country with jobs in hand. Others have had great success setting themselves up in fields where being foreign is an asset. The restaurant and tourist industries are particularly good bets, especially if you offer something that's unusual in Spain. However, you'll be facing economic ruin (and maybe ridicule) if you open a restaurant with the promise of serving up the best tapas in town. (Telling Spanish people that you can cook better than their mothers is more than a bad idea—it's close to a cardinal sin.) Know your strengths within the Spanish market, and use them to the fullest.

Self-Employment

Perhaps you, like Washington Irving, have a job that allows you to be mobile. Writers are not the only ones with that luck. Modern technology has made borders more flexible. If you have a laptop and telephone, you can communicate with people all over the world and in real time, too. As long as you're in a spot where you can have a DSL connection, you truly can create a virtual office. However, you might be interested in launching a business complete with physical space, employees, and local clients, and that requires a lot more consideration.

STARTING A BUSINESS

Some foreigners who have begun their own businesses have met with great success, but you should move forward cautiously. While Spain is cosmopolitan in many ways, it's also a traditional country. This means people are open to new ideas, but only once they're really, *really* convinced that a different way is worth trying. Here are some things to keep in

mind. First, think about capital. How much can you throw into your business and how long can you subsist without a profit? Consider location. If you intend to open a sushi restaurant, don't take it to a small town with an aging population that will be stunned by the idea of raw fish and traumatized by the fire in wasabi; Barcelona or Madrid would be better bets for that venture. Finally, think about employees. Figure out how many people you'll need to hire and calculate that cost—it's usually a substantial one.

Most people underestimate the expense of starting a new business and they overestimate the profits. To avoid that trap, consider both overhead and the amount you'll have to put up while you're finding your footing. Be sure that you have enough cash not only to launch your enterprise, but also to live on for a year at the very least. It could take a while before you begin to reap the rewards of your efforts.

Lastly, remember that you're the boss. That means that you'll have employees to look out for and each of them will be entitled to benefits including social security, bonuses, and the penalty for terminating an indefinite contract. (For more information on these benefits, see Benefits and Contracts in this chapter.) It's important to factor in those costs when tallying your expenses.

> While Spain is cosmopolitan in many ways, it's also a traditional country. This means people are open to new ideas, but only once they're really, really convinced that a different way is worth trying.

You might be able to secure a loan from a Spanish bank but they're conservative about lending to entrepreneurs, and that's doubly true when it comes to foreigners. The lesson there is this: don't move to Spain with the assumption that you can secure a loan to carry the costs of your new business. While you might strike gold with a loan officer, you'll probably receive modest financing at best. When going to the bank to check out options, be sure to have more than just a grade-A suit. Also take along a detailed plan of your proposed enterprise, and be prepared to offer security.

If you've done the math and you're prepared to make a go of it, then it's time to get the official stamp of approval. All self-employed people have to register with the appropriate college. In Spain, each career category has its own official body with the government and you'll need to join the appropriate one for your job in order to launch your business legally. Additionally, you may need to have your qualifications confirmed by the government. For example, a medical degree granted in a foreign country does not automatically allow you to practice medicine in Spain. (That's a good thing actually, even if it adds to your pile of paperwork.) The Ministry of Sport, Education and Culture accepts applications for *homologisacion*—the official recognition of your degree. Spanish embassies provide information on the qualifications needed in order to work in various fields in Spain. You should check into those specifics long before you make your move because you might need transcripts and letters from your alma mater and previous employers.

TYPES OF BUSINESSES

In Spain, as anywhere, some ideas blossom into rewarding businesses and others fall flat. The most commonly successful ventures in Spain are the following: running hotels, inns, restaurants, bars, cafés, shops that specialize in foreign goods, real estate, gyms, hairdressers, and social clubs. Hairdressers . . . . that's a weird one, right? Actually, it's just the sort of business that has strong potential. It's hard enough to convey what you want to your stylist in your own language. In a second one it's an excruciating effort. When foreigners with limited Spanish skills plop down in the barber's chair, their wide eyes and vague hand gestures essentially say, "I'm putty in your hands—go to town," and the result can be traumatizing. The opportunity simply to describe a desired haircut will be a big draw. If you set up a business that can provide that sort of service, and you do it in the right area—one saturated with native English-speakers—you could potentially thrive with just a pair of scissors and a little know-how.

The key to your success is being able to do your thing well. You won't develop steady customers if someone asks for a little off the top and you give them a butcher job. In other words, don't become a hairdresser if you don't know how to cut hair, and don't open a restaurant if you know nothing about the industry. However, if you have both the experience and you choose your location wisely, you'll be in a good position.

Similarly, gyms have a history of success in Spain. Many foreigners like taking kickboxing, yoga, and other classes, but these are harder to come by in Spain. Set up a gym in the right location and you'll have a built-in market. Real estate ventures in resort areas succeed because scores of English-speakers are buying homes along the Spanish coasts. Nobody wants to pony up several thousand dollars for a deal that was negotiated in a language that they don't understand. If you're bilingual and a real estate guru settled in the right place, you'll have real potential.

So that begs the question, why do some businesses fail? Sometimes you won't know. It might seem that all the elements were in place and yet the idea lacked that inexplicable alchemy that makes things work. However, sometimes you can pinpoint the problem exactly.

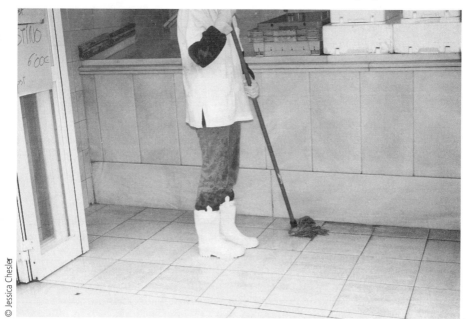

© Jessica Chesler

A woman employed in a fish store prepares to close up shop for the day.

One group of U.S. architects who set up shop in Madrid cashed out and moved back to the United States after a couple years of floundering. They had the skills and they hit a place where people want architects, so what gives? What those Americans failed to recognize is that in Spain, people will *always* give business to their friends and family before they hand it over to a stranger. Despite their expertise, the architects couldn't secure enough clients—they had no relatives and too few friends in the country, and because they were relying on a Spanish market for business, their social deficits made all the difference.

ESTABLISHING YOUR BUSINESS

Once you know what you want to do and where you want to do it, you'll be ready to roll up your sleeves and get to work. But before you get going, there are a few hurdles to prepare for. Spain's bureaucracy can exasperate even the most unflappable of people, but if you're entering the process prepared for some paperwork and long lines, that will help a lot. Some 85 percent of foreigners who embark on launching their own enterprise in Spain give up before the process is complete. Some undoubtedly change their minds along the way, but others lose their patience. In some ways, it's a good litmus test; if you can make it through the red tape, you very well might be able to make it in Spain. Also, keep in mind that there are approximately 1.5 million small businesses in Spain, and if all those people managed to make it through the initial stages, so can you.

Here's a big ray of sunshine. The Spanish government fully recognizes that overwhelming amounts of bureaucracy can push foreign investors away, and crucial steps have been taken to make things easier for you. You can now take care of everything from picking up documents to processing them in just one place—a *ventanilla única* (employment agency). To find the office nearest you, check online (www.ventanillaempresarial.org) or call the main number at tel. 902 100 096.

Your residency status will be a factor. Residents can begin their own businesses, and there's a special visa for those who want to do just that. (See Making the Move.) It's worth noting that you'll have to put up a lot of capital to show the government that you have what it takes. You'll probably be expected to put have about €120,000 ($150,000) in your bank account. Once you get the government's go-ahead, you very well might be faced with the demand that you employ a certain number of EU citizens, so be prepared for that, too.

At a kiosk on a Madrid corner

© Diana Berrent

BUSINESS PRACTICES

The Spanish way of doing business is not the same as it is in the United States. Some of the differences are minor—for example, you can expect more lunch and dinner meetings and fewer occasions on which you grab a sandwich and eat it at your desk. You'll also experience some frustrating moments when you approach certain situations in your usual way, only to discover that your methods—ones so successful in the United States—get you nowhere on Spanish shores.

For better or worse, Spain is not the capitalist juggernaut that the United States is. A good many people would rather have their nights free, weekends off, and lots of vacation time than be at the top of their field. One of the best things about Spanish culture is that free time comes before business. But when you're actually engaged in business this view may lead to some teeth gritting moments.

In Spain, the customer *isn't* always right, and if you offer to pay someone a little extra to have a service performed your way, you'll probably get absolutely nowhere with the tactic. The way someone offers you a service is the way you'll get it—no frills, no extras, no amendments. When one American wanted to shoot a television show in a certain Seville restaurant on a Monday night—a night when the place was typically closed—the owner flatly turned the producer down. So of course the American explained that the restaurant would by getting free publicity and all that was required was opening the doors and turning on the lights. That point was met with the response, "I don't need publicity—I have enough customers and I *don't* open on Mondays." That left the producer speechless and ultimately the show was shot elsewhere.

When you play your trump card and that card is more money or the promise of a bigger, splashier business, it's not necessarily going to work out in Spain—not if you're requiring that someone give up their free time. The upshot of that is that you can enjoy your time off, too. You'll have more vacation, you'll likely work fewer weekends, and you won't have to sweat pleasing each and every customer.

The Job Hunt

Arriving in Spain with employment set up is the ideal scenario, but if you're not in that lucky position you still have options. The most important thing to know is that speaking English is a boon, but speaking Spanish is just short of a must. With an estimated 266 million speakers, Spanish is one of the three most widely spoken languages in the world and it's the language of business in Spain—English is not. If you're not fluent in Spanish, your choices will be severely limited.

Given that, your résumé should be in Spanish and formatted like your U.S. one; begin with your most recent experience, detail the skills you acquired at each job, and be sure to include a section on language proficiency. On that last point, it's best to be honest lest you find yourself face to face with people you can't speak to.

With your résumé ready, the next step is to hit the personal ads and pursue all the channels available to land a job. The Instituto Nacional de Empleo (INEM; National Employment Institute) is the only job agency that can match people with a broad range of permanent positions, and help is given to residents, too. The regional offices have bulletin boards with postings, resource libraries, and employees willing to lend you a hand. However, many people argue that foreign residents take a back seat to Spanish citizens with the INEM, and that's one more reason to broaden your search; the more avenues you take, the better your luck will be.

Private agencies specialize in temporary positions, and Adecco (www.adecco.com) is one of the larger ones. When perusing the classified ads in larger cities, you'll undoubtedly come across some notices for

We Are the Young Americans

Apprentice, trainee, intern . . . call it what you'd like—the bottom line is that if you're an American citizen who's 21–30 years old, landing a job in Spain might just be a snap.

Along with Austria, Denmark, Ireland, New Zealand, and a host of other countries, Spain and the United States are both participants in the international trainee program. That means that if you've completed at least two years of higher education, you can find employment in Spain so long as it's within your field. The deal usually secures a yearlong arrangement (sometimes an additional six months can be tacked on), but it's a way for you to ratchet up some work experience *and* live in sunny Spain.

If that describes you and you're all set to pack your bags, but you don't know how to find an employer to take you on, try contacting the national trade association within your field. They often have information on companies or programs abroad that are eager to hire foreign trainees. Undergraduate students should speak to their home university and universities within Spain to find out what schools are open to foreign students.

You can also go through the International Association for the Exchange of Students for Technical Experience (www.iaeste .org). To get in on the offer, you'll have to be enrolled already as a full time student in one of several programs, including agriculture, applied arts, architecture, engineering, hotel management, horticulture, science, textiles, and even brewing. You won't rake in a pile of cash, but you will receive a cost-of-living stipend, valuable experience, and you'll be living in the land of paella—and that's invaluable.

headhunters. They can be useful contacts, too. Most specialize in a particular field but that narrowed scope is a very good thing if your career falls under the headhunter's umbrella. In addition to looking through the ads in *El País* and other national newspapers, don't miss the less obvious periodicals that also run classified ads. Particularly, *El Mercado de Trabajo* (www.mercadodetrabajo.com), a weekly paper that targets people looking for work, and global papers such as the *International Herald Tribune*.

Lastly, use the Internet. Monster.com has a Spanish site (www.monster.es), and Job Pilot (www.jobpilot.net) lists ads that apply to all of Europe. Be patient and know that many others will be using these channels—the Internet, newspapers, and agencies. You'll be competing with a lot of people, but if you're persistent and keep your search as wide as possible, you'll have a good chance of success. Fair or not, you'll have one extra thing working in your favor. U.S. citizens have a reputation for being hard workers, and go figure, that's something most employers really like. On the other hand, employers have to offer jobs to Spanish nationals first, European Union citizens second, and lastly anyone else—and that can make things rougher for Americans.

INTERVIEWS

Job interviews can be good, bad, and ugly, and I'm referring to the ones in the United States. That's also true in Spain. You might hit if off with your potential boss, or you may sweat through your Armani duds—that's just a universal fact of job hunting. That similarity aside, the process is almost—but not quite—the same.

Remember when you graduated from college and at your parents' urging, you bought your first suit? If you're a lawyer or an investment banker, those duds probably got a lot of mileage, but plenty of U.S. offices are more casual than they once were and thousands of first suits hung unworn in closets. Spain isn't quite so dressed down, and you'll want to look dapper for your interviews. Don't slap a flower into your lapel or wear a bowler, just err on the side of conservative. Ladies, I regret to inform you that stockings are de rigueur but you can avoid that loathsome nylon armor by wearing a pantsuit.

The next key difference is that it's unlikely that you'll know what salary is attached to a job before you're interviewed. While that might be the number-one question on your mind, don't blurt it out. Wait until the job has been offered before asking about pay. By that point, you might have been told the proposed salary but it's entirely possible that those magic numbers will be left unstated through the entire process. Once the job has been offered, you can and should negotiate—ask around to find out what the standard rate is for your type of job. Regardless of the slight increase that you might score, you'll likely be startled to see that the numbers are lower than you had hoped. Keep in mind that taxes and social security are included, and those additions take a big bite out of your checks.

BENEFITS AND CONTRACTS

Kiss your substandard HMO plan goodbye and welcome to Spain. If you're legally working a full-time job and you earn more than €421 a month, then your employer has to pay social security benefits on your behalf. Being a member of the system buys you access to the health care. You'll also be covered for work-related injuries, unemployment (you can take advantage of that if you've contributed to the social security system for more than 360 days within the past six years), and pensions (hey, there's no harm thinking about the future). However, benefits don't end with social security. You'll be given at least 30 days of vacation—yep, a full month. And two annual bonuses are commonly doled out—one in June and the other in December. While you will not have a set number of sick days, your boss has to pay you for days taken off due to illness. But if you exceed a certain number of days, the company will cease payment and social security will kick in to cover the cost.

You'll very likely be given a contract as well, and when you face that all-important piece of paper, there are a few things to know before you sign it. There are two kinds of contracts in Spain, short-term (usually for at least a year) and indefinite ones. The tremendous difference between the two kinds of agreements has nothing to do with what the contract actually stipulates regarding your job and salary.

More than 75 percent of workers younger than 25 have short-term contracts, and that's not a sign that they're viewed as untrustworthy—instead, it has everything to do with the law. When a worker with an indefinite contract is fired, the company has to pay a lot of money. The exact amount is worked out in an equation based on the duration of employment and the reason for the dismissal, but the bottom line is that an employer might pay a fired worker a full salary for as long as a year after the person was let go.

Unfortunately, a law designed to protect workers' rights has hurt the system as a whole. No company wants to be saddled with an inadequate member of staff so in order to dodge that bullet, short-term contracts have become the norm. Under those circumstances, workers can be let go without penalizing the employer. The terms within short-term agreements are the same except for the duration of employment. The hitch is that such contracts can only be renewed for up to three years. After that time period, the employee must either be hired as a permanent worker or fired altogether. I wish I could tell you that at that point, bosses hand out indefinite contracts like it's Christmas morning but unfortunately, that's not always the case. After three years, many employees are let go. In 2002, less than a third of all employment contracts signed were permanent ones.

Regardless of the contract that you have, you should know that the standard work week is 40 hours, and nine hours per day. However, that's merely a benchmark and it can vary according to the type of job you have. You should be given at least a day-and-a-half off per week (you'll almost certainly be given the entire weekend), and overtime is paid in either money or time off, and it's limited to 80 hours a year. However, the average worker's annual overtime logged in is about half of that. If the conditions stray from the standard, the alternative should be mutually agreed upon and written into your contract. In addition to your vacation, the country has 14 national holidays and all 14 of them are your playtime.

Labor Laws

The 1980 Estatuto de los Trabajadores (Workers' Statute) created the standard that's used today. Under the law, workers receive the promise of healthy working conditions, widespread rights, and a minimum wage. However, not everyone with a job benefits of the law. For example, part-time and seasonal workers enjoy few of the advantages outlined in the statute. Of course those working illegally (and they are legion) have no legal recourse whatsoever. But first things first—let's talk about what the laws promise.

WORKERS' RIGHTS

Discrimination based on gender, race, religion, age, marital status, political opinion, union membership, or social standing is illegal. Likewise, disabled people have equal employment rights and cannot be discriminated against provided that they are able to do the work in question. Children under 16 years old cannot work, and anyone younger than 18 is subject to special laws regarding overtime, nightwork, and hazardous conditions.

Each industry has its own union with both national and regional branches, and those groups help insure that working conditions, the practices of hiring and firing, and the details within labor contracts are

Off the Record

Although Spain has one of Europe's highest unemployment rates—11 percent— the country's economy is one of Europe's fastest growing . . . so how does that work? If you look for the key to that mystery, you won't see it—at least not on the surface. The numbers of people working in Spain are actually far higher than they appear on paper. It's estimated that 20–25 percent of workers in Spain earn cash in hand, so you won't find a trace of them on government records.

Spain has the second biggest cash economy in the developed world (Italy takes the prize), and while the government tosses out 500,000 as the probable number of those working off the books, the true number is almost certainly as much as twice that figure. If you assume that the majority of those involved in *trabajo illegal* (illegal work) are unskilled immigrants who arrive in Spain from developing countries, then you're quite right. You'll find most illegal workers toiling in agriculture and construction jobs. However, you'd be misguided to think that the epidemic is limited to just that one demographic.

The usual reasons a boss employs someone with a just a wink or a handshake rather than a legal contract aren't hard to guess—tax dodging and lower wages. Yet a surprising number of U.S. citizens and citizens of developed, non-EU countries also work jobs without passing through all the legal channels required by Spain. Although the practice is all but unheard of in big corporations, many small companies are willing to run the

all being adhered to. All that sounds great—and in many cases it is. However, not everything is rosy.

While fewer than a quarter of Spain's workers belong to trade unions, the Communist Comisiones Obreras and the socialist Unión General de Trabajadores have a lot of sway when it comes to establishing industry practices. In general, unions vehemently defend high salaries and the terms of employment, and while those are both worthy things to uphold, the battle has created two problems. Because so many employers find labor laws to be rigid, the illegal workforce has expanded dramatically and those who earn their livings illegally have no rights and no benefits. Additionally, the unions' demands have made Spain's labor market one of Europe's most expensive and as a result, multinational companies are picking up and moving elsewhere. Both Samsung and Philips recently closed Barcelona factories—in the case of Samsung, to open shop in Slovakia.

With increasing numbers of multinationals in the world and with offshore business practices becoming more common, labor practices have become extremely complex. Naturally, a country wants to encourage business but not at the expense of workers' rights. It's to Spain's credit that labor practices are so stringent, but the stark reality is that the laws cause some damage, too. Spain's unions are even unique within western

risk of employing a highly skilled employee who doesn't have a working visa.

That brings us to the topic of those risks. What are they? The government wants to put an end to the practice of unaccounted-for money changing hands and if either workers or employers are caught, the penalties can be mighty steep. Enormous fines for both the boss and the worker are levied, and some repeat offenders (meaning the bosses) have been sent to prison. Meanwhile, the illegal workers can be deported and prohibited from returning to Spain for three years.

Despite the potential repercussions, the practice of taking on illegal workers isn't likely to stop anytime soon—it fact, it very well might increase in keeping with the growing numbers of immigrants who are arriving in Spain. Moreover, such workers actually fuel Spain's economy rather than damage it. In most cases, they take on some of the hardest labor in the country while leaving the cushier jobs for the Spaniards. Yet that's not to say that the practice is one to applaud—it's not. Illegal workers have no rights whatsoever, their pay is usually below minimum wage, and should an employer conveniently forget all about payday, illegal immigrants have no course of redress. So while the unemployment rate is deceptively high, the gray numbers that make up the difference between the official stats and the true ones don't paint a pretty picture either.

Europe; more Spanish workdays were lost in the past 30 years due to union strikes than in any other EU country. Good? Bad? It's hard to say—but many speculate that something will have to give soon, or Spain will lose precious business opportunities.

MINIMUM WAGE

Spain does have a minimum wage but fewer than 500,000 people lived on it in 2003. That's really good because the rate is low given the cost of living—just €14.74 a day for an unskilled worker older than 18. (Ouch.) However, people keep their eye on those important numbers because when minimum wage increases, so do wages across the country. The most important aspect of minimum wage is that it sets the standard for salaries throughout the country.

Finance

Perhaps you've already heard the common complaints about the rounding-up effect. No? Well, you will hear grumbling about it once you arrive in Spain—or anywhere in euro-spending Europe, for that matter. The story of the rounding-up effect goes like this: For years, Spain had a currency called the peseta. Neighboring France produced francs, and Italy used the lira. In 2002 things changed, and arguably for the better. Twelve of the 25 member countries in the European Union have adopted a new currency—the euro. (The 10 more countries that became EU members in 2004 can join the euro zone once they have fulfilled the necessary conditions.) The implementation of a single currency was big news and its ramifications are still being felt. The switch to the euro was the biggest monetary changeover in history. The common currency suddenly opened up markets. Business, people, and capital could move more freely between member countries. In other words, the EU countries became stronger after being brought together by a common currency.

And the rounding-up effect? We're getting there. There are many reasons to applaud the amendments the European Union has brought but the road to a stronger, united Europe is a rocky one. The first problem people faced was in the details of the change. On January 1, 2002, Spain cashed in its pesetas and began spending euros. That means that every price set in pesetas—from lunch menus to the cost of cars—had to be converted. What did merchants do when they took out their calculators found that the conversion left them with a pesky decimal point? You guessed it—they rounded up. So every number was inflated except for one: workers' salaries. Suddenly everything cost more and yet people earned just as much as they had before. Most importantly, this story has a moral: Most everyone now thinks that euro-spending Europe is expensive, and that means Spain, too.

That sounds dire, right? It's not—there's good news, too. Thanks in part to EU assistance, Spain just celebrated its 10th consecutive year of uninterrupted growth. Furthermore, the pace of Spain's economic expansion is much stronger than other euro-zone countries. That's a par-

Declaring Money

Before you try walking through customs with a duffle bag full of Ben Franklins, there are a couple things that you should know. You can breeze in and out of the country with cash, checks, and even gold bars that amount to €5,999 ($7,499) or less. But if you try the same thing with amounts between €6,000–30,000 ($7,500–37,500), you might be in big trouble. You can in fact move that amount of money across the Spanish border, but you have to declare it. The government merely wants to know that everything is above board and that you're not an international drug dealer.

If your bank account was filled in small, undeclared increments and you need to re-export a large sum of cash, you should also declare it just to keep everything on the up-and-up. Here's how you take care of business: When entering Spain with gobs of money—that means €6,000–30,000 ($7,500–37,500)—you'll have to fill out a B-1 form at customs. When you receive amounts within those limits or pay such amounts to nonresidents outside of Spain, you should fill out a B-3 form—a simple slip of paper available at the bank that will require names, addresses, and the reason for the financial exchange.

So perhaps you're thinking that amounts greater than €30,000 ($37,500) are free to float across the border unchecked; dream on. The government will be a bit stricter when you start playing with digits that big, and non-EU residents have to receive prior approval to send or receive the cash. You can ask permission of the Dirección General de Transacciones Exteriores by simply completing a B-2 form at your local, Spanish bank.

So will you face a real mess if you accidentally forget to declare the cash? That depends on whether or not you think that having several thousand euros confiscated constitutes a mess. If you do, you should make a mental note to fill out the required forms.

ticularly big achievement given that for almost the whole of the 20th century, Spain was viewed as a backwater compared to the rest of western Europe. At one point, things were so bleak in Spain that thousands of Spaniards were forced to emigrate to neighboring countries in order to earn money. Those days are gone. Today, Spain is a contender.

Cost of Living

Is Spain really that expensive? That depends. People who are accustomed to notoriously costly cities such as New York or San Francisco usually think that the price tag attached to a life in Spain is downright reasonable. Yet others feel that the cost of living in Spain is higher than in the United States. Those voicing this opinion usually lived in more affordable U.S. towns before relocating to say, Madrid—Spain's most expensive city. The answer is further complicated by the fact that prices in one part of Spain vary from those in another part of the country.

Everything from rent to entertainment in Madrid and Barcelona is undeniably costly—more so, in fact, than just about anywhere else in the country. The prices in Spain's two biggest cities are rivaled only by the prices in resort meccas such as Ibiza or Mallorca. The towns there attract masses of wealthy tourists, so not surprisingly, restaurants, entertainment outlets, and landlords charge a lot on everything from food to homes. In smaller cities such as Granada, Valencia, and Seville, prices dip into the mid-range, while small-town life in Spain can be had for bargain-basement prices. Essentially, to say that the cost of living is high or low depends largely on your basis for comparison—both where you're coming from and where you're headed. Still, there are a few key things to know.

The days of the one-dollar-to-one-euro exchange rate are behind us and the euro has taken the lead. Conversion rates fluctuate daily but at the time of writing, one U.S. dollar was worth exactly €0.80. That's no problem at all for those earning euros, but if you earn your salary in dollars, the cost of living will jump up a notch so it's worth doing the math in order to figure out the real cost of things.

While you're in a better position if you're earning euros than you are if you're earning dollars, Spanish salaries are markedly lower than those in the United States. The majority of Spaniards live in their family home until they reach their late 20s or early 30s, and that's for financial reasons more than cultural ones. On a Spanish salary it's extremely difficult to save money for a down payment on a house while also paying rent. So most people need to budget themselves regardless of the currency they earn.

And while you're brushing up on your math, don't forget a little thing known as IVA or *impuesto sobre el valor añadido* (value-added tax). On a restaurant or hotel bill, the IVA is 7 percent. Not too bad. However, the IVA increases to 16 percent on retail goods. Often that tax is included in a quoted price but it's still a good idea to err on the side of caution and ask if IVA is included before plopping down your cash for a given purchase.

BALANCING YOUR BUDGET

In order to balance your budget, you'll have to keep costs down. That means knowing where to shop and, just as importantly, it means knowing what stores to avoid. For household goods, El Corte Inglés is so much more than a department store—it's more like a retail temple. I've asked for recommendations on where to buy items as disparate as socks, soy sauce, rechargeable batteries, and a pedicure, and in every case I've been directed to El Corte Inglés. Wherever you are in Spain, there's almost sure to be a branch near you. So now just a word of advice: if you can, you should avoid making the place a regular haunt. The department store is Spain's one and only, and with no competition out there, its prices have remained maddeningly high. Of course it's wonderfully convenient to have everything including real estate and packaged vacations for sale under one enormous roof, but the cost of that convenience is tremendous. You'll likely find that just about everything sold at El Corte Inglés is also for sale elsewhere and almost always at a lower price. In fact, Spain has a wealth of bargains and items such as beds, sheets, and wastepaper baskets can be had for less than in the States if you shop around.

As for groceries, El Corte Inglés has one of the broadest selections around but once again, at a higher cost. Old-school markets abound— the sort with individual stalls for meat, fish, produce, and dry goods. Small, independent stores with fresh albeit limited selections also have a secure place in every town and city. Both types of markets usually have low prices and if you stock your kitchen that way, groceries can cost as little as €70 ($88) a month per person. However if you don't bargain hunt, groceries will likely cost about €100 ($125) per person.

Not surprisingly, restaurants can vary a great deal in price. A three-course meal for two (with wine) at an exclusive restaurant in Barcelona or Madrid can easily topple into the triple-digits. One way to sample top culinary goods without breaking the bank is to take advantage of the *menú del día* (menu of the day). Spanish culture places great importance on lunch and you're often offered the meal on sale. Many of the nicer restaurants offer a three-course lunch (with a limited selection) for

© Nikki Weinstein

After Christmas, *rebajas* (sales) draw crowds.

as little as €10 ($12.50). True, that's a lot more than a sandwich costs—but it's also a great way to occasionally eat well for relatively little money.

Alternatively, you can dine at a quality mid-range place, where you'll spend about €15 ($19) a head. A wide variety of tapas bars and excellent budget restaurants are also available. Including such places in your dining out experience will invariably help you to manage your budget. Wine, beer, and liquor will quickly increase a bill in the United States but those items can be had for less in Spain. It's near impossible to spend less than $30 for dinner in New York if wine is included, but in Spain you can enjoy a high-quality meal at that price or even less.

Movie tickets go for €5–6 ($6–8). For entrance to a concert, expect to pay about €15 ($19) for smaller shows and as much as €30–40 ($38–50) to see internationally famous musicians play live. Theater tickets also range depending on the level of the performance and the notoriety of the show. Smaller venues charge about €10 ($12.50) while entrance to a show that's causing a critical stir will run about €15 ($19) for a cheap seat and €65 ($81) for a prime view.

Unless you're a Prada junkie, you'll find that in Spain you can dress for a whole lot less than you may be used to spending. Designer stores are as pricey as ever but chain stores such as Zara, H&M, and Mango make appearances in most Spanish cities and those shops are the ones with the real bargains. Zara specializes in convincing, designer knock-offs and it is *the* store of choice for people in their 20s and 30s. While the variety isn't great, the value is. Spain is not the land of the independent boutique in the way France is, but prices for clothing are low. That means a pair of pants or a sweater can cost as little as €20 ($25). Even chic stores such as Adolfo Domínguez sell their upscale duds for much less than the same items would cost in the United States.

Most Spanish cities have excellent public transportation and the country's trains are convenient and affordable. Consequently, cars are not the necessity that they are in much of the United States. If you're living in a city you can likely forgo owning wheels of your own, thus knocking all your car expenses right out of your budget. However you will need a car in smaller towns. The costs involved are as follows: a minimal fee for a driver's license—€13 ($16); the mandatory registration fee—€52 ($65); inspections for cars more than four years old—€26 ($33); insurance starting at around €135 ($169) annually for minimal coverage. The cost of a car itself is a little higher than it would be in the United States, in part thanks to IVA—that tax increases the total price. Gas also costs more but on the other end of that equation, you may find that your car has better mileage.

> *Unless you're a Prada junkie, you'll find that in Spain you can dress for a whole lot less than you may be used to spending.*

The cost of real estate runs the gamut. Naturally, luxury properties still cost a pretty penny but such homes can be had for less than the same house would cost in most of urban America. Of course, the better the neighborhood, the higher the price will be. But overall, you'll likely be pleased with the numbers you encounter. There is one important addition to note. You'll find yourself in a good position as a buyer if you're arriving in Spain with savings to put towards a home. However, if you plan to save for a down payment while earning a Spanish salary, you'll probably be in a stickier spot. The majority of Spanish wages leave little room for significant savings.

It's safe to assume that your telephone will total more than your U.S. phone bill did. Telefónica adds a 16 percent IVA to the total and you'll probably pay €25 ($31) on every bill just for basic service. On top of that, you are charged for each outgoing call—even local ones—and that means the total on a two-month bill can add up quickly if the entire family is using one line.

In Spain, local municipalities control the water and thus the cost varies from one district to another. However, most areas charge either quarterly or monthly for minimum consumption—that can be as low as €7 ($9) with a 7 percent IVA added.

Electricity bills also arrive bimonthly and a 16 IVA is added. Naturally bills fluctuate depending on how much electricity is used, but for two people sharing a modestly sized home, expect to pay an average of about €35 ($44) a month. If your home is supplied by gas, the bills also arrive every two months and are taxed at 16 percent. The bill will be about equal to your electricity bill.

Salaries for domestic help are relatively low—€650 ($813) is a standard monthly salary for live-in help to assist with babysitting and housekeeping every day but Sunday. If you're just looking for someone to give your home a good scrubbing once a week, that service typically costs about €8 ($10) per hour. Some people hire illegal immigrants for domestic jobs and that's a risky proposition. If you go the illegal route and are caught, the penalties are steep and you might have to go to court. It's much safer to seek nannies and housekeepers through official agencies, or at the very least to be sure that the person you've hired has working papers.

If you were paying for your own health insurance in the United States, you'll be delighted to count your savings on health care in Spain. Anyone contributing to the country's social security is entitled to the free or low-cost national health care service. For those who are not eligible for that benefit, private insurance is still wildly more affordable than it is in the United States. Coverage through an independent company typically costs less than €100 ($125). It can even cost as little as €50 ($63) a month and is available to, well, just about anyone willing to pay. Compare that to the monthly fees for a basic HMO in the United States and you'll see that those numbers look darn good.

Banking

It's more than advisable to open a Spanish bank account—in most cases it's a necessity. In Spain, people view checks as being almost as obsolete as horses and buggies. When it comes time to pay your monthly utilities, the total is usually deducted directly from your bank account. Some landlords require that rent be automatically transferred each month to their accounts. Additionally, if you use an ATM card from a Spanish bank, you'll be able to avoid paying service fees. U.S. banks have relatively few branches in Spain and you're far better off with a local account in order to avoid scouring a city for a lone branch of your home bank.

Spanish banks won't seem so different from their American counterparts—all the same basics are available. You can open checking and saving accounts, secure loans, use ATM machines, and charge just about everything to your debit or credit card (both issued by the bank). Still, a few minor differences do exist and in some cases foreigners are subject to different rules.

Most banks in Spain fall into one of two categories—clearing banks and savings banks. The difference between the two isn't in the services but in the ownership. Savings banks don't have shareholders; they were founded with charity in mind, and profits are invested in cultural and agricultural projects. Both clearing and savings banks offer the same services. Among the country's more popular banks are Argentaria, Banco Banesto, Banco Bilbao Vizcaya (BBVA), Banco Central Hispano, Banco Popular, Banco Santander, La Caixa, Caja de Madrid, and Caja Postal.

CURRENCY

One hundred cents amounts to one euro. Coins are easily distinguished at a glance. Each one is a different size, some are copper-colored, others look silver, and a few appear gold. Coin money comes in denominations of 1-, 2-, 5-, 10-, 20-, 50-cents, single euros, and two euros. The designs

© Nikki Weinstein

Prices hang alongside Spain's iconic legs of ham.

on one side of the coins indicate the country in which the money was minted. Paper money is uniform throughout the whole of the EU—there's nothing country-specific about it. Cash is also sized and colored to be easily recognizable with just a quick look into your wallet. The bills come in denominations of 5-, 10-, 20-, 50-, 100-, 200-, and 500-euros. Most ATM machines give out bills up to 50 euros and you'll rarely receive anything higher.

Exchange Rates

If you read the financial pages, you already know that the currency value can change from one day to the next. Exchange rates are fickle. Don't assume that the euros you can buy for a $20 bill on a given Monday will buy you just as many by the next Thursday. Many people still think that the dollar and the euro have a one-to-one exchange rate but in fact they don't—the euro is currently stronger. Over a short period of time, the change in rate is generally not dramatic but still, the dollar and euro are consistently changing in value and it's important to keep up with those developments. If you intend to wire dollars into your Spanish bank account, they'll be transferred to euros at the day's exchange rate and thus it's a good idea to transfer more money when the rate works in your favor. If you don't do that and you instead wire money at a low moment for the dollar, you can lose a fair amount in the process of a simple bank transaction. Moreover, if you don't keep up with the exchange rate you won't know what you're truly spending on anything.

OPENING AN ACCOUNT

If you hold a residence visa, you can open a checking account easily—just present your passport and foreigner identification number (the one printed on residence cards). Nonresidents can also open accounts with just a passport and a certificate of nonresidence. To get your hands on that mandatory piece of paper, go to the local police department and expect to wait in a line about as long as the ones at the Department of Motor Vehicles in the United States. Once you make it to the front of the line the worst is over. It usually takes about 10 days before the paperwork is processed. Then you can retrieve your certificate and take it to the bank to get things moving. However, for a small fee some banks will handle the issue of the certificate on behalf of their clients. To avoid a potential five-hour wait at the police station, it's well worth seeking that option.

Spanish banks can charge high fees for everyday transactions so it's advisable to inquire into expenses before setting up your account. Sometimes you can find a deal, and banks may change their fee policies, so

For a Real Steal . . .

When you arrive in Spain, well-meaning friends will advise you to hang onto your wallet, to watch your bag, to mind your cellular phone, to be careful at ATM machines, and they'll urge you to be especially vigilant in big cities. Why such cause for alarm? Petty crime is rampant in Spain. It seems that everyone has a story in which they were duped or else someone they know was.

Yep, I have a story, too, and I even play the starring role in it—sucker. While on the Madrid metro during rush hour, a visiting American friend and I were chatting away in English. When a guy standing nearby leaned in to ask the time, I didn't wonder why he chose to ask a foreigner

who, for all he knew, didn't speak Spanish. Instead, I happily obliged by answering. But he wanted to confirm down to the minute, so I double-checked my watch and again told him the time. While my friend and I thought we were doing the a guy a favor, someone behind me had unzipped my bag and helped himself to my wallet—cash, credit cards, and all. Until I stepped off the metro I was none the wiser.

Countless scams exist, and here are a couple of the big ones: you're on an escalator and someone in front of you trips, flails, and goes down. It's an acrobatic spectacle and you're likely the target audience for that show because while you're watching, the person behind you is prob-

shop around in order to make sure that you're settling on the most affordable option. Typically, you'll have 30 free transactions a year, after which you'll be charged a few cents per transaction. Some people have had luck waiving additional fees by speaking to the branch managers—it's certainly worth a try although there is no guarantee that you'll meet with success.

When setting up your account, bear in mind that most Spaniards have two last names. Many American have discovered that the bank erroneously filed their records under their middle names—undoubtedly innocent mistakes in which bank employees mistook middle names for last names. In order to avoid unnecessary confusion, just use first and last names on your account.

It's standard practice for Americans to hang onto one account in the United States while using another account in Spain. A good many U.S. citizens transfer money from their U.S. accounts into their Spanish ones, especially those who earn dollars while in Europe. When your greenbacks reach your local bank via wire transfer or traveler's checks, they'll automatically be converted to euros. Should you want to transfer euros to the United States that's also easily done.

A combined debit/ATM card comes with checking accounts. Debit cards function just as they do in the United States—you'll charge items as if you're using a credit card but instead of paying a monthly bill, the money is immediately deducted from your account. Your ATM card can

ably taking your wallet. Another common move takes place at ATM machines. You've just hit the requisite numbers and while you're waiting for your cash and card, someone steps up and kindly points out that you've dropped a 10-euro bill. You look down and . . . hey! What do you know? There are 10 euros on the ground. You thank your thief, bend down to pick up the fallen money, and by the time you've stood up again the supposed good Samaritan has made off with your cash, card, and even your PIN number if he watched you punch it in.

Of course you need to be cautious but also remember that not everyone is angling to pick your pocket and most peo-ple are quick to jump in and help strangers out. The bottom line is that you should be careful and if you are, you shouldn't face any problems. However, if in an unlucky moment someone does find a clever way to part you from your wallet, be prepared by keeping a spare credit card set aside as well as a small re-serve of cash. Lastly (and I know I'll sound like a commercial saying this), it's partic-ularly useful to have an American Express card even if you've lost the physical card itself. The company can overnight a new one out to you even on holidays or week-ends. As it turns out, you can actually leave home without the card—just have one in your name.

be used at bank machines throughout the country. The three groups that operate the machines are 4B, Servired, and Tarjeta 6000 and you can use your card with any of those systems. Your bank will have an affiliation with one of the three operating systems and service fees are waived when you use a machine run by that same system. However, a service charge is incurred every time you use an ATM machine run by a differ-ent group. You can deduct as much as €300 ($375) from your account in one day.

Bank loans are not difficult to secure so long as you're a resident and you can offer some collateral. Those who own homes in Spain tend to have better luck securing loans, but holding Spanish property is not a re-quirement. Interest rates span a broad spectrum depending on the bank, the amount requested, and the duration of the loan. Speak with officers at several banks before signing the paperwork in order to see what fi-nancial options are available.

CREDIT CARDS

Just as in the United States, most people in Spain are happy to put it on plastic. You'll have no trouble finding merchants who accept Visa, Mas-terCard and even American Express (though that card is less broadly ac-cepted than it is in the United States). Because Spain's rate of petty theft is so high, it's now required that customers present picture identi-fication with a credit card in order to avoid fraud. A U.S. driver's license or passport will suffice, but many stores turn down photocopied duplicates. You can have a credit card through your Spanish bank if you're a resident, but if you take your U.S. credit cards, you can continue to use them without any problems and many people opt for that.

If you have a credit card through your local bank you'll soon see that while it looks just like a U.S. one, it has one distinct difference. You can only spend up to the limit that you have in your bank account and no further. The upshot of that restriction is that you won't ever be burdened with credit-card debt. On the other hand, you won't be able to slap luxuries on your card if your bank account is running low.

Taxes

The Spanish dread paying taxes as much as anyone and just a short time ago tax evasion was so common in Spain, it was almost the norm. The system is less lenient today. The government penalizes tax dodgers with stiff fines and that has decreased evasion. Historically, taxation was lower in Spain than the EU average. That's still true although the disparity is smaller than it once was.

Although it's important to understand the tax system, bear in mind that laws are consistently amended and your individual finances and residency status can change things dramatically. The best way to handle a brand-new and completely foreign set of tax laws is to consult a professional who can help you stay within the guidelines of the law and even work the system in your favor.

SPANISH TAXES

The Spanish tax year runs from January 1 to December 31 and taxes must be filed between May 1 and June 20. The necessary forms for filing must be purchased. Some are sold in *estancos* (tobacco shops). Others are available exclusively from the Agencia Tributaria (tax office).

Three separate branches of the government have the right to impose taxes: the central government, autonomous regional governments, and local municipalities. However, income, capital gains, wealth, and inheritance taxes—four of the biggies—are all paid to the Agencia Estatal de Administración Tributaria, commonly known as the Hacienda (public finance department).

Ultimately, individuals might be responsible for paying as many as 17 different kinds of taxes including a garbage tax for property owners and a motor vehicles tax that applies to car owners. Even the tourist lounging at a Marbella resort will end up paying a chunk of change to the government in the form of IVA. Restaurant and hotels tack on a 7 percent increase due to IVA, and the tax is further bumped up to 16 percent for retail goods, rented car, and even services such as utilities. The general rule mandates that the tax on necessary goods such as food and medicine drops to 7 percent, but anything deemed unessential is taxed at 16 percent.

Income taxes are tricky and calculating the amount owed ultimately depends on whether or not you are a resident. For tax purposes, you're a resident if you live in Spain for 183 days out of the year or if the majority of your financial interests are in Spain. In either of those cases, you must pay income taxes on both earned and unearned incomes (the latter category includes investments, etc.). However, deductions are permissible and the rate of taxation can range from 17 to 45 percent depending on your net income. Now for some good news: You need not file at all if your taxes are being withheld and you earn less than €21,035 ($26,300). Nonresidents also might have to pay taxes and in those cases the sliding scale is discarded for a flat rate of 25 percent on all their income earned.

> *The best way to handle a brand-new and completely foreign set of tax laws is to consult a professional who can help you stay within the guidelines of the law.*

If you own property, you'll have to pay an annual property tax to the municipality where your home is registered—the rate fluctuates according to the cadastral value of the property. (That's the official value of the property and it's typically much lower than market value). Factors such as location and size of the land also affect the amount owed.

It probably won't come as a shock to learn that hiring accountants is a way of life in Spain. A huge portion of the Spanish population takes advantage of the services offered by financial professionals, but accountants are particularly useful to foreigners. A professional can spare you the burden of trying to figure out a tax system wholly unfamiliar to you, and they also know the system well enough to save you money. Numerous accountants throughout Spain cater to foreigners and many are bilingual.

AMERICAN TAXES

All U.S. citizens and residents must file their annual income tax forms regardless of where they live. However, that doesn't necessarily mean that you have to pay U.S. taxes. If you spend the majority of your time in Spain, it's the place where you earn your income, you're a tax resident, and your total Spanish income is $80,000 or less, you do not have to pay U.S. income taxes thanks to the Foreign Earned Income Exclusion. If you're worried that you'll be doubly taxed on an income exceeding $80,000, you can relax. Spain and the United States have a treaty to avoid double taxation. The details of that law are complex and you should speak to an accountant to know how to handle that.

Most bilingual accountants in Spain are more familiar with the U.K. tax laws than they are U.S. ones, but there are a few exceptions. One solution is to seek out financial assistance within the United States. A number of U.S. accountants specialize in taxes for expatriate people. Despite the ocean dividing Spain and the States, working with an American accountant is easily done thanks to email.

Investing

There are a couple of ways to invest in your adopted country. If you own property or run a business, that's one form of investment. Alternatively, you can create a financial portfolio with stocks, bonds, and the like. Both have their benefits but when it comes to the latter category, you should proceed with extreme caution.

MARKETS
There are two substantial reasons why you might want to invest in Spain. If it's your new home, you'll probably want to support it and that means financially, too. An investment in Spain is an inherently optimistic endeavor—it says that you believe in the country. The second reason to invest is strictly financial. When the dollar weakens and the euro strengthens, some people scramble to invest in the euro. Even people living in the United States want to protect their nest egg, and having holdings in strong currencies is one way to do that.

Spain has four stock exchanges—in Barcelona, Madrid, Valencia, and Bilbao—and a national securities commission. You can follow all their activity online (www.spainuscc.org/eng/blinks/finance.html). Among the more popular investments are shares, mutual funds, and bonds—pretty much what you'd expect. However, before you rush out to invest, take a deep breath and slow down. You'll have to do your research first.

HOW TO INVEST
Before handing over your savings, you need to know both the market and a little something about your financial advisor. Spain is notorious for scams it's not uncommon for tricksters posing as financial advisors to lose

every penny of their clients' money in swindles disguised as investments. Plenty of financially savvy people have been sold a bill of goods.

Anyone can become a financial advisor in Spain regardless of qualifications. When you choose an advisor, make sure that you request references and check them. Also ask for a documented track record. When you begin to invest, move slowly. Have a diverse portfolio and be sure that it doesn't contain all of your savings. Begin with modest amounts of money and once you see the outcome, you can add more. To find a financial advisor seek out recommendations from people you know. Plenty of professionals advertise, too, and if you go that route, enter the relationship cautiously and ask around to find out the firm's reputation.

DAILY EXPRESS

INTERNATIONAL
Herald Tribune

Bigger than Harry Potter
The latest global publishing phenomenon Page 14

How lean is your hierarchy?
Get the balance right – FT Summer School Page 9

PLUS: Bonds in crisis – has Greenspan lost his magic touch? Page 11

FINANCIAL TIMES
Thursday August 14

THE WALL STREET JOURNAL EUROPE.

BESTSELLER EVERY DAY
The Daily Telegraph

THE INDEPENDENT
EUROPEAN EDITION

DIE WELT

e, die von drei Gramm leben: Goldgräber in Sibirien / Seite 3

ddeutsche Zeitung

Allgemeine

Communications

N ever mind those old horror stories about people arriving in Spain and spending half a day trying to make an international call only to succeed in securing a line full of static. Those accounts are as obsolete as rotary-dial phones. Spain is wired, so phoning, faxing, and emailing is not a struggle. For lower-tech needs, the postal service is speedy and reliable. Moreover, city residents can fully modernize their homes with a high-speed Internet connection. That same option is hitting more remote locations all the time.

Telephone Service

All *fijo* (landline) numbers in Spain consist of nine digits and the first two or three of the set indicates town or city. That means that Madrid numbers begin with 91, Valencia numbers start with 96, San Sebastián uses the prefix 943, and so on. Those initial numbers are always included in dialing, even for local calls. Cellular-phone numbers in Spain always start with six and if you call such a number from a landline, you'll pay more than you would if reaching a *fijo* line. To contact a local operator dial tel. 1009, and to reach directory services, call tel. 1003 (for a charge of approximately €0.30 or $0.38). Spain's country code is 34 and precedes any Spanish number that's dialed from abroad. If calling another country from within Spain, 00 must be added before the country code and number. Dialing tel. 1008 will put you in touch with an international operator.

LANDLINES

When you set up a fixed landline, your provider will almost certainly be Telefónica. A few companies such as Jazztel and Madritel have recently begun to compete with Telefónica, and that's a great beginning to driving prices down. However, such corporations are miniscule by comparison and they're not yet in the position to serve the majority of customers. Although using the phone is easy enough, those moments of idle chat don't come cheap. Until recently, Telefónica was the national company and although it privatized in 1997, it still owns almost all of the country's phone infrastructure. That fact alone eliminates all substantial competition and means prices have remained as exorbitant as ever. Rates change constantly and occasional deals can chip away at the cost. But the basic facts are as follows: a line can be installed for €90 ($115) and for just a little more, you can rent a phone as well. Most people opt for the rental and pay the nominal monthly fee for the extra equipment. Bear in mind that the company's phones are never cordless. You can also buy a phone through Telefónica although if you want to own your telephone, you can save money by looking elsewhere—Telefónica sells phones at one price only and it's above average.

There are two ways to have a line installed. You can stop by one of the company's many stores—you'll recognize the trademark blue and yellow signs in towns throughout Spain. Be sure to take your passport and proof of address such as your lease or deed. Alternatively, you can dial tel. 1004 from any telephone to set up a time for installation. The company assures a wait of 7–10 days before installation. The lucky few receive service within that time, but others have wait for as long as a month. It's impossible to predict what your wait will be, but it's fair to assume that if you're in a city, you'll receive a line sooner than those in remote locations. In some unfortunate cases (albeit rare ones), the wait stretches on for what feels like an interminable amount

Most people have cellular phones but public ones still abound.

Cellular phones are easy to come by.

of time. If that occurs you can try to duke it out with a company representative, but a word of caution. Telefónica is a leviathan and stories of people winning arguments with the company are passed around like urban legends. Most people rely on cellular phones for the duration. Once your line is installed, the monthly fee for service alone tallies €12.60 ($15.75).

Bills arrive every two months and they're most often automatically deducted from clients' bank accounts. Personal checks are generally a thing of the past in Spain, and while most utility companies prefer automatically deducting the cost of bills each month, Telefónica all but requires it. Your only other option is to pay cash bimonthly at a company store or at one of two Spanish banks, Banesto or BBVA. To do this, there's no need to have accounts with the banks, just your phone number and the amount owed will suffice. A 16 percent IVA (value added tax) is added to the total.

Domestic Rates

Unlike in the United States, local calls aren't free. The day divides into two parts for billing purposes—peak hours and reduced hours. A local call placed 8 A.M.–8 P.M. (peak hours) costs €0.02 ($0.03) per minute. The same call made from 8 P.M.–8 A.M. (reduced hours) incurs a charge of €0.01 ($0.013) per minute. Calling another province will raise your bill a little more; a peak-hour call goes for €0.06 ($0.08) a minute while the reduced rate is €0.03 ($0.04) for every minute you're on the line. Dialing to a cellular phone costs a few cents more than the same call would cost to a landline. The precise difference depends on the recipient's company, but it's usually about 25 percent more costly.

International Rates

Making an international call without a special plan or phone card is break-the-bank pricey. While Telefónica offers some passing-grade plans, your best bet for low-rate calling is to rely on the *tarjetas telefónicas* (phone cards) sold at news kiosks and *estancos* (tobacco stores). The companies that produce such cards are myriad and new ones appear all the time. Be careful with those cards—some trap you by charging a steep connection fees while others don't, so read the fine print. The better brands of cards offer as many as 260 minutes to the United States for €10 ($12.50). Another good option is using a separate long distance carrier, such as Retevisión, reachable at tel. 015, or Uni 2, which you can contact at tel. 1414.

CELLULAR PHONES

Just like in the United States and pretty much everywhere else in the world, cellular phones are enormously popular in Spain. There were more than 26 million in the country in 2002 and that number is growing still. You won't have to look far to buy a cell phone of your own. They're sold in a variety of stores and the models run the gamut from the sleek and costly to the merely functional and shamelessly cheap. You'll undoubtedly recognize many of the same phone models that are popular in the United States. However there is one crucial difference: unless you have a special U.S. model, your old phone from home is no good in Spain. Europe operates on the GSM 900/1800 system and North America uses GSM 1900. Companies manufacture phones accordingly and the two systems are incompatible. Europe's phones are great for travel on the continent as most models can be used in other European countries. Unfortunately, the European system also fosters a huge market in stolen cellular phones, unlike in the United States where a phone isn't much good once it is disconnected from the service provider. Be careful. Leaving your phone on a table or bar top is risky behavior.

Phone Companies

When you buy your phone you'll invariably be assured trouble-free reception, but some companies are better than others depending on the area. To find out which company best services your part of the country, ask around (excluding those who want to sell you phones) and you'll easily find out which company you should go with. Among the more popular companies are Movistar (which is part of Telefónica), Amena, and Vodaphone.

Rates

Amounts per call vary but incoming calls are always free. As to payment plans, you'll have an option to sign a contract for a fixed rate or buy a prepaid phone—one that relies on cards to add credit. If you choose the latter option, tobacco shops, newsstands, department stores, and convenience stores all sell the necessary cards usually starting at about €10 ($12.50). Most companies also allow you to buy credit both online and at bank machines. A few contracts have a minimum duration of a year while others allow you to set the contract's time frame. Before signing a contract, ask about the dates so you don't find yourself stuck with an unnecessary financial obligation.

Email and Postal Service

Snail mail or email—it's all in Spain. The postal service is reliable and Internet companies abound. You can get fully wired for reasonable prices or go the old-fashioned route instead by mailing off brown paper packages tied up with string.

INTERNET ACCESS

A 2002 survey found that only 17 out of every 100 Spanish homes have Internet access, a lower number than in the rest of Europe. Internet access jumped in 2003, but still only 23 percent of homes are connected. That doesn't mean that it's hard to find Internet providers, but the choices are thinner than elsewhere and some of the remoter parts of the country don't yet accommodate DSL lines. That said, city residents have no trouble getting Internet connection and the prices are similar to those in the United States.

For a dial-up connection, the service itself is free but you do pay per call and that can be as much as five cents a minute. You can avoid excessive charges by using a *tarifa plana* (flat fee). That is, you pay a flat rate—usually about €20 ($25) a month—instead of shelling out with each call. However, some companies have hourly restrictions and limit the amount of time you can spend online each month. If you want a DSL line (that's ADSL in Spanish), the average cost is €40 ($50) a month, although initial service fees are tacked on to that. The most widely used companies are Wanadoo, Auna, and Terra (see Resources for contact information). Dubious companies will inundate you with offers of free Internet service, but beware; the service provided is 20th-century slow as those deals pass on an avalanche of publicity and ads along with their service. It's far better to go with one of the standard companies even though you'll have to pay.

> You can get fully wired for reasonable prices or go the old-fashioned route instead by mailing off brown paper packages tied up with string.

If you use a Mac, be sure to look into that before signing up for a service with any company as not all the Internet providers can offer you service. Companies are starting to become Mac friendly, but not all of them are there yet.

POST OFFICE AND COURIERS

Most post offices open for business on weekdays at 8:30 A.M., ignore the siesta and work until 8:30 P.M. Business hours on Saturday usually start at 9 A.M. and end at 1:30 P.M. But there is some variation in working hours and smaller villages have especially erratic hours.

Letters posted in Spain reach their U.S. destinations within 5–10 days and domestic mail is much faster. Unfortunately, that same pace slows considerably with packages. One way to circumvent the problem is to mail by *correo aéreo* (air mail) as the land-to-boat-to-land option can take weeks and sometimes longer. You'll have to shell out some extra euros for the service but if you choose that option, you do get what you pay for. If you're desperate for a same-day or next-day delivery at whatever cost, courier companies such as Seur will be happy to take your money and help you out. Seur delivers throughout the European Union, to the United States as well as to other counties—its U.S. sibling is Airborne Express. The company's offices are located throughout Spain, but not surprisingly, the bigger the city, the more Seur branches there are.

Within Spain, a letter costs about €0.26 ($0.33). Postage for the same to the United States costs about €0.75 ($0.94). Letters sent *certificado* (registered) incur an additional charge of €2.10 ($2.60) if they're sent internationally and if you want something sent *urgente* (urgent) you'll pay approximately €1.75 ($2.20) more. For postage alone, there's

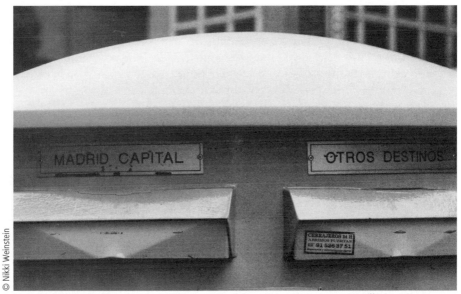

You don't have to go to the post office to mail a letter—you can just use a mailbox on the street.

no need to trek all the way to the post office and wait in line—most tobacco shops can also sell you the goods.

Media

Be it breaking news or celebrity gossip, you can read, hear, or watch up-to-the-minute reports and get play-by-play action. You'll find newsstands on just about every corner, the radio gets big play, and people watch a *lot* of television in Spain. You won't ever have to wonder what's going on in the rest of the world.

NEWSPAPERS AND MAGAZINES

Spain prints more than 155 daily newspapers. A few are national but the bulk of them are local. You'll also find a number of weeklies and foreign papers on news kiosks. Nationally, newspaper sales look meager (about one daily sold for every 8–10 people) but because Spaniards commonly share papers, the actual readership is much higher than that. The big three for daily news are *El País*, *El Mundo*, and *ABC*. All three are mainstream but political leanings vary. *El País* is farthest to the left, *El Mundo* takes the center, and *ABC* slants to right. Politics aside, all three offer solid coverage both nationally and internationally and the trio sell at most newsstands.

Among the many regional papers, a few of the better-known include *La Vanguardia* and *El Periódico* in Barcelona, *Sur* in Andalusia, *La Semana* and *Cinco Días* in Madrid, and *Deia* and *Gara* in Basque Country. If you plan to read those last two in their entirety, a good knowledge of Basque helps. Both periodicals feature articles in Spanish as well as the Basque regional language.

Towns with large populations of foreigners offer a wider selection of international and foreign newspapers, but even small towns usually have a smattering of English pages at their kiosks. *USA Today* lights up newsstands with its brightly colored pages and the *International Herald Tribune* (owned by the *New York Times*) is also easy to come by. The latter shares some of its articles with the *Times*, and although the paper itself is much thinner than its American parent, the *Tribune* offers a proportionally heftier version of foreign news and also includes an English-language insert of *El País*'s top stories. Both *USA Today* and the *International Herald Tribune* usually make it onto the stands the day of publication. Occasionally, you'll find a *New York Times*, *Washington Post* or another U.S. paper, but they're usually a few days old and sell for inflated prices.

> You'll find newsstands on just about every corner, the radio gets big play, and people watch a lot of television in Spain. You won't ever have to wonder what's going on in the rest of the world.

International magazines abound. Good places to look for them are El Corte Inglés, FNAC (the French department store), and VIPS (an all-purpose chain store). *The Economist* and international versions of *Time* and *Newsweek* are standard fare but even men's magazines, women's magazines, and an occasional *New Yorker* can be found if you patiently hunt through the shelves. Yes, the prices will be higher than you're used to paying back in the United States, but for the true media junkie, a fix of glossy pages can be well worth a few extra euros.

TELEVISION

If you typically complain about the sorry state of television in the United States, you won't find any relief when you kick back for a relaxing evening of talk shows and dubbed-over, three-year-old episodes of *ER* in Spain. In fact, the programming in Spain is a big step down on the quality scale. That might sound hard to believe but just wait until you catch a few of the ubiquitous talk shows—they make Jenny Jones look like PBS. Even so, TVs get a lot of play in Spain, both at home and in bars where people are likely to crowd around any television featuring a soccer game. As to the unfortunate programming situation, well, there

Pink and White and Read All Over

Nothing can help you jump into the office water-cooler talk like a dutiful study of the *prensa rosa* (pink press, a.k.a gossip rags), and a thorough examination of sports news doesn't hurt either.

Spain's ample *presna rosa* provides heavy doses of romantic rumors and tales of the inexplicably rich and famous (and really tan). It's likely that you'll begin your studies by staring at strangers in pictures and wondering who all those lovelies splashing in the Ibiza waves actually are. Don't worry. You'll soon have names memorized and gossip down pat. Before you know it, you'll be able to jump right into the chatter when the latest scandal is brought up.

The sports pages will give you all the latest soccer news, and by "news" I mean big controversies, such as the one surrounding Jésus Gil y Gil, the former mayor of Marbella and the now scandalous owner of Madrid's lovable losers, Atlético. Musings on Real Madrid's hottest player, David Beckham—the international megastar who came to Madrid in 2003—are also guaranteed to make it into the papers, as are straight-up stats.

If the idea of reading these periodicals leaves you cold, well, scoff if you must but conversations about the most recent soccer match and juicy celebrity pairings erupt all around—in the office, on the metro, at cafés. If you want to join in, these magazines and papers can give you the background you'll need.

Here are the details: *¡Hola!* will fill you in on the happenings of international superstars as well as Spain's celebrities. Fashion is covered and even small doses of politics get some ink on these pages. For gossip that's a little cruder but a whole lot more fun, check out *Semana*. Just as its name suggests, it's a weekly and it will fill you in on facts and rumor alike, sometimes not even bothering to differentiate between the two. *¡Qué Me Dices!* is yet another rumor-mill on the printed page. It's not exactly quality but you can't possibly hate a paper with a title that translates into "What Are You Telling Me!"—it's not asking to be taken seriously, so just enjoy it.

Sport delivers a hefty dose of information on exactly what its name promises and it hits the newsstands every day. *Marca,* another athletics-only paper, is also a daily and it seems to be the reading material of choice in bars and trains around the country.

Spend enough time pouring over these pages and you'll soon be able to wax on about the small but entertaining happenings throughout Spain—in other words, you'll be in the pink.

is some good news: while Spanish television is awful, there's always cable and satellite—and they change everything.

Under Franco's regime, television was regarded as a state public service and only one channel existed until 1965. Things changed in 1980 when control diversified and today, Retevisión (a private entity) oversees Spain's telecommunications system. Currently, television sans cable includes five main channels. The original two (now called TVE1 and TVE2) are still public. However, some areas have local channels that don't air elsewhere. For example TV3 and Canal 33, both broadcast solely in Catalan, while the channels ETB1 and ETB2 air in Basque Country. ETB1 is all-Spanish while ETB2 offers programming in Basque.

Spain's cable and satellite companies have been steadily expanding and merging in recent years. For now the main providers are Canal Plus, which features dubbed U.S. films as well as a variety of sports, and RTVE Grupo, which offers more entertainment and a hefty dose of news and documentaries. Canal Satellite airs children's shows, soap operas, documentaries, and more. Canal Satellite recently took over Via Digital and plans for the near future include more than 75 channels, 20 interactive channels and 50 radio channels.

Receiving international channels requires satellite or sky digital equipment—getting that is not usually a problem although those living in apartments sometimes need the approval of building management. Satellite brings in BBC channels and CNN Sky digital channels as well as a long menu of other options.

Videos and DVDs from the United States don't work in Spain, nor do televisions unless the box is multisystem. (The United States uses NTSC while Spain relies on the PAL system.) A few of the TV sets have an A/B switch that allows you to see some of the dubbed films and programs in the original language should you want to lose the dubbing. If you're just learning Spanish, the subtitle option offered for the hearing impaired on some televisions functions as great training wheels.

RADIO

Radio plays in just about every taxi, home, and store in Spain. Literally hundreds of stations broadcast throughout the country. That marks a huge change from the days of Franco, when the airwaves were heavily regulated and it seemed only the dictator's pals could get a license to broadcast. Radio Nacional de España (RNE) controls the state stations which include Radio 1, a straight-up talk-radio station with a focus on news, politics, society, and even some children's programming. Radio 3 places more of an emphasis on culture—both national and international as well as some music. Radio 5 is all news, all the time. Radio Clásica (also run by RNE) broadcasts classical music. Other privately owned stations fill the dial with pop music—especially the FM stations. The daily newspaper *El País* publishes a guide to local stations in its *Cartelera* section.

If you're craving the sound of English, you can find the BBC World Service on several frequencies including 6195kHz and 9410kHz. Voice of America requires a short-wave radio. If you have one, try 6040kHz and 9760kHz. The Internet has also expanded radio options as U.S. stations can be streamed online. This offers a nice taste of home, even if you have to listen to the morning traffic report in the late afternoon.

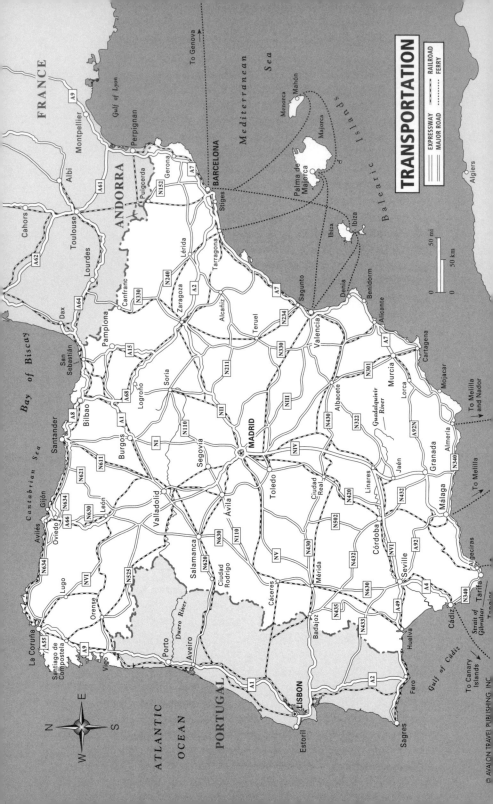

Travel and Transportation

S ome say Europe is a continent for train travelers, but they're really talking about the Europe of a bygone era. Although Spain's train service is far superior to its U.S. counterpart, the country's enormous web of roads is also intricate and far-reaching, and it seems as though new roads are always under construction. Cars are commonplace—arguably too commonplace in Madrid, which is choked with traffic during the days. However, you don't have to sit in a stationary traffic jam that's backed up for blocks if you don't want to. Spain's public transportation is excellent. All the country's major metropolitan areas have metros and buses that can easily move you from one corner of the city to another. But perhaps that's leaping ahead. Before you even think about how you'll get around Spain, you'll have to handle just getting into the country.

By Air

For a relatively small country, Spain is chock full of international airports including ones in Barcelona, Málaga, and Palma de Mallorca. But chances are good that Madrid's Barajas airport—the most trafficked in the country—will be your hub when it comes to flying in and out of Spain. The city's position in the center of Spain makes it an ideal jumping-off point to destinations all around Spain, and perhaps that's one reason why so many national flights go via Madrid. From the capital you can connect to all parts of Spain including the Canary Islands, Seville, Bilbao or just about anywhere in the world. The international flights at smaller airports are usually chartered planes or a few flights that shuttle off to Lisbon or London every day. For the most part, those airports are for national travel.

It might surprise you that Spanish people rely on air travel to move around the country, but the price for a ticket can be well worth it when you consider what's saved in time. For example, a flight from Madrid to Barcelona takes a little more than an hour but by train that same journey takes about five hours. If you find a well-priced ticket on a direct flight, why not fly? On the other hand, connections tack more time onto your trip so shop around and compare itineraries. Iberia is Spain's best-known airline and also its broadest reaching one, but it isn't the country's only company for air travel. Try Spanair or Air Europa for tickets, too—both fly throughout Spain. You'll have a few options so you can price your travel out and make sure that you're settling on the best deal.

National tickets can add up fast if you're booking to a holiday destination with little advance notice. Plan ahead, especially during the summer, Christmas, and Easter when it seems as if the entire country is vacation-bound. To find deals, check out sales advertised in newspapers or just walk into any travel agency—and there are plenty of them around. Don't overlook the Internet either. That's where most of the good finds will be hidden. Rumbo (www.rumbo.es) manages to offer tickets for less than most agencies. Viajar (www.viajar.com) also does a good job, and eDreams (www.edreams.es) is another popular travel site.

Looking online will likely turn up the best offers for international fares, too, and Ryanair (www.ryanair.com) and Easyjet (www.easyjet.com) specialize in shockingly cheap flights throughout Europe. You'll have to book well in advance to get in on one of their super-low fares. But if you do that you might be able to buy yourself a round-trip ticket to London for just 20 euros.

By Train

The sort of elegant train travel that requires stiff leather luggage and high-balls in the evening is a thing of the past. You'll no longer find well-heeled folks convening in the dining car over cocktails as Cary Grant's and Eva Marie Saint's characters did in *North By Northwest*. European trains are no more chic than American ones simply because they're European. As far as style goes, the continent's trains are a lot like Amtrak's. These days a good rail system means an efficient one and that's exactly what Spain has.

The country boasts an impressive network of trains that cover 9,138 miles of track and hit 2,500 stations. Renfe (Red Nacional de los Ferrocarriles Españoles) oversees the country's trains, and by all accounts the company does a good job of it. However, aside from a handful of high-speed lines, the trips can be slowed down by multiple stops. The bus will almost always be faster and less expensive—but then again, the bus will also be a tad less comfortable and it won't have a sleeping berth or a place to buy snacks.

> Although Spain's train service is far superior to its U.S. counterpart, the country's enormous web of roads is also intricate and far-reaching, and it seems as though new roads are always under construction.

Your ticket price will depend on the type of train you're taking. A trip that stops at every station en route will come fairly cheap. For a more direct route, the price will jump up a few notches. If you're not going far, look into the *cercanías* (outskirt) lines. Destinations further afield will require the regular lines. For the latter, you can opt for either *turista* (first class) or *preferente* (second class). To speed up your trip, look into a *regional exprés* (regional express) line if you can. If that's not an option, you'll have to stick with the *regionales* (regional) line—one that stops frequently.

Prices change all the time and, of course, they'll run a broad spectrum. However, here's a general idea of what it costs to ride the rails. A trip from Madrid to Barcelona goes for €33 ($41) at its cheapest and €59 ($74) at its priciest. A trip from Valencia to Málaga costs €45.50 ($57). Traveling from Seville to Cádiz can be as little as €8.40 ($10.50) and as much as €18 ($22.50).

The high-speed trains run from Madrid to Seville, with a few stops along the way, and Madrid to Lleida, also with some extra stops. A Madrid–Barcelona line is currently under construction and it should be operational by 2006 or shortly thereafter. Naturally, shaving time off your journey comes at a higher price. A ticket from Madrid to Seville

In Spain's cities you'll find excellent public transit, like Madrid's well-marked metro system.

will run you between €65 ($81) and €117 ($145), depending on the class you choose. You can hit a compromise between price and speed with what's known as the Talgo trains. They're more comfortable, prettier, and faster than the regular ones, but they only make limited stops between major cities.

Just as the speed of the trips varies, your experience inside all of those trains will not always be the same. Opting for a nicer (read: faster) journey will also bring a few perks such as movies and a newer and plusher atmosphere. Budget trains can feel bare-bones and worn. However, you can always shell out a few euros to travel in relative style. For overnight trips you can pony up some extra cash to travel in a *trenhotel* (sleeping-car train). Your options break down into three different classes: *turista, preferente,* and *gran clase* (better than first class). If you opt for the least expensive choice you'll be sitting up or lying in a bunk bed in a shared berth. In second class you'll have a sleeping car, and if you go for the deluxe version, you'll get a shower. A trip from Barcelona to Málaga begins at €52.50 ($66), costs €91.50 ($114) at the mid-level, and *gran clase* goes for €127.50 ($160).

Children, young adults, and seniors receive discounts on tickets but if you're eligible, you must request the slashed price—don't assume it will be offered to you when you buy your ticket. Tots under the age of four can travel for free, and children 4–11 years old travel at 40 percent off. Young adults aged 12–25 receive discounted rates on international tickets. Seniors aged 60 plus who are also residents can buy a Tarjeta Dorada for €3 ($3.75). This enables you to buy tickets at 25–40 percent off, depending on your day of travel.

You cannot buy your ticket on the train and if you board without a pass, you'll be subject to a nasty fine or even being booted off at the next station if that stiff penalty is the conductor's inclination. However, Renfe makes buying a ticket in advance easy enough. You can buy via telephone, although you'll have to collect your ticket at the station within a certain number of days of the purchase. Alternatively you can opt for the home delivery system if you live in Barcelona, Madrid, Seville, or Valencia. It might be easier to buy through a travel agent or one of Renfe's offices. Those storefronts are in the business districts of most cities and plenty of towns. If you're traveling during a holiday or popular vacation time, it's an especially wise idea to buy in advance since trains can book up quickly. There's no extra cost for your foresight. It only requires an advance trip to the office or train station.

By Bus

Anyone who's ever been on a Greyhound knows that bus travel is never as relaxing as going by train. However, it's a lot cheaper and it's often faster. And sometimes in Spain it's the only option. If you're headed to a tiny town without a train station, you may have to take the bus to get there.

Several companies operate Spain's buses and they usually operate out of the same station. However, in bigger cities there might be two stations so find out in advance which one is right. Smaller towns might not have a station at all. The bus will pull up in front of a café or bar and it will depart from the same place. In such cases, tickets can likely be bought inside or very nearby. To find out where that is, just ask anyone local and they'll surely know.

If you're headed to a tiny town without a train station, you may have to take the bus to get there.

Apart from holiday travel, you probably won't have to buy your ticket days in advance but you should arrive at the station with ample time to battle the long lines. It's a drag to miss your bus and discover that the next bus leaves six hours later. (Believe me, I know.) Call or stop by the station beforehand for scheduling information—buses don't necessarily leave hourly.

To chip away at your ticket price you can choose a non-express bus if such a route is available. It's always less expensive to buy round-trip, too, although if you won't be returning the next day, you should make sure that the ticket is still valid for the return leg—sometimes they expire quickly. If you're going a long distance, you'll likely have a break or two just long enough to go to stretch your legs, make a bathroom run, and buy a sandwich. Bus service is sporadic on Sundays and public holidays, so plan your journey accordingly.

By Car

A car is only a necessity in small-town Spain. Everywhere else it's a luxury. Still, a car can be a big asset even in a big city—with your own set of wheels you won't have to rely on public transportation to ferry you in and out of town and you can leave for weekend trips at a moment's notice. Nothing is perfect though and the down side will be battling city traffic and fighting it out for parking spaces if you don't pay rent on a private spot. If you're up to the task, here's what you need to know.

Stick-shift cars are the rule and mammoth SUVs are not the cars of choice in Spain. Sure, you'll see a few of the monstrous vehicles around, but in Spain, less is more and cars are usually small enough to navigate narrow medieval streets when necessary. Size has diminished even further in recent years and scores of city dwellers own Smart cars. Haven't heard of them? They're itty, bitty, candy-colored vehicles that slip easily into unfathomably small parking places and zip through streets at something close to breakneck speed. Those cars are not meant for highway driving—just one glance at them will tell you that. However, they're broadly adored alternatives to public transportation and best of all, they come cheap. If you buy one, don't expect to carry any passengers in the back unless they're tiny and extremely flexible. Other popular (and roomier) choices include Renaults, Volkswagens, Fiats, and the like. You'll see Mercedes and BMWs, too, as well as the odd Ford or Chevy, but American cars are rarer than European and Japanese models.

More than 25 companies run gas stations in Spain including a few international ones, but Repsol and Cepsa are two of the country's most successful. When you pull over to fuel up, you can expect to pay a lot; although gas prices in Spain are lower than in many European countries, they're still higher than the prices in the United States. If your car takes *gasóleo* (diesel)—and many Spanish cars do—you'll shell out a tad less than you otherwise would. Prices fluctuate dramatically according to oil tariffs, taxes, and international relations—prices differ between gas stations, too. However, as a general rule a 98-octane breed of gas is the most expensive and a 97-octane is just slightly behind it in cost. The latter was brought into Spain recently to replace leaded gas, which was banned in 2002. In most stations you can pay with either cash or credit cards.

Once you've bought your car keep one thing in mind before you decide to take it out for a spin. Spain's safety record is not impressive. Despite good conditions, Spain's roads are Europe's deadliest and in 2002 alone, 4,026 people died while driving. That's a frighteningly big number for a country of only 40.5 million people. Spaniards drive quickly and aggressively and that means that you should drive defensively. Yet the promising news is that over the course of the past 10 years, drivers have become more cautious, the use of seat belts has increased, and the number of driving-related fatalities is beginning to drop

DRIVING

The high rate of accidents has nothing to do with Spanish roads—they're among Europe's best. That stated, the smaller and more remote the street, the patchier the pavement. Illustrated signs usually have clear meanings and you'll see that speed-limits, passing zones, mountain passages with dangerous curves, and the like are all fairly well marked. As a result, foreigners quickly adapt to driving in Spain.

The main roads have been laid out logically. Madrid is the country's epicenter and highways wind out from there to points east, west, north, and south. However, not all highways were created equal. When you hit the road, you'll soon discover that owning a car isn't the only thing that costs money. You'll have to shell out to drive your car, too. Spain's *autopistas* (toll roads) are some of the continent's most expensive. You might have to pay as much as €14 ($17.50) at tollbooths, and prices go up with the temperature—summer is the most expensive season. You can slash the cost by 10 to 25 percent if you buy a *tarjeta de la autopista* (toll-road card). To pay, you'll either have to insert the card in a slot at the toll or if indicated, just pass on through—your license plate will automatically register. En route you'll pass service stations with bathrooms, phones, and basic restaurants. Those amenities spare you the expense of having to exit and reenter for pit stops. It's undoubtedly due to toll roads' high prices that some Spanish people avoid them when they can and take the back route instead. That national tendency has a big upshot. Traffic on the *autopistas* is a little lighter than the norm and those routes are safer to boot.

Carreteras (freeways) run parallel to some of the highways and they're a more economical alternative if you don't mind the traffic—because they're free, they're crowded. *Autovías* (highways) are speedy and they also cost nothing at all, but they have crossroads and so you'll have to take a little extra care when driving.

On any road, a sign reading *cambio de sentido* (change of direction) indicates an opportunity to turn around via an overpass or underpass. If you're on a main road and you run into trouble, be it a flat tire or an overheated engine, know that an emergency telephone will be planted on the side of the road somewhere nearby; they're every five kilometers. Just pick up the receiver and you'll automatically be connected to the local police department. If you want to use your cellular phone instead, just dial the operator and ask for *auxilio en carreteras* (roadside assistance). If you're able to, park your car on the side of the road, place emergency triangles 30 meters behind and in front of your car and then—and this part is very important—get out of the car and head well away from passing cars. It's not safe to sit in your vehicle while you're waiting for help to arrive.

Driver's Licenses

The legal age limit to drive is 18 and that extends to foreigners, too. If you're already licensed in the United States, you can rent a car—even tourists can do that. However, if you're resident of Spain, you can only use your U.S. license for six months from the start-date of your visa and you must have official written translation of the license. You can obtain the translation at the Spanish consulate in the United States. In Spain, you can go to the Real Automóvil Club de España. Before six months has passed, you'll have to trade your old license in for a Spanish one. (Naturally, people with tourist visas cannot have a Spanish driver's license.) In order to get a Spanish license, you'll have to take the following documents to your local Jefatura Provincial de Tráfico (Department of Motor Vehicles):

- your passport
- a completed application for a driver's license (that can be picked up from the Department of Motor Vehicles)
- a photocopy of your residency card along with the original documents (you'll receive the originals back as soon as the office clerk compares them to the copies)
- a certificate attesting that you're both psychologically and physically capable of driving (you'll have to go to your local driver's checking center for that)

Driving Quiz

While this quiz isn't as rigid as the government's, it covers some of the most important things that you'll need to know when you hit the road. So buckle your seat belts, start your engines, and take out your number-two pencils.

1) In the trunk of your car, you should have a spare tire, tools, and what else?
A. a flare gun
B. a sleeping bag in case you have a breakdown and you need to spend the night in your car before help arrives
C. two red warning triangles
D. windshield-wiper fluid

2) If you wear glasses, what should you keep in your car?
A. maps with extra-large font
B. a little screwdriver for emergency repairs
C. reading material to keep you occupied in traffic jams
D. an extra pair of glasses

3) Who needs to wear helmets?
A. people on motorcycles and mopeds
B. drunk drivers
C. clumsy people
D. pedestrians

4) Who has to wear seatbelts?
A. children younger than 10
B. everyone in the car
C. people in the front seats
D. people in the backseats

5) What kind of cellular phone can you use while driving?
A. That's a trick question— you can't use a cellular phone in the car.
B. the kind that have digital cameras so you'll be prepared if you see something scenic
C. hands-free ones
D. Nokias

Answers: 1) C. 2) D. 3) A. 4) B. 5) C.

- two updated 35 x 25 mm photographs
- a written declaration stating that: you don't have any major moving violations on your record and your license has never been suspended; your U.S. license and its Spanish translation are both authentic; you don't already have an EU driving license
- your U.S. driver's license or a photocopy of it

Rules of the Road

Before moving on to traffic rules, there are a couple of things you should know about your car. You're required to keep an emergency stash in the trunk: one set of headlight bulbs and whatever you need to change them, two red triangular warning signs that you can pick up from the Ministry of the Interior, and a spare tire and its accompanying tools. You don't actually have to know how to use any of that (although it's a very good thing if you can), but if you're pulled over without these items in your trunk you can be fined. You should also have your car registration in the glove

Reading the Signs

Most road signs in Spain are self-explanatory and a few—such as *Stop* and *Yield*—are even the same. Still, plenty of mysterious ones are out there and it's a good idea to get the skinny on their meanings. To American eyes, one sign suggests driving off a dock, another appears to encourage drag racing, and yet another suggests turning in two directions at once. As you might have guessed, the real messages in those pictures are more logical than they appear—so here's a breakdown of Spain's strange signs.

The shapes signs take are no arbitrary detail. They specify what sort of sign you're reading. A diamond indicates priority, red triangles warn you of an upcoming change in the road or danger, and blue-rimmed circles tell you of a particular rule. Circles with red borders specify a restriction—those signs' pictures indicate what you *shouldn't* do. More simply put, blue means, "do the thing in the picture" and red means, "*don't* do it." The most crucial thing to note is that you won't see a diagonal slash through a circle when a sign indicates a prohibition. Instead, the circle will merely have a red margin.

So given that information, let's revisit that sign of a car driving off a pier. The picture is on a red-bordered, triangular

sign, so the shape and color signify a warning. What exactly does it mean? A dock is nearby and you shouldn't drive off of it. (Sound advice.) What about the apparent drag racing sign—the one of two cars depicted side-by-side in a red-rimmed circle? That means no passing; and if you see a circular sign with the same image and a diagonal slash through it, you're exiting the no-passing zone. How about the picture of two arrows pointing in different directions? Traffic moving in the direction of the red arrow has to yield to traffic coming from the other direction.

While we're demystifying signs, let's talk about speed limits. A number in a circular sign will tell you what the speed limit is, and a number with a diagonal slash through it tells you that you've left the speed limit's zone. A circular sign with a number on a shaded background tells you the recommended *minimum* speed.

Now that you know how to interpret the more baffling signs, it's a good idea to follow their directions—if you don't, you can expect other drivers to beep their horns, shake their fists, and shout out that you're *loco* (crazy). That being said, don't expect every else to follow the rules.

---

compartment, evidence that your car is insured, and your license tucked into your wallet.

Speed limits run the gamut depending on the type of road. On the *autopistas* the limit is 74 mph (120 km/h). On autovías you can drive up to 62 mph (100 km/h). Drivers on *carreteras* can go no faster than 56 mph (90 km/h), and in cities or urban areas the speed limit is 31 mph (50 km/h). If you don't remember all of those numbers, don't worry too much—the limits are well posted.

Most traffic laws are either the same or similar to those in the United States, but it's of course helpful to know the differences. Fines range from €91–602 ($114–753). The highest ones are given for the most dangerous infractions; in those instances licenses can also be suspended. Violations that incur the most severe penalties are:

- driving more than 19 mph (30 km/h) above the speed limit
- driving while under the influence of drugs or alcohol (the legal blood-alcohol limit is 0.05 percent)
- refusing to take a Breathalyzer test
- exceeding the number of people permitted to ride in the car by 50 percent
- reckless driving
- driving at nights with the lights off

Other important laws include the following:

- Cars must have seatbelts and the driver and passengers must wear them.
- Children younger than 12 have to ride in the backseat unless the front seat is fitted with safety equipment or they're in a car seat.
- Drivers may only use cellular phones with a hands-free system.
- People who wear glasses must keep an extra pair in their car.
- Helmet laws apply to people on mopeds or motorcycles.

The government has been working towards making Spanish roads safer, and the result is that the penalties for traffic violations are stiff. A police officer can demand that you pay any fine up to €300 ($375) while you're stopped, so travel with a loaded wallet. If an automatic traffic camera catches you speeding, the ticket will arrive in the mail. Radars are occasionally used, too, so if you're driving too fast, you may be pulled over.

If you're innocent of a traffic charge you'll have 15 days to appeal by writing a letter to the traffic authorities. Although you can write your letter of contest in English, doing so won't help plead your case. If you can't write the letter in Spanish yourself, ask a bilingual friend to help or hire a professional translator. If your dispute is not settled in your favor, you'll have a month to appeal the decision but you should hire a lawyer for that because the dispute might end up in court.

RENTING, LEASING, AND BUYING A CAR

You'll find few differences between renting a car in Spain to renting in the United States and you can even go through Hertz, Avis, or a number of international companies that you may have already used before. Drivers must be at least 21 years old, although some companies require that drivers be 23 years old. Any airport that sees a significant number of tourists passing through will have a few desks reserved for rental car companies and you can walk right up, take care of the paper work, and, provided there's a car available, drive off. You can also request to pick up and drop off through rental agencies in town. However, it's a good idea to book in advance, not just to insure that you have a car, but also to lower the total price. Wherever you go to rent a car, you'll be charged exorbitant rates for an automatic rather than a manual. If you know how to drive stick shifts, you should request one.

You can call a rental car company directly but one agency that offers especially good deals is Auto Europe (www.autoeurope.com). They manage to find bargains through major, international companies. Spanish companies usually offers slightly lower rates than the name brand ones do. In all cases prices drop on the weekends. A 48-hour, economy-car rental with Hertz costs about €63 ($79)—that's before insurance and value-added tax (IVA) are tacked on. The same rental for two weekdays costs €89 ($110) euros before the extras are added.

If you want to buy your own car, you'll need a resident's card. If you do have one, buying is fairly easy, although cars in Spain are slightly more expensive than their U.S. counterparts. That's mainly due to the sales tax slapped on. If you buy through a dealer, you can sign on to a monthly payment plan, but if you buy directly from the seller you'll likely have to pay in one lump sum. Most foreigners choose used cars. If you want to do that, too, look for one that is still within its warranty period—the car will probably be in better condition. Also do a background check on the car to be sure that there are no outstanding payments. Even debts unrelated to the car can be pinned to the vehicle and if you were to buy unaware of that, you would assume the responsibility for those debts. Regardless of whether you buy through a dealer or an individual seller, you should make sure that you receive the following documents:

- registration
- the current ITV test certificate and a photocopy of the same (the ITV is the Spanish equivalent to the safety-inspections tests required by some U.S. states)
- a *ficha técnica*—that's a mandatory technical form that the previous owner or dealer should have
- a transfer-of-ownership form
- a road-tax receipt and a photocopy of the same
- a receipt for the payment of transfer tax (4 percent)

It's just bad business sense to lease a car and few people do it. While leasing is a way of life in the United States, there are significantly few companies who provide the service in Spain and those that do charge exorbitant rates. You're better off buying a car and then selling it later.

TAXI SERVICE

Taxis are ubiquitous in Spanish cities and you flag one down the same way you would in New York City—just raise your arm and hail it. Madrid has more than 15,000 taxis, Barcelona isn't far behind with a fleet of 10,500 cabs, and smaller cities have their share, too. If you can't find an available car (and you'll know that one is free if the light on top is on), you can look for a taxi stand along the side of the road—they're marked with signs. During rush hour and at the end of weekend nights when everyone is leaving bars to head home, there's no guarantee that you'll find an available cab. Other times, a long line of taxis will be parked at the curb by stands and in those cases you should take the first one in the line.

The minimum fare changes depending on the city but it's usually €1–2 ($1.25–2.50). A ride can add up if you're sitting in traffic, but in most cases the fares are low—certainly lower than in many other parts of Europe. Taxi drivers are required to carry €12 ($15) in change but they often don't. (It won't help to point out that they're supposed to have change—believe me, that tactic will go absolutely nowhere.) You should make sure to have small bills because in many cases the driver won't have change and you'll have to run into the nearest shop or café to break a bill while the meter is still running.

By Boat

Pleasure cruises aside, you'll only travel by boat if you're heading to the Balearic Islands, North Africa, or traveling between the Canary Islands. A few companies compete for passengers and you can learn about prices and schedules either online or through travel agents. You can buy tickets through both those avenues, too. Because ferry companies compete for business, prices remain fairly low. To go to Ibiza from Valencia (a 3.5-hour tour) in tourist class will cost no less than €48 ($60) one-way, but prices go up from there depending on the distance traveled, the boat chosen, and the class of ticket. If you tack on car passage and sleeper berths, the total can rise well over the €200 ($250) mark. A trip to Ibiza from Barcelona takes between 8.5 and 10.5 hours and is even costlier. With most ferry lines you can rein in costs by opting for a slower passage. Crossing the Strait of Gibraltar to reach North Africa from southern Spain is a remarkably short trip—less than an hour—and ticket prices are relatively low. You can find a ticket for about €50 ($63) round-trip.

Usually your choice of boats will be broken down into a few categories: extremely fast, kind of fast, and not that fast. Every company has its own names for those kinds of boats. One company has a "Fast Ferry"— that's a big boat that goes to the Balearic Islands in relatively little time. The same company offers passage on the "SuperFerry," which, while speedy, isn't quite as super as the other one. To find out about prices and travel times you'll have to call or look online because the boat options are numerous and ferry names can be deceiving—they all sound like they recently won the America's Cup.

When it comes to ferries there are a couple rules of thumb. The more you take with you, the more expensive your ticket will be. For example, should you want to take your car along, you'll have to tack a large chunk of change onto the cost of your ticket. If you want a cabin for an overnight passage, you'll pay more than if you're reserving just a seat. You should book far ahead in the summer—the tourist season—when tickets can sell out well in advance. In the off season you'll find bargains but the ferries will run relatively sporadically so be sure to plan your trip according to the schedule.

Again, shopping around is a good idea but you can also book in advance with Trasmediterránea (www.trasmediterranea.es) which has all but cornered the market on business between the mainland and the Balearic Islands. Ferrys Rápidos del Sur (www.frs.es) does a good job of shuttling people back and forth from the south of Spain to Morocco.

© Nikki Weinstein

Housing Considerations

Whether you're coming to Spain for just a few weeks or for the rest of your life, you're going to need a roof over your head. Finding housing is the issue that people sweat out the most before arriving and there's no wondering why. House-hunting is stressful enough in your own country. When you toss a foreign language and a new set of laws into the mix, the prospect can seem downright overwhelming. Your list of initial questions might seem endless now but rest assured that every query you have has an accessible answer. Once you arrive in Spain and begin your search you'll find that the reality of finding housing in Spain is no more complicated than it is in the United States.

Before even considering contracts and deposits, you'll probably want to know a little bit about the market. What you should expect to pay varies from one city to another—even within a given town, prices range dramatically between neighborhoods. However one thing is true throughout the country: prices have gone up. In 2003 alone, prices rose by more than 15 percent and a house in Spain now costs about five times what it cost in 1985. Moreover, it's expected that prices will continue to rise—at least through the near future. Don't panic though—there is good news for you, too. Houses are not prohibitively expensive and in 2003, the number of people taking out mortgages also rose by more than 23 percent. Furthermore, homes in Spain have historically been cheap when compared to those in bigger U.S. cities. Even given the rising prices in Spain you might be pleased with the numbers that you find. Additionally, a Spanish home could make an attractive investment if you intend to live in the country for a while.

Rent prices have also increased, especially in Madrid and Barcelona where you'll find competitive markets. Both cities have fewer vacancies than people interested in letting a place and the financial result of that discrepancy is clear—everything is pricier than it used to be. However, the rents still fall below those in cities such as New York and San Francisco. In Spain's smaller cities and rural locations, housing is still considered affordable—just a few hundred euros a month can secure an apartment far superior to what the same money would buy in much of the United States.

RENTING VS. BUYING

So you've been to Spain before, you already know the town where you intend to live and it feels just like home. The waiter in your favorite café always remembers your order without being told, and you rarely refer to your map because you already know the streets by name. Should you take the plunge and buy a place? Probably not—or at least not immediately. No matter how well you think you've gotten to know a town during prior visits, the same place will seem different when you're a resident. What strikes tourists as rustic and peaceful will likely be that much more enchanting when you live there, but after a few months you might surprise yourself by feeling an acute longing for the rush of city life. In that case, perhaps you'll want to make a move. Alternatively, if you're smitten with Barcelona and you plop down money for an apartment in the center of all the action, you might find that while the city offers every attraction that you had hoped for, you just can't shut out the noise. Perhaps you erred by moving into one of the city's busiest neighborhoods—a great choice for some people but evidently not for you. In that case you might want to move to a more residential district. One American found a teaching job at an international school in Madrid a few years back and shortly after arriving, he spent his savings on an apartment and became a homeowner. Within a year he discovered that he preferred life in Barcelona—a city he'd begun to visit more and more frequently. When a school in Barcelona offered him a job, he jumped at it. Unfortunately, in order to make the move to his new city he had to sell his home and he ended up losing a fair amount of money in the process.

Ultimately, vacations to Spain don't provide enough knowledge for informed decisions on real estate and until you live in a place for at least a little while, you simply don't know what you'll think of life there as a resident. When I moved to Madrid I knew exactly which neighborhood I wanted to live in and I was lucky enough to find an apartment there. While I can't complain about my choice, I would have decided on a different part of town if I had known the city better—I was lucky that as a renter I wasn't committed to anything but the lease on my place so I never felt buyer's remorse. If you rent a place you can bide your time and learn the various areas of town without rushing. In just a short period you can see how different neighborhoods are evolving and eventually you'll know which one feels right for you. At that point you'll be in a good position to buy. After renting a place for a while you also might learn that you'd prefer to live somewhere else in Spain entirely, and as a renter it's easy enough to pick up and move. However, as a homeowner you could lose a chunk of cash if you make that same decision after a short trial run in a home that you bought.

> No matter how well you think you've gotten to know a town during prior visits, the same place will seem different when you're a resident.

Sentiment aside, it might seem wise to stake your claim in the market while prices are going up. Yes, buying a home can be a good investment but the key ingredient is time. Why? You'll have to pay about 10 percent of the total price in expenses and that's cash that you won't see again. The money put into your home can be recouped as the market goes up but until prices climb enough, you should hang onto that property. If there is a chance—even a small chance—that you'll want to sell your new property shortly after purchasing it, you'd be wise to rent instead.

Renting

If you're not prepared to put up the money needed to buy a place, or if your stay in Spain is temporary, then you'll be ready to learn the renter's market. No need to worry, there's little that will surprise you if you've already rented in the United States. Homes are usually found through

A narrow street in one of Granada's best neighborhoods, the Albaicín

© Jessica Chesler

the same avenues you've used before—word-of-mouth, ads, and agents. Contracts are the norm and as long as you have a lease, the law assures basic tenant's rights.

However, there is one thing to know before you begin house-hunting: "unfurnished" has a whole new definition in Spain. An agent might open the door to reveal just walls, a floor, and doors. Amenities such as refrigerators, light fixtures, and towel racks do not necessarily come with a let apartment. Some people—especially those looking for short-term stays—avoid unneeded hassles by specifically seeking out furnished places. Finding a furnished apartment isn't so difficult and you'll find that everything including the kitchen sink is tossed in. Detached houses rarely come furnished, but there are a few of those homes around. Before you even begin to look at property, decide whether or not you want a furnished place or not and limit your search accordingly. After all, why waste your time viewing homes that you know you won't take?

FINDING THE RIGHT PLACE

There are several ways to find vacancies and none of them are so different from methods used in the United States. If you're passing an appealing residential building and you see a sign reading *se alquila* (for rent), stop by and inquire within. Ask around, too. If you know people in the country, they might have heard of an upcoming vacancy through a friend or colleague. Start reading the paper for something other than the news—both Spanish dailies and even most English-language newspapers run columns of listings with every issue, and those ads might turn something up. If you see a listing that looks promising call right away so you don't miss out on the chance to view the property—especially in Madrid and Barcelona where a home can be rented the same day that an ad for it appears in the newspaper. Occasionally people find places by asking porters in the buildings that they like if apartments are available—it's a long shot but you might get lucky. A real estate agent will provide a smoother but slightly costlier route to a home. Not all agents deal in rentals but plenty do and some even specialize in them. Loads of agencies advertise abroad and on the Internet but you can also find an agent by walking into an office with the sign *Agentes de Propiedad Inmobiliaria* (real estate agents) hung out front. The standard rate of commission falls between half a month's rent to a full month's rent.

When you begin to look at homes, take your time, get a feel for what's out there, and don't jump at the very first place that you see just to get the process over with—you might regret it later on. Consider

Cracking the Classifieds

So you bought a stack of newspapers, ran to the nearest café, started reading, and that's when you discovered that the ads are all in Spanish! No worries. The following guide will help you decode the text.

aire acondicionado—air-conditioning	*fachada*—facade
amueblada—furnished	*gardín*—garden
antigüedad—older	*gastos incluidos*—utilities included
armario—closet	*lavadero*—washing machine
ascensor—elevator	*m²*—square meters
aseo—half-bath	*muy luminoso*—plenty of light
baño completo—complete bath	*nuevo*—new
buhardilla—attic	*parking*—parking space
calefacción—heat	*piscina*—pool
cocina—kitchen	*piso 3*—third floor
comedor—dining room	*reformado*—renovated
como nuevo—like new	*salón*—living room
dormitories—bedrooms	*suelos de parquet*—parquet floors
embaldosado—tiled	*terraza*—terrace
empotrados—built-in	*ventana*—window

issues such as noise pollution, proximity to bus lines, and metro stations. Being in the center of town has advantages but will the street noise come in through your windows? What would your morning commute consist of? Would you feel safe walking home late at night? Does the apartment have a good amount of natural light? Once you've found a place that feels right and meets your criteria, you'll be ready to sign a lease.

LEASES

Spanish law distinguishes between short-term and long-term contracts. The former is any lease that will expire within a year or less. It specifies the condition of the home, the date on which rent must be paid, and the date on which the tenant must move out. Those are the standard contracts used in vacation rentals and they're the leases signed by foreigners in Spain for a short period of time. However, long-term leases are a little more complicated. Any rental contract that exceeds a year is by definition a long-term lease, and its standard duration is five years. Annual rent increases are made according to the consumer price index so they're usually minimal. A five-year commitment might sound uncomfortably binding but those contracts usually work in the renter's favor. Few people encounter difficulty breaking their leases and you shouldn't have any trouble either as long as you give sufficient notice. However, landlords can only reclaim their property after the five-year term.

Long-term leases come with another big perk. If your landlord decides to sell the place, by law you must receive the first offer on the home. You may or may not be interested in buying at all, but it's worth knowing that you do have priority over everyone else including the landlord's family. You'll be given 30 days to reply to the offer and if you discover that the place was sold without an offer having been made, you have a month to annul the sale of the home. Likewise, if the property was sold at a lower price than the one your landlord offered you, you can cancel the sale.

Even if you're not interested in finding a place that might lead to the possibility of buying, you'll still want to handle the contract the right way. Any lease, be it short- or long-term, should specify the duration of time that you'll live in the home as well as the amount of monthly rent that you'll pay. Those are just the basics but you also can ask for all kinds of amendments to the lease. For example, if new fixtures are in place in an otherwise unfurnished apartment, the landlord might want you to cover that cost. It's common to negotiate a point like that, and even the amount of rent is sometimes open to debate. Naturally, your success in that dialogue will hinge on the housing market. If you're renting in an area where apartments are hard to come by, your landlord probably won't budge on the rent. Still, why not try? Before putting pen to paper, be sure to check for damages, too, so you won't be held accountable for them later on. Test the oven and examine the floorboards—really scrutinize the place. If something is broken when you sign the lease make sure that it's either fixed or, if it's a problem that you can live with such as a crack in the ceiling or a loose floorboard, detail it in the contract. Tenants must pay for gas and electricity unless otherwise outlined in the lease, and if you live in a community with a shared pool or garden, you might be expected to cover the community fee. The landlord usually pays real estate taxes but it's a good idea to include that into the lease anyway.

When you sign the contract you'll have to put down a month's rent as a deposit—very occasionally more is requested but the law specifies just one month's rent. If you turn the place over to your landlord in the same condition it was in when you moved in, your full deposit should be returned to you.

There's every reason to think that things will go smoothly but in the case of a conflict, you should know your basic rights as a tenant. You landlord has a legal responsibility to keep your place in good, livable condition and the owner should never use the apartment for any reason while you're living there. However, if problems arise as a result of your actions or even due to daily wear such as marks or nail-holes in the walls, you should either repair the damages yourself or be prepared to give up a chunk of your deposit when you move out.

Buying

So you've gotten to know the market and you're ready to make a piece of Spain your very own. The hardest part of the process is finding the right place. If you've only looked as a renter before, you'll be viewing property with a slightly different perspective when you're prepared to buy. You're not only on the hunt for a place that you'd like to live in but you'll probably want the assurance that you're making a sound investment. Once you get a feel for the market, you'll have more confidence in the choice you make both as an investment and also as a home.

The most notable difference between home sales in the United States and in Spain is in the unwritten part of the transaction. In some cases everything moves according to the letter of the law, but in many cases the numbers on paper don't reflect true amounts. You should never encourage a transaction to move in an illegal direction, but

In Spain's south, doors swing open in summertime.

Historic buildings are often adorned with gorgeous old doors.

don't be surprised if the seller or agent talks openly about avoiding taxes. One document that might look wildly off is the deed—perhaps you'll see that the home's dimensions on paper appear to be much smaller than the actual house is. That's a deliberate discrepancy made to save money. The practice of altering those numbers is so commonplace that when third parties (i.e., bank employees) see a deed that has been altered they'll often ignore the issue. A seller might also request that a portion of the sale be given in cash or *dinero negro* (black money) in order to avoid taxes. For years, operating in that manner was the unwritten rule of Spanish real estate but things are beginning to change and the government has become stricter. Still, fudged numbers and cash exchanges are alarmingly common when compared to the United States. If a seller or agent suggests a shady alteration to a document, you don't have to comply—after all, you're probably not moving to Spain with the hope of becoming embroiled in legal problems.

FINDING THE RIGHT PLACE

Browsing through advertisements in the newspaper and looking at listings online provides a good start to understanding Spanish real estate. A simple Web search on real estate in Spain will turn up countless pages and most of them full of property descriptions, pictures, and prices. Once you're ready to move forward, begin speaking to different agents about the properties that they have available. All registered agents in Spain belong to the Agente de Propiedad Inmobiliaria and can show you their certificate and registration number. You'd be wise to work with licensed agents; if you don't do that and something goes wrong, you'll have little legal recourse. A good agent should also offer you a wide selection of properties to view but even so, speak to more than just one agent in order to broaden your search.

> The most notable difference between home sales in the United States and in Spain is in the unwritten part of the transaction.

Once you've found a place that interests you, speak to people who live there and find out how the neighborhood has changed in the past few years. Is it evolving in a direction that you like? Consider some of the same issues that renters also need to think about: map out your daily commute, take into account the natural light, and whether or not you'll be comfortable with the level of street noise. You'll want to make sure that both the neighborhood and the house feel right to you.

FROM MORTGAGES TO MOVING IN

Once you've thought it over and decided to buy the place, you'll have to dive into the details. Now it's time to finance the property and hammer out a contract. If you'll be mortgaging the house—and most people need to—you can apply for the loan at a Spanish bank. The maximum mortgage for nonresident foreigners is 60 percent of the total price and for residents it's 80 percent. In order to determine your percentage, the bank will consider your earnings and naturally the property will have to be valued. The house is not assessed according to the current market value, but according to rebuild cost per square meter—in other words, what it would cost per square meter if you were to rebuild the house.

Before signing the contract you should stop by the Property Registry to get all the details on the house. Specifically, you'll need information on the owner and the full size of the property as it's officially recorded. The report should also include any outstanding charges, legal restrictions of use, and court orders for seizure of the home if any exist. Make sure that mortgage payments are all up to date and also obtain proof of that from the owner.

Since you're already verifying things, there are a couple additional points to check on. Confirm that payments on the municipal real estate tax are current—if they're not, you'll be responsible for covering the outstanding fees plus their penalties. If the house is part of a community that requires payments, speak to the community administrator to see that everything is financially squared up with the previous owner and also request an official statement from the seller attesting to that same fact. (That should be provided anyway.) Lastly, you'll have to request a tax-identification number (NIE) if you don't already have one—that can be taken care of at the police department and the number allows you to pay your taxes.

In theory, you'll only need to pay one tax but in practice most people pay two. The buyer always pays the transfer tax upon signing the contract—that's 6 percent of the purchase price. You'll likely pay the capital gains tax, too—although the law stipulates that the seller pay that, it's usually agreed that the buyer assumes the coverage of it.

There are just a couple more costs. You'll have to pay a fee to the Property Registry in order to have the deed filed in your name, and you must sign the contract before a notary (who will also add his or her stamp and signature). You'll also have to pay the fee for that service. Spanish notaries do everything that their American colleagues do and much more. They're lawyers who have additional degrees and they represent the state when overseeing everything from drawing up wills and deeds to executing contracts. In many cases they write the deed in addition to signing it, and they'll often offer legal advice to both the buyer and seller.

Now it's time to sign and make the place yours. Before adding your signature, make sure that the contract includes the amount, rate, and the terms of the mortgage. Also confirm that a description of the home is included, that the property is free of outstanding charges, and that you and the seller are both named. At the end of the transaction you'll be given the keys and as soon as you register the property, everything will be complete—the home will be yours.

BUILDING

Newly constructed properties are springing up all over Spain and foreigners own a good portion of them. That's especially true of the southern coast in Andalusia where many retirees snap up vacation homes that might only exist as brand-new blueprints when they're bought. Organized developments make the process of building a home easier and if you go that route, the developers will handle the majority of the details. However, plenty of people choose to take on the construction process independently and if you're among them, you'll have to know how to go about it from purchasing the land to moving in. You should hire an attorney to oversee the process and read all the contracts, but you should still familiarize yourself with everything.

In contrast to the Spanish housing market, the cost of land and labor have actually gone down a little bit in recent years which means that you can build a slightly nicer home than you could buy. However, you should only take on the task if you're the kind of person who can snap into a Zen-like calm in the face of red tape and inexplicable delays, because you'll inevitably face your fair share of hold-ups. Chalk it up to the Spanish philosophy of *mañana* (tomorrow) or just plain bureaucracy, but there's no getting around it.

After scouting out the land you want, you'll have to confirm that the house you have in mind can be built there—not just literally but also legally. The government classifies all of Spain's terra firma in one of three ways: land for development, green zones, or rural areas that cannot be built-up. Plots available for development are further restricted—a building must be a certain size in relation to the land itself. To confirm that the plot of land will suit your needs, you'll have to have a solid idea of what you want your house to look like and you'll also need to know its dimensions.

Town hall provides a few more particulars on the land. Zoning restrictions might apply. For example, perhaps the land can be developed but if a public bike path crosses the property, you'll have to make sure that the path remains unobstructed. Town hall will also be able to insure that no major roads or other obtrusive construction are planned nearby. Err on the side of caution and request written permission to build everything from the house itself to road access. Also obtain a *nota simple* (simple note) from the Property Registry confirming the details of the seller and that the land has no outstanding charges on it. Once you have that information, you're ready to move onto the mortgage, which works exactly like it would if you were buying a house. The sales contract is also as it would be in any other case—signed before a notary whose services you'll have to pay for. If the value of the land has increased since it was last purchased, a capital gains tax might apply. (As with buying a secondhand home, the seller and buyer usually agree that the buyer pays that tax despite the fact that it's legally the seller's obligation.) After your lawyer looks the contract over, you'll be ready to add your John Hancock and make the land yours.

Now it's time to begin construction and for that you'll need a building permit. You can make that request at town hall but you'll need to present detailed plans of the home, so unless you're an architect yourself, you'll have to hire one. You'll also have to hire a builder and you should work with a licensed one so you have legal recourse should anything go wrong. The contract with the builder should state the payment terms, the date of completion, a description of the job, and the financial penalty should the home be finished late. The home should be insured while it's under construction, and the builder usually takes out the policy. For future reference, you should know that you'll have six months from the signing of the deed to have the builder make corrections to substandard work should any alterations be necessary. Now construction begins.

Flash forward a few months to the time when your new home has been built. Before you pack your bags and prepare for the move, you'll have to register your property now that it exists, so you should get a Certificate of the Termination of the Building from the architect. Take that paper to a notary who can write a declaration of a new building. The next stop will be town hall where you can get a License of First Occupation. With that done, the property will have been registered for tax purposes and for the connection of utilities. However, that does not mean that your property is fully registered.

Now that you have a home, you'll need a deed for it. As soon as the notary oversees the singing of that and adds an official stamp and signature, you can take a copy to the Property Registry to be filed. Oh . . . one last thing. You can start living in your new home as soon as you're ready.

RESTORING

If you want to make alterations to your property—even something as minor as adding a terrace or garage—you'll need permission. Don't worry too much about that, it's simple enough to get the government's official thumbs-up on alterations. For a small fee, town hall can provide you with the necessary license to amend your property. If you're not planning on building an enormous, purple windmill or interfering with someone else's property, you'll probably get permission. However take note: many people either ignore the fact that they need to get permission or they simply don't realize that they have to. In many cases those people have been slapped with huge fines and they're sometimes forced to remove the offending addition. Take caution and go through the extra step of getting a license for restorations.

Household Expenses

The price of owning a house can be divided into two categories: the cost of buying and the costs spent while living in your home. The substantial expenses in the first group include the capital gains tax that has to be paid for the value increase of the property since the last sale and a transfer tax

The Rain in Spain Does *Not* Fall on the Plain

If you're used to hosing off your driveway, scrubbing down your car, and taking long, leisurely showers, you'll want to amend your ways once you reach Spain. Water bills have begun to soar in recent years, and there's good reason for that. The country is a parched land and current water supplies are stressed to the breaking point.

While Spain is hardly a rainy country, the real problem lies in the distribution of resources. Some provinces are the land of plenty, others suffer, and regions squabble over resources. A national plan that can shuttle water from the lush north to the scorched earth in the south is badly needed. For years, the government was woefully deficient in raising conservation awareness, and it was only after a severe drought in the mid-1990s (the century's worst) that ads warning people not to waste water began to pop up. Despite the new conservation efforts, people in Spanish towns and cities consume about 80 gallons of water a day—that's one of the highest rates in Europe.

Not long ago, the government drew up a national hydrologic plan to correct the issue, but the plan has yet to go into action. As things currently stand, the northeast is literally awash in water (it's a place where residents always have an umbrella at the ready) but the Mediterranean coast fares less well. In the Costa del Sol, wastewater is recycled and used to irrigate crops and keep the golf courses green and healthy. But when the local population increases tenfold during the high season, the region's water resources are stretched to their brink; some farmers' very livelihoods are on the line when supplies dip too low.

Ironically, the Canary and Balearic Islands—places surrounded by ocean—have some of the biggest problems in the country. The Balearic Islands rely on more than 20,000 wells to dredge water up from the ground, and the Canary Islands use desalination plants to quench the population's thirst.

Hopefully the government's hydrologic plan will kick in soon and the problem will be amended. But until then, you might want to keep your bills in check, be an *amigo* to the earth, and forgo watering your lawn.

(6 percent of the purchase price). If you're buying new construction you'll also have to pay a seven-percent sales tax and a stamp tax amounting to 0.5 percent.

The cost of living in a house includes upkeep—you'll have to fix things that break from broken pipes to wiring problems. Those fees can add up on a poorly maintained property. However, the biggest cost will be your mortgage and homeowner's insurance. The insurance premium is based on the size and value of the house as well as of your belongings. While Spanish law does not require that you have a policy on your home, if you have a mortgage the bank will almost certainly demand that your house be insured at least against fire. Some people also have to pay a community fee for the upkeep of shared amenities such as a pool or yard. Costs vary depending on the total number of properties and the size of your unit, but the range usually starts at about 0.075 percent of the shared community cost and can go as high as 0.1 percent.

Utilities are the last price you'll have to pay for domestic maintenance. Depending on where you live, that might not cost much. If you're settled in the south where winters are mild, then you're heating costs will be minimal. Of course, you'll want air-conditioning running straight through the infernal heat of summer, and that will increase your overall payments. If you're in the mountains you'll have colder winters but more temperate summers, so the costs will ultimately remain about the same. However, if you're living in Madrid or on the Spanish tableland in the center of the country, you'll have cold winters, hot summers, and your utility bills will be a good portion more than they would be elsewhere.

UTILITIES

Before you worry about paying utilities, you'll have to make sure they're hooked up. Electricity is an easy one to handle. Just call or stop by the local company's office to sign a contract. You'll need to bring along your passport and the previous owner's contract. Bills come bimonthly. If you're in a major city you might rely on gas. To set everything up, just call the company, have the meter read, and sign a contract. Again, a form of identification is a must. Parts of Spain are dangerously parched and thus water is heavily regulated. Your local municipality will manage your water supply so call the good people who work there to get things started. You'll have to pay fees during the course of the year in addition to a connection fee which might be as low as €50 ($63) and as much as €300 ($375).

Prime Living Locations

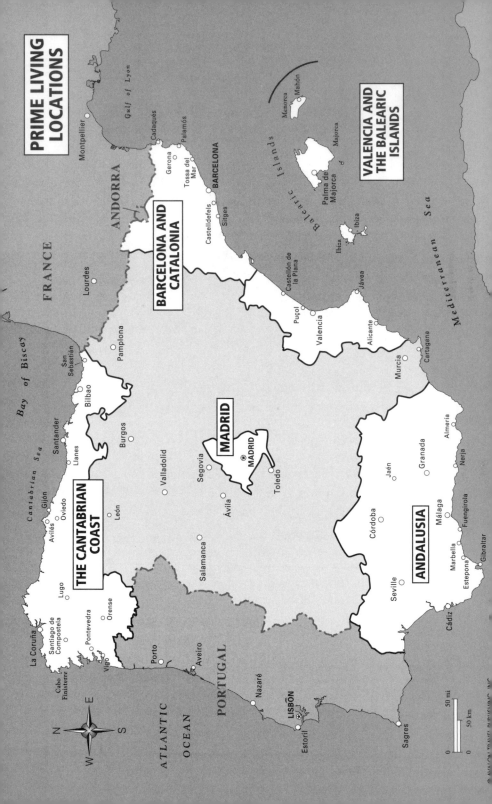

PRIME LIVING LOCATIONS

VALENCIA AND THE BALEARIC ISLANDS

BARCELONA AND CATALONIA

BARCELONA

MADRID

MADRID

THE CANTABRIAN COAST

ANDALUSIA

FRANCE

ANDORRA

PORTUGAL

ATLANTIC OCEAN

Bay of Biscay

Cantabrian Sea

Gulf of Lyon

Balearic Islands

Mediterranean Sea

Montpellier
Lourdes
Pamplona
San Sebastián
Bilbao
Santander
Llanes
Burgos
Oviedo
Gijón
Avilés
Lugo
La Coruña
Santiago de Compostela
Pontevedra
Vigo
Orense
León
Valladolid
Salamanca
Ávila
Segovia
Toledo
Cabo Finisterre
Porto
Aveiro
Nazaré
LISBON
Estoril
Sagres
Cádiz
Seville
Córdoba
Jaén
Granada
Almería
Nerja
Málaga
Fuengirola
Marbella
Estepona
Gibraltar
Murcia
Cartagena
Alicante
Jávea
Valencia
Puçol
Castellón de la Plana
Ibiza
Ibiza
Majorca
Palma de Majorca
Menorca
Mahón
Castelldefels
Sitges
Barcelona
Tossa del Mar
Gerona
Palamós
Cadaqués

N
W E
S

0   50 mi
0   50 km

Overview

Talk to anyone living in Spain and they'll likely tell you that they've found the country's most idyllic spot—and the funny thing is they're often right. Those who want a slower pace, backcountry living, and a lot of greenery will be thrilled to wind up on the craggy coast of Galicia. But for anyone who craves the manic pulse of long nights out that don't end until sunrise, Madrid is undoubtedly to place to be. There's one thing that's certain: Spain offers a seemingly endless array of possibilities and each one is distinct. Although the following chapters don't cover every town in Spain, those most populated (by Spaniards and foreigners alike) are mentioned, as are some of the most desirable country destinations.

MADRID

Spain's capital appeals to both young and old, urbanites and suburbanites—the city is as varied as you'd expect any European capital to be. This is the seat of politics and the center of culture. Every neighborhood is bursting with tapas bars and restaurants offering a range of fare that includes hearty and traditional dishes, and modern creations inspired by old classics. There's no doubt that Madrid has drawing power, but add to the list the notorious nightlife and it's little wonder that people from even the remotest corners of Spain choose Madrid when they seek out big-city life. If you have young children, you'll find life easy in any part of the city but you'll also discover more space in the suburbs. Those who choose to live in one of the communities in the outskirts will find less noise, houses rather than apartments, plenty of schools, more grass, and less pavement. However, plenty of folks prefer to duke it out for space right in the urban center where all the action can be found. Now, just one thing to note: because Madrid is the country's most popular city, it's also the country's most expensive one.

BARCELONA AND CATALONIA

Barcelona is unequivocally Spain's most international town, and it's home to a flourishing community of expatriates. The late-night clubs attract a slew of European party-seekers, many of whom are recent arrivals to the city. Artists are moving to Barcelona in droves, and even lovers of the great outdoors enjoy life in an urban space with nearby beach-and-mountain access. Families also do well in Barcelona; the city offers a choice of international schools and parks abound. Much like San Francisco in the United States, Barcelona offers the best of both worlds—city living with nature still within reach. Yet Barcelona is pricey—Madrid is the only place in Spain that's more expensive.

> *If you prefer a quieter life near the beach but you also want to be a short train-ride away from a sophisticated urban area, you would do well on the Costa Brava.*

Head north from Barcelona and you'll quickly find yourself in rural Catalonia. The majority of those who choose this spot are retirees, but nature enthusiasts of all ages will find a playground right outside their front doors. At first glance, the Costa Brava seems to be filled with built-up resorts, but a closer look at the area reveals a few rustic towns full of history, where Catalan is the reigning tongue. If you prefer a quieter life near the beach but you also want to be a short train-ride away from a sophisticated urban area, you would do well on the Costa Brava. This is an ideal place for people who want to kick back in luxury. Sitges—a decent-sized town south of Barcelona—is a popular spot among beach lovers, partiers, and commuters who want a little distance from the big city. The town mellows out during the off-season but in the summer months it's in full swing and that's precisely what so many Sitges residents adore about their home.

VALENCIA AND THE BALEARIC ISLANDS

Valencia is the place to be if you want the comforts of a decent-sized city without the frenetic tempo of a huge metropolis. It's the country's third-largest city and though it's not exactly beautiful, it compensates by throwing great parties (especially Las Fallas de San José, a spectacular street party that rages on for five days every March). It also offers heavenly stretches of beach, and paella that beats any other. Houses and apartments cost less than the going rate in both Barcelona and Madrid (prices are mid-range for Spain). Those who live here often boast that their lifestyle is not only more affordable than for residents of other cities, it's also more peaceful. Just outside the city, you can find commuter towns with sprawling villas and a few solid international schools to boot. From Valencia, traveling south along the Costa Blanca you can dodge the concrete high-rises and instead find bucolic, coastal towns and small urban areas such as Alicante—a place that provides every amenity you'll want including entertainment, restaurants, and Internet connections. However, Alicante offers fewer cultural outlets than Spain's big cities. The population along this stretch of Spain is growing quickly and property prices reflect its popularity; but if you secure a villa along the Costa Blanca, you'll find a beach lover's paradise.

Some people forgo the mainland for life on the nearby Balearic Islands, and if you're considering that move you should be up for a constant party. The islands are known for their nightlife but if you chose your home wisely, you can settle in a spot that stands apart from the masses of tourists and yet you'll still be ideally situated should you want to enjoy the resort culture offered in this part of Spain.

ANDALUSIA

Although many don't know it, when most people picture Spain, they conjure up an image of Andalusia: green, rural, the birthplace of flamenco, and a region with deep ties to Moorish and Roma culture. Seville and Granada—the area's two biggest cities—are entirely different from one another. Seville exudes a stately elegance and, not surprisingly, it's a tad conservative. Granada is a bit rougher around the edges; it's more casual, attracts younger people, and has a more intimate air to it. Throughout Andalusia, the weather is hot in the summers, temperate in the winters, and the pace of life is decadently slow. Yet in Seville, Granada, and the Costa del Sol, you can find a variety of movie theaters, health clinics,

Although many don't know it, when most people picture Spain, they conjure up an image of Andalusia: green, rural, the birthplace of flamenco, and a region with deep ties to Moorish and Roma culture.

restaurants, and the like. Outside the resort towns on the coast, you'll find a smaller selection of international schools than you would in Madrid and Barcelona.

The Costa del Sol is Spain's most famous tourist-magnet and it still attracts hordes of foreigners, but most are just looking for a brief getaway to the beach. Still, plenty of people find this place alluring enough to stick around for good, and they have an easier time at adapting than those who live elsewhere in Spain. Some communities are almost entirely populated by northern Europeans, and you could end up in a town where speaking Spanish is optional. Is this a plus? A minus? You decide. You'll find plenty of international schools and amenities that range from the useful (think grocery stores and a long list of doctors) to the out-and-out deluxe (think mud wraps, golf courses, and decadent massages).

THE CANTABRIAN COAST

If you want to plunge deep into Spain's backcountry, Galicia is the place to do it. The northwest corner of Spain jutting out over Portugal is a pocket of forests, rivers, mountains, jagged coastline, gray mists, and serenity—and it's unjustly overshadowed by Spain's more celebrated areas to the south. Yet plenty of those who live here enjoy Galicia just the way it is: a wild arcadia and a relative secret. Most foreigners who live in Galicia do not seek out urban life—they prefer country living. This is one of Spain's poorest regions and as you might expect, services are harder to come by and perks such as DSL lines are more difficult to secure than they are elsewhere. Naturally, clinics and hospitals are around but your choices of doctors will be limited. Yet such drawbacks are acceptable to those who choose to make Galicia home because what's lost in ease is gained in natural beauty. Despite the rainy weather, this is arguably Spain's most gorgeous spot.

The small regions of Asturias and Cantabria pull in small numbers of foreigners seeking quiet lives near the beach and mountains. Oviedo and Santander—both modestly sized cities—are particular favorites among those seeking life in this area. In both places you'll find schools, theaters, and some other cultural perks, but best of all, nature is still blissfully nearby.

Basque Country is the most famous locale among Spain's northern lures, and most people drawn to the area head straight for the coastal city San Sebastián (Donostia in Basque). The region is broadly distinguished by its temperate climate, a thriving industrial sector, and the Bay of Biscay, which pulls in surfers from the whole of Europe thanks to its fierce waves. The regional language—one with no known connection to any other—also makes San Sebastián unique. Fewer expats live here than in the south. But those who do make their homes here adore the relative quite, the proximity to nature, and the elegance and culture that's available in San Sebastián. However, the cost of living is significantly higher than it is in the rest of the north.

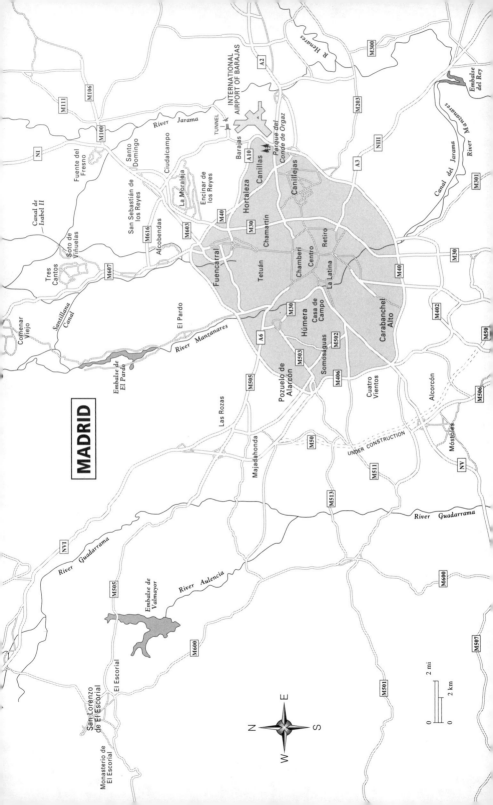

Madrid

Madrid is as vibrant and forward-looking as it is infused with reminders of the romantic, old Spain that Cervantes wrote about in his signature novel, *Don Quixote*. Originally a Moorish fortress that dates back to the 10th century, Madrid wasn't much of a town until 1561 when Philip II moved his court here from its previous spot in nearby Toledo. Since then, the city has developed into a cultural Mecca. Smack in the center of the country, the city looms on the *meseta* (tableland), a high, flat stretch of fertile earth that's sun-scorched in the summer and downright chilly in the winter. The mercury has been known to dip below the teens and on rare summer days it can soar above 100°F. The city is also surprisingly high; at 2,120 feet it's Europe's highest capital. But the area's geographical extremes are only one piece of this intricate city's rich personality.

By European standards, Madrid suffered a late start, and many point out that this city lacks the history-steeped physical beauty of places like

A Madrileño boats around the lake in El Parque del Buen Retiro.

Paris and Rome. This is a fair point, although even a cursory visit shows that Madrid has plenty of architectural triumphs to boast of, most especially in the center, which houses both the Royal Palace and the Plaza Mayor. Yet Madrid has an altogether different appeal, and for those who choose to live here, it's one that's equally as powerful as outward appearance. Madrid truly *feels* like the center of Spain. During the day, the streets buzz with the palpable sensation of business being conducted, local and national politics being argued, tourists marveling at the works of Goya and Velázquez in the Museo del Prado or wandering through the Parque del Buen Retiro. Come nightfall, galleries host openings, theaters fill, taverns grow rowdy, families pack into restaurants, and clubs grow jam-packed with all those who are determined to stay awake until dawn. With three million residents, the city is Spain's most populated. Throw in the outer suburbs, and the population of the region numbers 5.53 million people. Madrid caters to people with a broad range of interests. From the artistic to the political, it's all here.

Given all its enticements, many Americans (and in fact people from all over the world) have chosen to make Madrid a long-term home. Of the approximately 74,000 Americans living in Spain, it's certain that a vast number of them are in Madrid, though there are no reliable statistics on

The Public's Garden

Take a stroll through El Parque del Buen Retiro on any summer Sunday and you might think that every resident of the city is there enjoying the capital's great, green space. Families stroll five abreast, children sit in the sun eating ice cream and watching puppet shows, couples row rented boats around the lake, and tarot card readers predict the future for anyone willing to shell out a few euros for the service. Given how egalitarian the area is today, it's worth noting that it wasn't always so. The park opened as a royal garden that was decidedly for the monarchy. What's more, the park was built to fashion a bragging point; the royalty wanted a gorgeous triumph that might help put Madrid on the map.

In the 1630s when Spain's empire was quickly slipping away, Philip IV decided to flex some muscle and show off Madrid—a capital to suit the glorious empire that the king wanted to hang onto. The only snag in the plan was that Madrid wasn't that glorious—not then anyway. As a modern city it was young, it didn't have much of a river, and to the embarrassment of Madrileños, their city had been founded by the Moors. So the royalty decided to enhance the city's stature by making Madrid beautiful and what is now the Parque del Buen Retiro was born as part of that plan.

Until the 17th century, the area surrounding El Parque del Buen Retiro was untamed land. So some of Europe's most illustrious gardeners were called on to turn 300 acres of near wilderness into a verdant masterpiece complete with a lake. The result was stunning. Soon after, Philip IV's right-hand man, Count Duke Olivares,

built the Palacio del Buen Ratiro for the king. However, the public only gained admission to the gardens in 1767 and then, only certain portions were available. In 1868, the park fully opened to the citizens and with that change the royal gardens officially became a park.

Today, the area can boast newer attractions, too. In 1790, Charles III built the Observatorio Astronómico. The neoclassical building is one of Madrid's prettiest and it still contains a working telescope. In 1887 the Palacio del Cristal—the glass structure on the south side of the lake—was constructed to house exotic flowers in the winter, and floral exhibits are still hosted there today. A monument to Alfonso XII was erected in 1902 and it still stands over the lake. One of the park's most unusual attractions is also one of the least noticed. A statue called Angel Caído (Angel Falling) was added to the park's collection in the 19th century. This is the image of Lucifer falling from heaven, and it's said to be the only public statue of Satan in the world.

For all the history hidden among the trees and monuments, few people take notice and there's good reason for that. The best aspects of the park aren't hidden in the footnotes of its history. The area's very best feature is that it manages to draw just about everyone in the city. Despite the fact that it's now a public place Philip IV's ambitions for the park worked out . . . in a way. Today, El Parque del Buen Retiro truly is a beautiful spot that befits a celebrated city.

El Parque del Buen Retiro is sprinkled with gardens and fountains.

© Nikki Weinstein

just how many. However, there are unquestionably fewer Americans in Madrid than there are people from other countries such as Germany and England. While some *extranjeros* (foreigners) might find themselves immersed in a community of their fellow citizens, Americans won't. That reality comes with a distinct benefit: new arrivals from the States won't find a soft landing pad of comforts from home, so they have little choice but to mix into the city's predominant culture, and for most people living abroad that is the main point of the experience.

The Lay of the Land

When people say that Madrid is in the center of it all, they truly mean it. The city isn't the figurative heart of the country nor is it kind of near the geographical center—it literally *is* the middle of Spain. To be more specific, the sprawling square Puerta del Sol marks the spot and it's referred to as "kilometer zero." From that nucleus all the nation's roads wind out. When you're driving along in Andalusia or Galicia and you come across a kilometer mark on the side of the road, the number you see tells you just how many kilometers you are from Puerta del Sol. The area surrounding Sol is the oldest part of Madrid.

Just north of Sol, you'll find the Gran Vía. This broad avenue lined with businesses, stores, and teeming with pedestrians merges into the ritzier Calle de Alcalá. A historic route once considered Europe's most magnificent street, Calle de Alcalá has plenty of bragging points such as the 19th-century Banesto building and the Círculo de Bellas Artes, which gently hints at a kind of modernism that's more commonly seen in Barcelona. Both streets run through Madrid, bisecting the city into the southern and northern zones.

Housing

While Madrid is expensive, the going rate for shelter is less than it is in places such as New York, San Francisco, Paris, and London. Yet that distinction is little consolation to people earning Spanish salaries. Most people in such a position make big concessions in order to live in the capital. Throughout Spain, it's the norm for people to remain at home with the family while in university and sometimes well into their 30s; the reason is mainly economic although culture surely plays a role, too. Those who do move into their own places typically share them with a few *compañeros de piso* (roommates) in order to chip away at the price tag of independence. The fact is, rent can account for as much as 50 percent of a Spanish salary in Madrid and if you're getting your cash from elsewhere, you can still expect rent to take a big bite out of your bank account.

Vacancies are not difficult to come by, although the desirable ones don't exactly abound, either. A good place to begin your search is in the newspaper *Segunda Mano* (www.segundamano.es) under *Inmobiliaria* (property) which lists *venta de pisos* (apartment sales) and *alquiler de pisos* (apartment rentals). The paper can be found at most local newsstands. Online resources like Guía de Madrid (www.guiademadrid.com) also have listings. Some people prefer to hire a service to manage the headache of relocation and one company that comes particularly recommended for the job is Crown Relocations. While most of their clients want to live in Madrid and Barcelona, they've helped people move to cities throughout the country. Another option is ignoring the ads and going through an agent—if you do choose to go through an *Agente Inmobiliario* (real estate agent), the normal cut taken for the service amounts to about half a month's rent.

> The majority of apartments are not cramped, especially to those expecting apartments like those in New York and Paris where cubbyholes pass for real estate.

An improved economy in Spain has given more people more money with which to invest. Lately, the stock market has been a shaky bet but that's less true of property and it doesn't take Alan Greenspan to explain the consequence of that—prices on both purchases and rentals have been increasing at an alarming rate. So what does a place in Madrid really cost? That answer depends on the neighborhood and the unit itself, but the monthly rent in the city center can begin as low as €700–1,300 ($875–1,625) for a two-bedroom. A three-bedroom apartment usually exceeds €1,500 ($1,875) per month, and if the building is prime it will top that number by a lot. Although apartments priced on the lower end of that scale can be found, they're true steals. Sale prices also change drastically according to the building, but for the city center, you should expect to pay anywhere from €225,000–850,000 ($281,000–1,063,000) for a two-to-three bedroom place. Pricing a place by the square meter or foot is a fallible technique as one meter of apartment in a swanky neighborhood or an attractive, older building costs far more than the same in a working-class area or building in need of renovation, without an elevator or air-conditioning.

The good news is that you'll get a good amount for your money. The majority of apartments are not cramped, especially to those expecting apartments like those in New York and Paris where cubbyholes pass for real estate. For a two-bedroom place in the city, 200 square feet (60 square meters) is the average. Some places are much smaller of course, some much bigger. However, one word of warning: if you fall in love with a place for its aged charm, remember that everything about the place is likely older, including the pipes and wiring. You might have a few more hassles in that regard than you would in a newer place.

Finally, as the old adage goes (only slightly amended), you can't judge a home by its doorway. Walk through the streets in Madrid and you'll find endless numbers of stately, old doors crafted by artisans and suggesting splendor within. In many cases, the beauty of the interior matches that of the exterior but in just as many cases, it does not. Madrid may be young when measured against other cities in Europe, but it's still a town that's been around for a long time. Plenty of the buildings have been altered multiple times over and it's impossible to know what an apartment will look like until you view its interior.

WHERE TO LIVE

No matter where you live—city center or suburbs—you'll find everything you need right in the neighborhood. Madrid is a huge urban space and people live and work in all neighborhoods. That means that the city is dense with grocery stores, Internet cafés, restaurants, and the like. The suburbs have all of those same things right in town—the only difference is that you might have to reach those places on wheels rather than on foot.

Don't worry about seeking out a place with a launderette nearby—you'll almost certainly have a washing machine in your house. (That's right—no more lugging loaded laundry baskets around town!) Unfortunately, you probably won't have a drier and instead you'll rely on clotheslines and drying racks as everyone Spanish does.

The Center

When people refer to this cluster of neighborhoods, it's easy to think that the word *centro* (center) refers to the entire country and not simply to the city—here, the pulse of Spain beats that powerfully. Each of the *barrios* (neighborhoods) that make up this area blend gradually into the neighboring territory and yet each still retains its own personality. Puerta del Sol and Gran Vía are places you'll inevitably grow to know well if you're living anywhere near Madrid. Together they make up the city's commercial hub and tourist nucleus. This part of town is always crowded, often exciting and decidedly not the place for those with acute noise-sen-

Plaza de Oriente

You'll know Puerta del Sol when you see this landmark sign.

sitivity. Puerta del Sol (or just "Sol") is home to Madrid's proud symbol—that's a statue of a female bear eating from a *madroño* (a tree with fruit that resemble strawberries). Sol also marks the place where a city gate once stood thus giving the area its name, "door of the sun." Rent for a two-bedroom apartment on one of the residential streets just off of Sol costs €700–1,300 ($875–1,625). To buy would cost as least €225,000 ($281,000) and prices go up from there.

Los Austrias and La Latina border Sol to the east and south respectively. Both neighborhoods are part of the city's most historic area. They're picturesque and marked by twisting streets, brightly colored doorways, and attractive plazas. Los Austrias (The Austrias) might seem like an strange name for a Spanish *barrio,* but there is logic to it: the first generations of Habsburg Royals built this area and though the architecture hardly hints at the family's roots, the name pays homage to the royal lineage. The Plaza de Oriente where one finds the Royal Palace is, many argue, the stateliest corner of the city and not coincidentally, the Parliament is just around the corner. Aside from in the Palace's plaza (which has a few buildings catering to politicians and the ultra-rich), homes are priced as they are throughout the center. You can expect to pay €700–1,300 ($875–1,625) per month for a two-bedroom, and

€225,000 ($281,000) and higher to buy. Depending on the building and the unit, you might pay *a lot* more.

Heading south, you'll find the Plaza Mayor, another notable landmark that has been around since the 17th century when Philip III commissioned the building of the site. (Naturally, that's him seated on the horse in the middle of the plaza.) If walls could talk, the Castilian-baroque ones surrounding the plaza would have the city's most colorful stories. This is the site of Madrid's early bullfights, executions during the Inquisition, annual parties and concerts galore. Today the plaza continues to be a central meeting spot for Madrileños (Madrid residents) and the site of regular fiestas. South of the Plaza Mayor is La Latina—a glamorously, gritty magnet for the beautiful set on the political left. Both Los Austrias and La Latina are popular with 20-somethings and 30-somethings who don't mind some noise drifting in through their windows, but want less of it than the steady din that emanates from Sol. Again, the building and quality of the apartment means everything when it comes to prices, but you likely won't pay less than €700 ($875) a month for rent, and you might pay a good deal more. Purchasing prices begin around €225,000 ($281,000).

The Rastro and Lavapiés are enjoyed by day but because of the reputation for crime in this area (an exaggerated reputation, say some), many people steer clear of the neighborhood at night. Both of these are considered the most multicultural neighborhoods in the city, and they're also among the most historic. Though a little dilapidated these days, the architecture shows off that rich past. Each Sunday, Madrileños and visitors alike crowd into the Rastro for a flea market that dates back centuries. You're unlikely to find a hidden treasure buried in the piles of kitsch and mass-produced junk that fill the stalls lining the streets, but simply walking around and taking part in the tradition is the main point. Most of those who live here are attracted to the notion of living in the center for less money. This is the one part of the city where prices dip down below the average for the center. You might rent a two-bedroom place for as little as €600 ($750) and buy one for €175,000 ($219,000).

Just north of the Gran Vía, Chueca and Malasaña are considered the most avant-garde *barrios* in Madrid. Until recently, Chueca was the closest thing the city had to a red-light district but for better or worse, recent gentrification has forced the prostitutes and drug-addicts to the outskirts. Chueca has an active gay scene though that is only one aspect of this dynamic neighborhood. It's also full of shops selling fashion-forward clothing, cafés with minimalist art, and restaurants where entrées are served with mango sauces and other modern creations. Not

The Guy Who Put the *Vida* in Movida

You've probably heard of Pedro Almodóvar already—he's the guy who directed *Women on the Verge of a Nervous Breakdown, All About My Mother, Talk to Her,* and a host of other movies. You've probably heard that his films are artsy, and maybe you've also heard that people either love his work or they hate it. But what you might not know is that Spain's darling auteur was part of an entire movement in the late 1970s and early 1980s.

While it might seem surprising that the 1980s even *had* movements, the decade you likely remember for glut and shoulder pads was a bold period of awakening in Spain. Franco was dead and buried, blatant sexuality and subversive creativity began to blossom, and Movida was born. The creative movement was most visible in the arts, but really the artists themselves were part of Movida—the very way in which they lived their lives was a part of the art they created. Almodóvar was more than just there as a witness—he was the group's heart and soul.

The great director started out in Madrid by selling secondhand junk at the Rastro. Soon he had cross-dressing nightclub act and not long after that, he was running around the city with a Super 8 camera. His early flicks give a good dose of Movida's spirit.

In *Pepi, Luci, Bom and Other Girls on the Heap* (1980), *Labyrinth of Passion* (1982), and *Dark Habits* (1983), Almodóvar depicts drug-taking nuns and cross-dressing judges. It's not hard to catch his drift—Franco's Spain was decidedly gone and thanks in part to Almodóvar, its foundations began to crack in Madrid first.

In its heyday, Movida had its own magazine and gallery, and the central figures of the movement occupied city bars until the wee hours. These days, a few of those iconic individuals are still around. You'll see Alaska, although you probably won't recognize her from her screen moments in *Pepi, Luci, Bom and Other Girls on the Heap.* The singer-cum-club-owner's presence is most strongly felt on gay pride day when her anthem *Bailando* (think "It's Raining Men" only in Spanish) blasts from floats winding through the city. The Movida photographer Alberto Garcia-Alix continues to exhibit his work and even more impressively, he show up at openings and events throughout Madrid. Although he looks like he could use a nap, he's still partying like it's 1982.

While the movement itself is over, Movida helped catapult Spain into a new era—one in keeping with the rest of western Europe. Just take in the gay bars in Chueca, the bohemian flair of Malasaña, and the all-night clubs throughout the city, and you'll see that the movement mattered then and it matters still—Movida was the first sign of Spain's fully modern incarnation.

surprisingly, the area's recent overhaul has succeeded in raising home prices, too, but they don't exceed the average for the center as a whole. Rent for a two-bedroom begins around €700 ($875) but you're far more likely to pay about €1,000 ($1,250) a month. To buy the same sort of place prices begin around €220,000 ($275,000) and they can be much more expensive.

Slightly north of Chueca, Plaza Dos del Mayo functions as Malasaña's epicenter. Despite the effervescent feel that the plaza and its surroundings

© Myriam Weinstein

Strolling through El Parque del Buen Retiro

exude today, this was a run-down area following the Civil War. At one point there was even talk of decimating the whole city section and starting anew but those plans never came to pass and Malasaña had a second-wind during the heady, artistic post-Franco days. There's still something of that atmosphere there today and while not the most architecturally interesting spot in Madrid, Malasaña's ultramodern aura does more than enough to compensate. Malasaña's property prices are on average the same as Chueca's.

North of Center
Plaza de Colón, the city's salute to Christopher Columbus, functions as an unofficial gateway to Salamanca and Recoletos in the northwest part of the city and what is hands-down the most posh part of town. Unlike the neighborhoods south of Sol and just north of the Gran Vía, these locales attract more families and more corporate transfers than other districts. The streets radiate elegance and not only because of the designer stores that line them. The imperial Parque del Buen Retiro borders this area, the buildings (while not as old as the ones in Los Austrias, La Latina, and Lavapiés) are stunning, the restaurants are among the city's most cosmopolitan, and yet, for all its magnetism, Salamanca is blissfully quiet at night. To buy a two-bedroom €450,000

($563,000) is the bottom end of the price range and there is no limit. For rentals, €1,100 ($1,375) might be obtainable for a two-bedroom, but that would be a bargain and you're more likely to pay about €2,100 ($2,625) a month.

Prices in Chamberí are also inflated (though slightly less so than in Salamanca and Recoletos where people pay for proximity to the center). However, Chamberí is ideal for those who don't want to be in the middle of the city but also don't want to be far from it. Chamartín began as a working-class neighborhood. Perhaps it has personality and charm today because it enjoyed a more interesting beginning than neighborhoods whose rows of modern houses rose as a utilitarian answer to urban sprawl. Today the demographic has changed and this is an upscale area that caters to families.

> *The imperial Parque del Buen Retiro borders this area, the buildings are stunning, the restaurants are among the city's most cosmopolitan, and yet, for all its magnetism, Salamanca is blissfully quiet at night.*

Suburban Madrid

The word "suburb" conjures up a particular image in the United States—one of split-level, clapboard houses with working fireplaces, emerald green lawns, and a white-picket fence thrown in for good measure. As in the United States, Spanish suburbs were built during boom-years to provide relief from overcrowded cities and the essential benefits are the same in both countries: proximity to the city center, family-oriented communities, a little more breathing space, and a lot more tranquility. Most suburbs have a small commercial area and a few restaurants to that cater to local residents and spare them the hassle of traveling into the city for everyday necessities. However, while American and Spanish suburbs are similar, they're not quite the same. For example, free-standing houses exist in Madrid but attached townhouses (or "terraced houses") are more common. Likewise, most swimming pools are either public or private in the United States—whereas here they're often shared among the members of a given community.

The quality-of-life benefits in the outskirts are numerous, yet there are some negatives, too. Suburban dwellers complain most about Madrid's unbearable traffic, a phenomenon most infuriating on Friday and Sunday evenings, but the daily dose of congestion is so excruciating that some people who work in the city spend about two hours in the car every day. The stream of cars slowly chugging into the city each morning and back out in the afternoons is a natural result of Madrid's enormous suburban population. These communities are no afterthought. More than two million residents call Madrid's outer district home. There is some variation between the neighborhoods. Some feature more luxurious, detached homes with lawns and others have townhouses and with small communities that share swimming pools and gardens. All the outlying districts are relatively new. The housing boom in Madrid began full-force in the 1980s, but some are newer than others.

Northern Communities: The northern suburbs La Moraleja, El Soto de la Moraleja, and Encinar de los Reyes are enormously popular with foreigners. The commute into the city center averages 20–45 minutes (depending on both distance and traffic) and the area boasts a solid selection of bilingual schools. Several British schools are nearby, including one boarding school. There's a Spanish school with an English curriculum, and you'll find a Montessori School as well as the city's only Jewish school.

The perks are ample. Buses connect these suburbs with the city. Local residents tee up at one of two private golf clubs. Running errands is made easy thanks to the local markets and shopping centers. These days, finding vacancies in La Moraleja—a mere 10-minute drive from northern Madrid—is a challenge. However, some people get lucky. Real Madrid's new star-player (and international heartthrob) David Beckham and his wife Victoria (the artist formerly known as Posh Spice) secured a McMansion in the elite La Moraleja. If you also strike gold and find a place, it will likely be a detached house averaging 2,500 square meters. Townhouses are smaller and more economical but because this suburb has mainly detached homes, the prices are higher—rent averages €2,500 ($3,125) for a two-bedroom and purchasing prices usually begin around €500,000 ($625,000) and head up from there.

El Soto de la Moraleja and El Encinar de los Reyes both offer access to the same schools and community benefits as la Moraleja but for less money. Apartments and terraced houses are the rule here and there's currently new construction in Encinar de los Reyes, which was a U.S. Air Force base in its first life. A two-bedroom townhouse might be rented for €1,400 ($1,750) and can be bought for €300,000 ($375,000).

Northeast of Madrid, Aurturo Soria and the Parque Conde de Orgaz also attract many foreigners with apartment blocks and terraced houses, the British primary school nearby, the selection of nursery schools, and the local bilingual school. These suburbs are accented with trees and all shades of green. Homes here tend to go for similar prices to those in El Soto de la Moraleja and El Encinar de los Reyes.

A little further north from the city center, Santo Domingo, Ciudalcampo, and Fuente Del Frenso have detached houses for less than they cost in La Moraleja. But these homes have another price: the agonizing

30–50 minute drive to the city center. When you aren't coming or going behind the wheel of a car, this part of town is a pleasant place with decent shopping, a few local clubs with golf courses, tennis courts, and even horseback riding. A two-bedroom home can be rented for prices beginning around €1,600 ($2,000) and can be bought for €250,000 ($313,000) and more.

The newer quarter, Soto de Viñuelas is becoming an increasingly populated due to the fact that a British school is there. Yet it's still relatively new and thus short on resident services. A good amount of property is available here at rates similar to El Soto de la Moraleja and Encinar de los Reyes. You'll find detached houses here as well as townhouses.

Western Communities: Because the American School of Madrid (K-12) is here, so are a lot of Madrid's American families. These residential zones blend into each other more subtly than the ones in the north, so they have more amenities. If you have young children, you will certainly visit this part of town for the water park, the shopping malls, and the ice-skating rink.

Somosaguas and Habitúmera lie further from the city-center than some neighborhoods, but they're also more Americanized than other places. Many of the houses are unattached and some even come with their own swimming pools. A decent number of markets and stores carry both necessities and luxury items. In addition to the American school, there's a Montessori School, a British school, and a choice of Spanish schools, all of which also attract families. A two-bedroom home typically rents for at least €2,000 ($2,500) and can be bought for prices beginning at €400,000 ($500,000).

Ponzuelo offers plenty of shopping opportunities but if you live in this suburb, you'll face a nasty commute (sometimes more than an hour each way) and have fewer school options, although there are a few bilingual schools as well as some well-regarded Spanish ones. Its popularity among Americans is mainly due to the luxury houses that go for slightly lower prices than the homes in nearby Somosaguas. One month's rent for a two-bedroom unit can be €2,000 ($2,500), which is a reasonable price for an independent home. The asking price to buy typically starts at €400,000 ($500,000).

Although Las Rozas and Majadahonda are also lacking community international schools, their popularity is on the rise. They're both a relatively heavenly 20–40 minutes drive to central Madrid and they're also affordable. Detached homes, townhouses, and apartments can all be purchased and rented here. If you have a family and are not intent on educating your children in an international school, the resident Spanish schools are known to provide a solid education. To rent a two-bedroom, the range can be anywhere from €1,500–4,000 ($1,900–5,000). To purchase the same sort of place, the range is similarly expansive: €300,000 ($375,000) and upwards.

REAL ESTATE AGENTS: MADRID

You won't be at a loss to find real estate agents to help you in your housing search, but here are a few that come particularly recommended. Relocation agencies are also listed.

Real Estate Agents

Coldwell Banker
Gran Vía, 86
Grupo de ascensores 3, planta 2
28013 Madrid
tel. 91 454 97 49
www.cbeurope.com

Intromadrid
Calle Mesena, 104
28033 Madrid
tel. 91 766 06 61
www.immomadrid.com

M&M
Avenida de Machupichu, 19
28043 Madrid
tel. 91 388 25 96

Roan Asesoramiento Inmobiliarios
Plaza de la Castellana, 120
28046 Madrid
tel. 91 395 83 00
fax 91 561 76 56
www.roan.es

Relocation Agencies

Crown Relocations
Ctra. de Mejorada, 1
Planta 1
28830 Madrid
tel. 91 485 06 00
fax 91 673 80 02
www.crownrelo.com

Madrid Experts
San Bernardo, 89
Piso 4, Izquierda
28015 Madrid
tel. 91 445 66 22
www.madridexperts.com

Relocations España
Calle de Arturo Soria, 263 B
28033 Madrid
tel. 902 190 317
fax 91 384 39 01

Getting Around

It doesn't take long to get a feel for the city's layout—Madrid is compact and easily navigable by one of the 11 metro lines. The metro operates 6 A.M.–1:30 A.M. daily; a single fare costs €1.10 ($140) and a 10-journey ticket goes for €5.20 ($6.50). If you ride daily, investing €33–81 ($41–101) for a monthly pass will save you money. The pass has the added bonus of covering bus-fare, too. The price of the card depends on what zone you want but keep in mind that the broader the area, the higher the price. Just one warning: *abono transportes* (monthly passes) are valid for one calendar month—the first of the month, not the date of purchase, counts as day one. An identity card and two passport-size photos are needed when buying the pass.

City buses, overseen by Empresa Municipal de Transportes de Madrid are used just a little bit less than the metro, but not by much. Most buses run from 6 A.M.–11:30 P.M. daily. You rarely have to wait more than 10 to 15 minutes for one to come. Fare costs €1.10 ($1.40) for one trip on *las líneas normales* (regular lines), and a monthly pass is €22–63 ($27.50–79). As with the metro, the price depends on the elected zone.

Barcelona and Catalonia

Catalonia (Catalunya) begins in the eastern part of the Pyrenees mountains—that imposing wall of natural beauty that kept Spain isolated for centuries. From that hilly border, the region stretches to the Mediterranean coast, down along the Costa Brava, through Barcelona and the Costa Dorada, where it abuts the border of the Comunidad de Valencia (Community of Valencia). This part of Spain became something of an artistic hothouse back when local boys Pablo Picasso, Joan Miró, and Salvador Dalí earned their reputations. Today the region has maintained its forward-thinking legacy and its international standing as an artistic hub. The cultural offerings of the area are quite a magnet, but the region's natural riches are an equally powerful lure to Spaniards and foreigners alike.

The Pyrenees beckon vacationers with a wealth of enticements. Sparsely inhabited medieval towns nestle into arcadian valleys and impressive skiing and hiking trails are tucked into the mountains. The idyllic beaches grow packed with masses of oiled-up tourists during the

The Spirit of Independence

If Catalonia is your destination, there's one thing you need to know, according to many of the locals: this is all Spanish land now but it is not truly Spain. Instead, they'll tell you that this is *Catalunya*. While that distinction is insisted upon with a stubborn tenacity that is so . . . well, Spanish, the point is a fair one. Catalonia is unique and its rich history attests to that point.

In 218 B.C., the Romans arrived in Spain. Evidence strongly suggests that around 230 B.C., Hamicar Barca (Hannibal's father) began a settlement called Barcino on the Mont Taber, a well-situated hill that rises up between two streams and lies near the coast. (Today, that's in the Barri Gòtic district of Barcelona and the original Roman temple has been replaced with a cathedral.) By 15 B.C., the Romans fully occupied the surrounding territory and officially governed the people. The town wasn't much to speak of at first, but the course of the next several centuries saw Barcino transformed into an economic powerhouse thanks mainly to its maritime trade and fertile plain. Eventually, Catalonia thrived with Barcelona as its capital and the area became its own, independent dynasty that at its height—between the 13th and 15th centuries—extended its power as far off as Sicily. However, at other points, Catalonia suffered occupations from Romans, Visigoths, Franks, and crippling Moorish invasions. Eventually the rule of Spain took hold completely when the region lost a key battle in 1714. Although some cultural flavor from Catalonia's various invaders was adopted (it's often said that Catalan sounds more French than Spanish), the sweet taste of independence is fondly recalled and for many, it remains the ideal.

Many Catalonians still bristle at the mention of Spain's rule but one need not look too far back to understand why. In the 1930s, after making a couple of pushes for nationhood, the powerful revolutionary spirit of the area was redirected to focus on the Spanish Civil War that was then erupting throughout the country. Barcelona became the capital of republican Spain in 1937—a move that brought bombing raids and other fierce attacks upon the city from the Nationalist forces. The republicans eventually lost the war and when General Franco took control of the country in 1939, he continually punished Catalonia for so vehemently fighting his forces earlier. In an effort to cleanse the area of its republican spirit, thousands were shot in the war's aftermath (executions took place into the 1950s), and Catalan was outlawed in public. Publishing houses and libraries were searched for books printed in the regional language and such publications were then burned. Street and town names were changed to Spanish, and all talk of independence was forcibly silenced.

The country changed from a dictatorship to a parliamentary monarchy shortly after General Franco died in 1975, and at that point the status of Generalitat was once again granted to the area. In 1980, Jordi Pujol—a conservative nationalist who had been imprisoned under Franco's rule—became the president of Catalonia (a position he held until 2003). Streets and signs have returned to Catalan, the local language has a strong place in classrooms, on television, and on the radio, and the sound of Catalan fills the streets. Although the status of Generalitat allows for some autonomy, Catalonia remains under the Spanish flag and battles between the local government and the national government continue to rage on in mellower forms.

summer months before the crowds suddenly thin out again for the rest of the year. And then there's Barcelona—the pride of Catalonia. Spain's second largest city is the country's design capital, an architect's dream, a fashion hot spot, and currently in the midst of a culinary renaissance that's won the notice of food critics from around the world. Many argue that the city had a second wind when it hosted the 1992 summer Olympic Games, and more than a decade later, Barcelona shows no sign of slowing down. It's no wonder that people are moving here en masse—Catalonia and its notorious city seem to offer a little something for everyone.

Barcelona

Barcelona is more than 2,000 years old, and it wears its age well. Medieval churches and remnants of the old city walls dot the streets and tradition is strongly felt and proudly maintained. Yet the city exudes a fresh, modern air, too. Old cafés in tiny plazas serve as meeting spots where people sit in the shade of linden trees. Chrome-accented restaurants with ocean views host boisterous crowds until long past midnight. Antoni Gaudí, a key figure among the *modernistas,* built outrageously shaped buildings that have come to symbolize the city they adorn. The Rambla—that centuries-old promenade running through the heart of town—attracts scores of tourists and locals alike.

Things weren't always so prosperous. Just a little more than 10 years ago, Barcelona was run-down—just a shadow of the destination point it is today. Preparation for the 1992 Olympic Games gave the city a badly needed face-lift, and those changes still serve Barcelona well.

Since the early 1990s, the locale has hosted several international events that range from the World Buddhist Conference in 1994 to the International AIDS Conference in 2002. Barcelona devoted itself to the much ballyhooed (and nebulously defined) Fòrum Universal de les Cultures 2004, a 141-day extravaganza that focused on issues of peace, sustainable development, and cultural diversity. Such mammoth events provide great fuel for the city's economy but they're hardly Barcelona's only source of income. Thanks in part to its excellent harbor, the city is one of the most important trading and manufacturing hubs in the country and ships continuously head out to sea loaded with cargoes of cork, fruit, cotton, wool, and silk products.

Barcelona's many attractions draw attention and the city's enormous population of foreign residents attests to that. Among people from other countries, this is the most popular destination in Spain and

Sant Jordi

Did you know that Barcelona's patron saint (George, or Jordi) is also the patron saint of syphilis sufferers? Perhaps that's why Barcelona celebrates the guy in full, romantic fashion. When Dia de Sant Jordi rolls around every April 23, women give their fellas books, and in return the guys give roses to their sweeties. The event is no small thing—publishers specifically work their schedules in order to launch new titles on that day, and the entire city is transformed into a blanket of vendors hawking books and blooms. By all means, jump into the festivities by handing out love tokens, but before you do, there are a few more things to know about Saint George.

Rumor has it that the guy was a quite a dragon-slayer but in fact, the word "dragon" was possibly (some say probably) a misunderstanding of emperor Diocletian's name. The despotic ruler was fiercely anti-Christian and Saint George was a pretty religious man as you might have already guessed. Interestingly, the slaying part of the story goes a little differently in that version. It's believed that Diocletian had Saint George (a Roman soldier) killed for defending Christianity.

Yet before that fateful event, George was put to death on three separate occasions. Once he was chopped into small pieces, another time he was buried deep in the earth, and he was also consumed by fire. Miraculously, he licked all three events. (While no saint had it easy, enduring three brutal deaths before the final one is a particularly rough hand to be dealt—it seems fair that he's adored now.)

As it turns out, Barcelona is not the only place that appreciates the saint. He's also the patron saint of Portugal, England, Germany, Lithuania, the Greek army, knights, archers, boy scouts, and sufferers of skin diseases. Despite all that devotion, on Valentine's Day, 1969, Pope Paul VI deemed the worship of George optional, but in 2000, Pope John Paul II plucked him from the sidelines and put him back on the Saints' calendar.

It's also worth noting that Shakespeare, Cervantes, Wordsworth, and Rupert Brooke all died on Saint George's day—April 23. Perhaps that's just a coincidence but it's an awfully convenient one. After all, you'll now have a few good wordsmiths to consider when shopping for books for your main squeeze.

it's estimated that 4,000 Americans are currently living in Barcelona. The fact that so many have already settled in means that the new arrivals will find a tremendous support system. If you want to live here and speak English more than Spanish, you can do that more easily here than in just about any other Spanish city. But most people who move here aspire to mix in and not just with people from home.

THE LAY OF THE LAND

The city itself lies on the Pla de Barcelona (or the Barcelona plain), about halfway between France and the Valencia region. The land is only about 14 feet above sea level, although a few hills, such as Mont Taber, rise up above that average height. The region's population totals 6.3 million, 1.5 million of whom live in Barcelona proper. (That number more than doubles to 3.3 million if you count the whole of the greater Barcelona area, outskirts and all.) The land grows steadily flatter towards the south of the region, especially along the Costa Dorada. The temperate Mediterranean climate promises winters so mild that 40°F is the average low, and the air carries strong hints of warmth again as early as March. The summers are kind by Iberian standards. The average high is 82°F, although July and August can make people sweat with occasional scorchers at the 99°F mark.

Local Language

Just how important is the region's language, Catalan? That answer depends on what you want out of your stay in Barcelona. While Catalan was once the dominant tongue, the city is bilingual today and Spanish and Catalan are spoken in equal amounts. Many foreigners choose to ignore Catalan, and while that's a perfectly workable decision, people who have made Catalonia their long-term home will say that in order to fit in and make friends, learning to speak Catalan is a good idea. Classes are offered in abundance, and those classrooms fill with foreigners and

© Nikki Weinstein

Food on display at the bustling La Boqueria market on the Rambla

even Spaniards who have relocated to Catalonia from other parts of the country. Ultimately, speaking Catalan has many benefits but it is by no means a necessity.

WHERE TO LIVE

People live in all corners of the city, and although housing is not considered pricey if compared to, say, London or Paris, the city is among Spain's most expensive (just a little bit behind Madrid) and it's growing costlier each year. You'd be wise to allow more time for your apartment search than you might in a less popular location. While you'll certainly be able to find a place on short notice, if you look under pressure, you might end up paying a higher price for the luxury of settling in quickly. Old homes abound and thanks to Barcelona's rapid expansion in recent years, you'll also have no trouble finding a modern apartment if that's your preference. Having said that, the condition of units varies, even among newer homes.

The average monthly rent is €300 ($375) for a share. Several papers and websites list available rooms, including *Metropolitan* and Loquo (www.loquo.com), an all-around invaluable resource. Anyone who has used the Web-based Craig's List in the United States will be pleased to know that Loquo is a nearly identical site for the Barcelona community. In addition to apartment listings, you might find a dog for sale, a chess partner or a used bicycle. Students and those on a tight budget can use the Habitatge Jove (www.habitatgejove.com) as a resource. The local government-run organization helps young people find rooms, placement with host families, or available apartments. The website requires more than a little patience, but most people have success with this service.

As in the rest of Spain, unless an apartment is listed as furnished, it's not. That might mean it has no amenities at all, even refrigerators, stoves, or curtain rods. If you move in to this sort of apartment for a short-term stay, you might want to rent furniture. Several companies offer that service, and you can find listings for them in the yellow pages. If you're in search of a good relocation service to help with everything from house-hunting to setting up a bank account, several companies in Barcelona can lend a hand. Especially high marks are given to Olympic Advisors and Easy Relocation. (See Real Estate Agents: Barcelona in this chapter.)

As Barcelona has grown more crowded, housing prices have escalated accordingly. There is no set price for a square meter of house—that amount changes by a lot depending on the neighborhood and the condition of the home. However, there's a general rule that's used to approximate prospective rents: €600 ($750) per bedroom for high-end units, and €300 ($375) per bedroom for low-end to mid-range units. In the city-center's choice neighborhoods, you can expect to pay at least €1,200–1,400 ($1,500–1,750) per month for a two-bedroom apartment. To buy a spacious apartment in a choice area or building, you'll pay €200,000 ($250,000) and upwards for a roomy two-to-three bedroom unit in an attractive building. The prices do vary throughout the city but not much. If you find a run-down place in a well-heeled neighborhood, you'll pay about the same as you might for a bright, palatial apartment in a less desirable area.

The Center

When people refer to the Ciutat Vella (old city), they're talking about a cluster of neighborhoods at the core of which lies Barri Gòtic. This historic quarter is about as old as Spain gets. The Museu d'Història de la Ciutat located in Barri Gòtic takes visitors below ground, down to the city's first layer of history—Roman times. You begin your tour by taking in the impressively intact ruins of the Roman settlement, Barcino—floor mosaics, public baths, and all. As you travel a walkway that slowly spirals up, each step is a hop forward in time. The exhibitions reflect the gradual movement of the calendar. Roman artifacts give way to Catholic relics until eventually you arrive back at street level—the 21st century.

> *There's no predicting what's around the next corner in this tangle of streets, but whatever it is, modernity and history are sure to mingle as if their unlikely combination is nothing unusual.*

Outside the museum, the district's long timeline is just as evident in a display that's far more jumbled and twice as enchanting. Among the labyrinth of streets you'll find endless treasures, from modern art collections to sleepy cafés where old men play dominos.

Ciutat Vella is the city's political center and Plaça Sant Jaume is home to both the Palau de la Generalitat (the seat of the regional government) and city hall. Like so much in Barri Gòtic, the square has been refurbished endlessly and now looks younger than its true age. There's no predicting what's around the next corner in this tangle of streets, but whatever it is, modernity and history are sure to mingle as if their unlikely combination is nothing unusual.

On the western side of the Rambla lies El Raval—an area once famously known as the city's seediest district and a place that still retains some of that flavor. This neighborhood is built along the lines of the 13th-century city walls, and until a little after that time, this area was rural land. But the city population was increasing and El Raval then developed into crowded working-class neighborhood that absorbed spillover from the growing population in the oldest part of the city. In fact, the name El Raval derived from an Arabic word that means "outside the city walls" and referred to urban expansion. Today, the neighborhood attracts a mix of immigrants (about 30 percent of this neighborhood's residents come from outside Europe). El Raval has also grown into a hot spot for a host of new bars and restaurants. Despite the attractively bohemian image that these new businesses have brought to the neighborhood, crime continues to be a problem, and for that reason many people shy away from living in El Raval.

The docks of medieval Barcelona jut off of La Ribera and they're the reason for this district's name, which literally means "waterfront." The shore lies farther away now but the area—northeast of Barri Gòtic and across Via Laietana—has retained its original spirit. El Born and Sant Pere, two neighborhoods within the district, were once home to the merchant class—the top tier of society—and today they both still exude a prosperous air. The web of historic streets dotted with boutique museums and historic gems do more to bedazzle tourists than any other area in the city. However, La Ribera has not been without its troubles. In 1714 the Spanish definitively took control of Barcelona and upon that landmark event, the King's forces demolished a large section of the neighborhood in order to build the Ciutadella—a fortress that came to be a despised symbol of Spain's rule. Eventually the fortress came down and that blight on Barcelona's history was softened when the Parc de la Ciutadella was built in the Ciutadella's place. Today the park is a cherished oasis of greenery in the thick of the city.

The old part of the city is a desirable place to live and except for in El Raval, where prices are a little lower, you can expect to pay about €1,200–1,700 ($1,500–2,125) a month. If you're buying, you'll spend €275,000 ($344,000) and upwards.

Barcelona's character has always been bound to the sea, but that's easy to forget when you're immersed in the maze of the urban blocks that make up the center of the city. For a reminder of the seafaring essence that has been part of Barcelona since its inception, head to Barceloneta. The neighborhood is still every bit the working-class spot it's always been. The city built the neighborhood in the 19th century to house the long-displaced residents from La Ribera's leveled corner. A grid-system of roads was laid down, utilitarian, block-housing sprung up, and an inner-city fishing village was born. Barceloneta is no prettier today than it ever was, however, it's hung onto every bit of its authenticity. The local parties give a taste of Barceloneta's culture. Carnaval here includes sea-lore inspired street theater and an age-old tradition that has revelers burying sardines in the sand. The neighborhood has a distinct hipness to it in the way that gentrifying, working-class areas often do. Add the ocean proximity and you probably won't be surprised to discover that the area isn't cheap anymore. Rent on a two-bedroom place will likely be about €1,200–1,500 ($1,500–1,875) a month. If you're buying, you'll spend €250,000 ($313,000) and upwards.

A little more than 10 years ago, Vila Olímpica was nothing but an ignored, industrial stretch of land. Now it's a vibrant neighborhood just off the water, further evidence of the breadth of the changes brought to the city by the 1992 Olympics. Just two years were spent furiously constructing this area and 2,000 new apartments were among the many additions. Originally intended as affordable housing, those apartments became luxury homes instead—no doubt the elevation in price is a result of the area's new desirability. Port Olímpic was built for the Olympic sailing events and now it's a luxury marina peppered with popular bars and some of the city's best restaurants. A Frank Gehry sculpture of an enormous, copper fish is the port's landmark and yet another pretty feature in this attractive spot. If all those benefits don't pull you in for some kickback time, Passeig Marítim, the rambling promenade that connects Port Olímpic to Barceloneta surely will.

Port Olímpic is more Spanish than international, and that's its greatest appeal. Prices for a two-bedroom apartment begin around €200,000 ($250,000) and climb from there. Rent for an equivalent unit can cost €700 ($875) a month.

In the 19th century, Barcelona faced yet more overcrowding and the city's answer to the problem was L'Eixample, the neighborhood just north of Plaça de Catalunya. The urban planner Ildefons Cerdà designed the area with all the practicality that befit his time and the avenues were laid down in an easy-to-understand grid full of straight lines and clean angles. The streets are broad, stately, and marked with upscale stores and fine restaurants. Moreover, the area is so chock-full of landmarks that it earned the praise of UNESCO (the United Nations Educational, Scientific and Cultural Organization). Among the many sites are two by the city's favorite son, Gaudí: La Pedrera and La Sagrada Família. The latter, a cathedral, is the architect's most notorious structure; it's still a work in progress (in other words, less than half finished) and it likely won't be completed for another several years—or more likely, decades.

Despite the many tourist magnets in L'Eixample, visitors are not the only ones who fill these streets. Many locals make their home in one of the many apartment buildings here, and those who do are usually proud to name their address. Vacancies aren't easy to come but should you find an available place, it will cost about what it might if the apartment was in El Born or Sant Pere. The area appeals to a variety of people—20-somethings, 30-somethings, and even families who want to be in the city proper in a commercial location. Monthly rent on a two-bedroom place averages €1,200–1,500 ($1,500–1,875). To own a place, you'll spend at least €250,000 ($313,000) and apartments might even cost a whole lot more.

Montjuïc, the hill overlooking Barcelona, has undergone endless reinvention since the city's early days. The neighborhood's name means Jewish Mountain, and most agree that the moniker comes from the medieval Jewish cemetery on the premises. Big moments in the area's history include the 1929 World Exposition. This event that brought new development to Montjuïc as did the 1992 Olympics, which held some competitions here. However, the neighborhood has also seen more than its share of grim moments, too. In the 17th century, the Spanish capped the mountain with a fortress that loomed over the city and reminded residents of Spain's rule. The already loathed monument became far more detested when it became the site of post-Civil War executions. Today, Montjuïc prominently displays pieces of its history, but more than anything it's a modern neighborhood full of parks (both the theme and green variety) and an endless array of museums and monuments. The area isn't as hip a neighborhood as some, but it is every bit as comfortable. Rent for a two-bedroom apartment is approximately €700 ($875) a month, and prices for the same sort of set-up begin around €200,000 ($250,000) and climb from there.

Gràcia is home to countless urban hippies and hip urbanites; but Birkenstocks or not, plenty of the residents are upscale. This *barrio* offers artistic flare without necessarily skimping on luxury and for many, that's an ideal combination. Gràcia, just north of L'Eixample, joined the city's map in the 19th century but it had been around before then as a separate village. The area has long been known as a bastion of radical thought and there was a time in the last century when anarchism and communism were the norm for the area. It's impossible to mention Gràcia without noting that it has a square named Plaça John Lennon. Okay, I actually *could* talk about the neighborhood without mentioning the Beatle's piece of terra firma, but why ignore such a fun fact—especially one that typifies the character of the area.

Today, a lot of the neighborhood's residents are attracted to the low-rise buildings, choice restaurants, and the wealth of cultural outlets that include two not-so-blockbuster cinemas and a well-regarded theater. But the most famous attraction in this neighborhood is Gaudí's justifiably notorious Parc Güell, which amazes visitors with its fantastic, colorful sculptures. However it's not just tourists strolling through the park's greenery—Parc Güell provides city residents with a welcome reprieve from the city cement. Rent on a two-bedroom place begins around €700 ($875) a month. To buy a place, prices in Gràcia start at €250,000 ($313,000) and climb from there. The better units can cost more than €500,000 ($625,000).

Zona Alta translates into "upper zone." When you see the area, its name makes sense—the residents around here are usually in a higher socioeconomic bracket. The neighborhood is located on the western edge of the city and it breaks down into four separate areas: Sant Gervasi, Sarrià, Pedralbes, and Tres Torres. There are numerous benefits to living in this part of town and that's especially true for families. Zona Alta is about a 10-minute drive to the center of the city—a blissfully short commute when compared to the average daily drive that many suburban dwellers contend with. Even so, some residents opt for public transportation. The area is accessible to the city by buses and trains.

Many of the blocks in the area have communal facilities that might include pools, gardens, and parking garages. Yet for all those benefits, the neighborhood still manages to be an urban one complete with the restaurants, upscale shops, cultural venues, and a smattering of Gaudí works that help keep this part of town beautiful. Three of Barcelona's most popular international schools are located in Zona Alta: an American school, a bilingual Spanish school, and a French school. The schools' proximity is the main reason that the district has become so popular among expatriate families. Newer apartments are the most prevalent sort of housing, although some stately, old houses can be found in Sarrià. Zona Alta's biggest drawback is that the neighborhood pulls in foreign families in the city for relatively brief periods of time. Not only is the neighborhood less Spanish, but also a good many of its residents are transient. Prices average €500,000 ($625,000) and monthly will be approximately €1,700 ($2,125).

Suburbs

Urban sprawl has expanded Barcelona's borders and the result has worked in the suburbs' favor. The divide separating the urban center from many of the outlying residential neighborhoods is shrinking. For suburbanites, such proximity to the city's culture and conveniences is a boon. For some, daily commutes have also been cut down as the city has crept closer. However, there is still some distance between the city and the suburbs, and a car is necessary for most.

Sant Just and Esplugues de Llobregat—two neighborhoods adjacent to each other—are so nearby Barcelona that they could be considered part of the city. However, because both districts are poorly served by public transportation (most residents have cars), they've maintained an aura of independence from Barcelona proper. Rent and housing prices are high, but the good news is that you do get what you pay for. Most homes are detached or semi-detached although a few apartments are also available. Many of the local families chose these spots for their prime access to two international schools, a German one and an American school. The spectacular views are yet another advantage to the districts—Sant Just and Esplugues de Llobregat are situated on a hill and the vantagepoint offers breathtaking vistas of the city. Throughout the area, rent averages €1,200–1,500 ($1,500–1,875) a month, and for deluxe places, you can expect to spend more. If you're buying, you'll spend no less than €250,000 ($313,000) and a few places top the €400,000 ($500,000) mark.

Not only is English a foreign language in Castelldefels, even Spanish is less heard than it once was. This neighborhood—just 11 miles south of Barcelona itself—is a big hit with expatriates, most of whom come from northern Europe. There's a good reason for the area's popularity: it's a magnificent beach-town and it pulls in hordes of day-trippers during the summer months. Despite the fact that this suburb doubles as a vacation destination, rent and home prices have remained relatively stable which is good news for those who choose to live here. The excellent train service is another bonus—it takes about 20 minutes to reach the city center. Unfortunately, travel by car is less convenient and rush-hour traffic can keep commuters on the road for as long as one hour in each direction. Foreign families put up with that headache in order to enjoy the town's attractions as well as the opportunity to enroll their children at a popular international school located in Castelldefels. You can expect to spend about €1,000–1,300 ($1,250–1,625) per month on rent. If you're buying, you'll spend no less than €215,000 ($269,000) and possibly a good deal more.

Romans lived in Sant Cugat del Vallès and in the 8th century, the town housed a Visigothic monastery. But much of the evidence of that assorted history was razed when the Moors invaded the area.

There are still hints of the early past in Sant Cugat del Vallès, but more than anything, the town is a comfortable (if slightly pricey) suburb that caters to year-round residents rather than people who come and go with the seasons. Both apartments and houses are available, and the prime access to public transportation is one of the greatest benefits to living in the area—it's just 30 minutes to the city by train and an hour by bus. Driving, the commute is slowed by traffic but it usually takes just a little more than half an hour to reach Barcelona by car. You'll pay at least €1,200 ($1,500) per month for a two-bedroom home, and €800–1,000 ($1,000–1,250) is the average rent for an apartment. You can expect to pay a minimum of €275,000 ($344,000) for an apartment, although prices can be twice that amount. Homes begin to sell at about €300,000 ($375,000).

REAL ESTATE AGENTS: BARCELONA

You'll find no dearth of people willing to help you settle in, but here are a few recommended agencies.

Real Estate Agents

Home BCN Real Estate Solutions, S.L.
Calle Aragón, 233
1-1B
08007 Barcelona
tel. 93 272 27 67
www.homebcn.com

Fincas Viscasillas & Asociados
Calle Tres Torres, 28
Bajos
08017 Barcelona
tel. 93 205 71 03

Grupo de Empresas Prasa
Avenida Roma, 6–10
08015 Barcelona
tel. 93 226 69 49
fax 93 226 65 82

Relocation Agencies

Crossing Cultures
Calle Josep Carner, 5
08193 Bellaterra
tel. 93 580 87 29
fax 93 580 04 76

Easy Relocation
Avenida 300, 45–47
08860 Castelldefes
tel. 679 18 23 82
www.easyreloc.com

Olympic Advisors, S.L.
Calle Plató, 6
Atico 1
08021 Barcelona
tel. 93 414 40 00
fax 93 414 40 99

GETTING AROUND

You don't need a car to live in Barcelona proper—it's only a necessity in suburbs that aren't connected to the heart of the city by public transportation. In fact, the city's system of metros and buses is among Spain's best.

The metro has five lines, and each is identified both numerically and by color. All lines operate 5 A.M.–midnight Monday–Thursday, 5 A.M.–2 A.M. Friday–Saturday, 6 A.M.–midnight Sunday. A single ride goes for €1.05 ($1.30), but if you're a regular rider, you might as well shell out a little extra for a multi-journey card in order to get discounts over longer periods of time. Options include the T-10 card, which gives you 10 trips for about €6 ($7.50); the T-Familiar, which offers 70 trips within 30 days for €36 ($45); the T-Mes, which provides unlimited travel within 30 days for €38 ($47.50); and the T-Trimestre, which allows you to ride the rails as much as you please for three months for €103 ($130). You can buy tickets in the station, but they're also sold at newsstands, tobacco shops, Servi-Caixa ATM machines, and lottery stands.

The buses begin running around 6 A.M., and the drivers usually quit for the night around 10:30 P.M. Monday–Saturday. Sunday service is more sporadic than normal. The fare is the same as that on the metro, but only single tickets can be bought onboard, although you can use a special-rate card if you already have one.

The Costa Brava

This run of coast begins at Blanes, 37 miles north of Barcelona, and stretches north for 125 rugged miles until the Costa Brava hits the French border. The region earns its name, the Wild Coast, thanks to its rough beauty, accented with coves, inlets, fishing villages, and pine forests. The combination proved breathtaking enough to inspire artists such as Dalí, Picasso, and Chagall. A look at recent history shows that the Costa Brava has also been a huge hit with sun-worshippers. Mass tourism arrived here in the 1950s, and beginning in the 1970s, some of the more handsome spots in the area were swallowed up by concrete highrises and generic resorts. If such tourist playgrounds don't have the sort of homey atmosphere you're looking for, then you should avoid Lloret de Mar. However, a few choice spots have been preserved from the ravaging effects of mass-development. The coastal towns are about an hour away from the Pyrenees, close to Barcelona, and a short drive away from resorts that offers golf, shopping, and spas. The area attracts a large retiree community but younger people are beginning to move to the area, too, probably because it's ideal for outdoor enthusiasts. Winter ski resorts are tucked into the nearby mountains, hiking trails wind through the area, water sports can be enjoyed on the beach, and the resorts provide a good number of golf courses.

THE LAY OF THE LAND

The most powerful attraction of the Costa Brava is the ocean, but the nearby hilly terrain doesn't go unappreciated. While the highest peak of the Pyrenees mountains is found in Aragón (Pico de Aneto measures 11,200 feet), the Catalonian summits aren't too shabby, in many cases exceeding 9,000 feet. At its lowest point Catalonia reaches sea level. The fact is, the combinations of a mountainous interior and a pretty if slightly wild coastline is exactly what makes people fall for this stretch of Spain—within the Costa Brava, you'll find pleasantly varied landscapes.

> *The region earns its name, the Wild Coast, thanks to its rough beauty, accented with coves, inlets, fishing villages, and pine forests. The combination proved breathtaking enough to inspire artists such as Dalí, Picasso, and Chagall.*

The mountains hide an impressive collection of Romanesque churches and monasteries—all architectural relics that nod to the region's golden era in the 11th and 12th centuries when the Moorish threat subsided and Catalonia was allowed to flourish. The Parc Nacional d'Aigüestortes offers hikers a lush dreamland of glacial lakes, granite hills, and dramatic waterfalls, and Baqueira-Beret is a snowy destination point for skiers and snowboarders. In fact, the winter resort is the Pyrenees' largest one. Its slopes are favorites of King Juan Carlos and his family.

Local Language

While Catalan is even more broadly spoken in the small towns of Catalonia than in Barcelona, the areas outside the city also have denser expatriate populations who speak their own languages with each other—namely English. Learning some Catalan is a good idea if you want to mingle with the locals, but it's not an absolute necessity—you can get by with just Spanish since everyone in the area also speaks it.

WHERE TO LIVE

It's long been said that bargains are still available along this part of Spain, but that has begun change and prices are increasing. You'll find that prices are akin to those in Spain's Costa Blanca and other areas popular with foreigners. To look for a relative deal, look at property away from the water or without a view—the prices on such places are far more reasonable. However, access to water is one of the most sought-after features of a home along the Costa Brava, and the prices below are for such properties.

That having been said, where do people settle in? Tossa de Mar is a popular spot. With a population of 17,320, Tossa de Mar is among the larger of the Costa Brava's seaside towns. The medieval old-city comes complete with still-standing defensive walls and towers that date back to the 12th century. This part of town exudes an old-world charm that's enhanced by the sea breezes blowing through the stone streets. The village has grown in recent years, and now includes a newer section that caters to tourists. Some say the expansion is a blessing and others claim it's a curse, but the good news is that while old and new Tossa are adjacent, they're still separate and you can choose which of the two distinctly different corners of town you prefer. You can buy a seaside two-bedroom apartment for €150,000–250,000 ($188,000–313,000) and a palatial villa for about €400,000–600,000 ($500,000–750,000).

If you want immediate access to the water and the pleasure of living in a small seaside town, Cadaqués could be the place for you. The village itself is an exquisite vision of whitewashed homes and olive groves laid out in a half-moon sprawl that surrounds the bay. Although Cadaqués boasts a tiny population of just 1,810 residents, those numbers expand considerably come summer when the tourists descend. Nonetheless, the town maintains its authenticity and if you think that you see hints of Dalí's rocky dreamscapes in the scenery surrounding this bayside town, you're not imagining the likeness. Dalí's family vacationed here when the artist was young, and traces of Cadaqués appear in many of his paintings. Two-bedroom apartments fetch €150,000–250,000 ($188,000–313,000), and more deluxe villas (think marble, wine cellars, and enormous swimming pools) go for about €400,000–600,000 ($500,000–750,000). If you're willing to forego some of the extras, you can find smaller detached homes in the €200,000 ($250,000) range. A month's rent on a spacious unit will begin at about €1,400 ($1,750) and for more decadent places you can spend several hundred more a month.

Palamós, a small town (population 15,000), offers the best of the Costa Brava; the medieval fishing-village is near the mountains and thanks to protected areas that restrict development, the area has been preserved from tourism's more ravaging effects. Palamós attracts plenty of tourists yet it mainly caters to year-round residents who enjoy the more resort-laden places nearby. Within a stone's throw, you can find golf courses and spas. Housing is similarly priced to Cadaqués; that means that a two-bedroom apartment will go for about €150,000–250,000 ($188,000–313,000), and sprawling villas with all the frills will sell for approximately €400,000–600,000 ($500,000–750,000). If you're renting for just the summer season, prices will be exorbitant but winter prices are lower. A month's rent on an enormous unit (and there are a few of them around) will begin at about €1,400 ($1,750).

To say that Gerona is lovely simply does not do the town justice. Gerona lies on the Onyar River, slightly inland from the coast. In many ways the town, which has a population of 17,080, is a miniature city complete with architectural marvels and cultural events. Best of all, the small city maintains a neighborly feel and thus it offers its residents the best of both worlds—lively culture in a small-town setting. The river bisects the town into two sections: the old quarter which boasts historical artifacts from Romans, Jews, Moors, and even Charlemagne's army which once beset the city. The newer quarter sprung up over the course of the 19th and 20th centuries. Gerona is the largest city in northern Catalonia and has its own airport—albeit a tiny one. The town is connected to Barcelona by train, although the hour-and-a-half commute is long for those who expect to ride the rails to and from work; Gerona has plenty of benefits but it's not well situated as a commuter town.

The city's popularity has increased and so too have homes' prices. A few years ago you could have bought a rambling old farmhouse for €150,000 ($188,000) and fixed it up. Sadly, those days are gone. You should expect to pay the same prices that you would for the coast's seaside towns. In other words, a villa will rent for about €1,400 ($1,750), and it will sell for €300,000 ($375,000) on the low end and €400,000–600,000 ($500,000–750,000) on the high end.

REAL ESTATE AGENTS: THE COSTA BRAVA

Van Den Hout Enterprises
Calle Aragó, 463
Pral. 7
08013 Barcelona
tel. 93 265 35 15
fax 93 265 35 15
www.vdhenterprises.com

Real Estate Costa Brava S.L.
Plaça del Mercat, 29–30
Sant Feliu de Guixols
17080 Girona
tel. 972 32 24 10
fax 972 32 69 71
www.immospain.com

Brava-Casa Real Estate International S.L.
L'Escala
Calle Ave Maria, 19
17130 L'Escala
tel. 972 77 58 28
fax 972 77 24 55
www.bci-immobilien.de

Costa Brava Centro Informativo Inmobiliario S.L.
Calle Josep Tarradellas, 1
E-17310 Lloret de Mar
Girona
tel. 972 36 95 05
fax 972 37 31 94
www.costabrava.de

GETTING AROUND

While you'll be able to walk around most of the towns in the Costa Brava and you can rely on mass transportation to reach nearby places, most people have cars. The area is not an urban one, and having the mobility and flexibility of your own transportation offers a tremendous amount of freedom.

Sitges

Just a half-hour drive from Barcelona is Sitges—the crown jewel of the Costa Dorada (the coastline south of Barcelona). The modestly sized beach-town is a world unto itself. In the summertime, when crowds of clubbers and sun-worshippers arrive, the town's population swells considerably from its normal population of 17,600. Come winter, Sitges hunkers down for a relatively quiet rest. However, even in February this place emanates life—just see the town's riotous Carnaval for proof of that.

> In the late 19th century, Sitges began to attract an artistic crowd. That bohemian flavor is still present today (just visit the town's two nudist beaches for evidence of that).

In the late 19th century, Sitges began to attract an artistic crowd. That bohemian flavor is still present today (just visit the town's two nudist beaches for evidence of that). Sitges is especially popular with young people and the local gay population is one of Spain's largest per capita. The town offers every luxury from gourmet food to extravagant homes, and the steep, jagged coastline is beautiful to boot. So what's not to love? There is one big drawback to making your permanent home here: a huge number of the town's residents are seasonal, and as a result, there's a palpable lack of community here.

THE LAY OF THE LAND

Although the landscape of Costa Dorada is not considered Spain's finest—the scenery is flatter and less varied than it is in other areas—the area is home to a few choice spots and Sitges is broadly considered the supreme among them. The beaches are the area's best features. They extend for miles and the sand is fine and golden (hence the area's name, the Golden Coast). The Ebro River delta lies at the southern end of the coast, and the protected area attracts hundreds of birds. To the north, the Garraf National Park offers both hiking and mountain biking.

Sitges itself is compact and easy to navigate on foot for those living in the center. The Església de Sant Bartomeu I Santa Tecla church is the town's main landmark, and it is the midpoint between the main beach (in the southwest) from the more tranquil beach, Sant Sebastià (in the northeast). The old quarter is further inland from the church, and small housing communities lie even further back in the scenic, hilly outskirts.

Local Language

Along the interior you'll hear a lot of Catalan, and while that's also true in Sitges, you can get by with just Spanish. However, Catalan is a boon, just as is the case throughout the whole of Catalonia.

WHERE TO LIVE

The center of town attracts a mix of people from young singles to retirees—it's both the heart of Sitges and conveniently located to stores, schools, and the like. However, if you want a single house you'll have to look elsewhere. An apartment in the center of Sitges costs about the same as one in Barcelona: €600 ($750) per bedroom for high-end units, and €300 ($375) for low-end to mid-range places. High-end properties will rent for €1,200–1,400 ($1,500–1,750) per month for a two-bedroom apartment. House prices begin at about €200,000 ($250,000) and from there they increase—in some cases, by a lot.

If you're more interested in a single-family house, Zona Vinyet and Leventina are popular spots. The first area lies south of the church and the latter is to the church's north but both are scenic, good for families, and priced similarly. The low end for rent on a two-bedroom is €1,200 ($1,500) and those numbers can escalate by a lot. To buy, you'll pay about €600,000 ($750,000) or more—for the nicer properties, much more.

REAL ESTATE AGENTS: SITGES

Finques Farreras
Passeig de la Ribera, 10
08870 Sitges
tel. 93 894 35 04
fax 93 811 31 28
www.afarreras.com

Key Star
Paseo de la Ribera, 27
08870 Sitges
tel. 93 811 46 14
tel. 93 894 16 58
fax 93 894 16 58
www.keystar.org

GETTING AROUND

You don't absolutely need a car in Sitges, but it helps to have one. The city is compact and easy to navigate on foot (or by bus if you live by the edge of town), but you'll be able to move more easily if you do have your own transportation. You very well may leave your wheels untouched for days on end, but they'll be useful to have for visiting nearby areas.

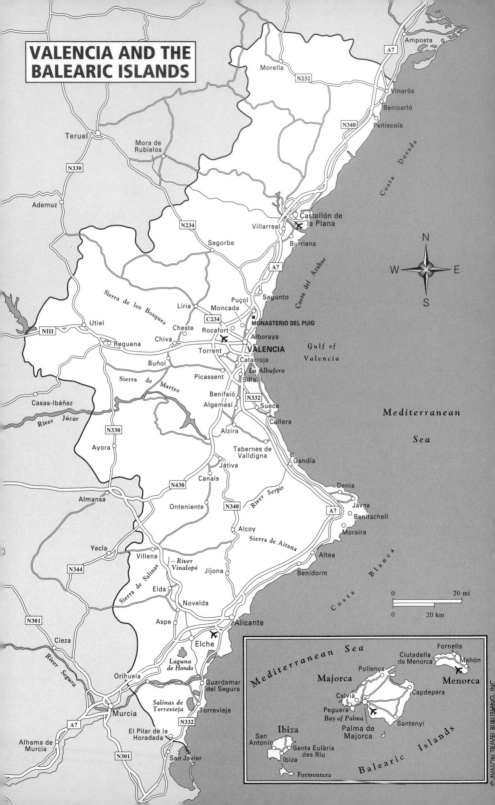

Valencia and the Balearic Islands

James A. Michener begins his tome *Iberia* with a description of being escorted by boat from his ship through the deep blue Mediterranean waters off the Costa del Azahar to the tiny town of Burriana. Once on land, he traveled through sweet-scented citrus groves to Castellón de la Plana where he flirted with young women at a town fiesta and saw his first zarzuela (a brief, light opera), and by evening's end he had fallen head-over-heels in love with Spain. The next day Michener hopped on a train and headed south for Valencia City. After just one night on the country's southeastern coast he was besotted and wanted to see more.

Michener isn't the only American to have fallen for Spain's south-eastern coast. People still do it all the time. Although the places Michener wrote about in 1968 are far more modern today, the charm and natural beauty that he described are still present—you just have to know where to look for them. You can avoid the concrete high-rises and garish resorts such as Benidorm, and instead hit more authentically

Valencian towns where the local festivals are riotous affairs that include elaborate displays of fireworks, a few bulls, and mountains of paella. Along the Costa del Azahar and the Costa Blanca you'll find fragrant orange groves, sandy beaches, and azure waters. Further inland you'll discover small towns with Gothic architecture and walking trails winding through the hills.

Valencia City is Spain's third largest urban area and although it's known for being an industrial center where tiles, paper, toys, and cosmetics are made, it's also a cultural center and home to a community of artists. The city is varied, vibrant, and those who live there have long felt that it deserves more acknowledgment than it gets. Not only is Valencia home to the Holy Grail and paella—Spain's signature dish—but it's also home to the impressive art museum, Museo de Bellas Artes, and to a number of ceramic studios. Moreover, when the ultramodern Ciudad de las Artes y de las Ciencias was built in 1996, the new arts and science complex made the definitive point that Valencia is a sophisticated city with its eye on the future. Yet for all the local commerce and the dedication to the arts, the city feels intimate and even a tad rustic; it's often said that Valencia is the biggest small town in the world. Who knows? Maybe the Mediterranean breezes blowing into the region of Valencia influence the culture, because people in this part of Spain take it real easy.

Even if you're merely passing through, you'll undoubtedly notice a strong sense of regional pride. The tone isn't as political as it is in Catalonia or Basque Country, but like the residents in those areas, people in Valencia and the Balearic Islands literally speak their own language—Valenciano. (Naturally, Spanish is also spoken.) The region's history is another point that proves that this part of the country is indeed unique. The Romans ruled Valencia for 700 years; soon after that, the Moors controlled the area for five centuries, and the crown of Aragón edged into the area during the Reconquest. Yet during the 15th century the region found its footing and became a thriving force with one of the most powerful ports in the Mediterranean. Valencia finally flexed its muscle.

Through the centuries the region suffered the rule of marauding invaders and yet it made good on the cultural and agricultural riches that were brought by the foreign occupiers. In its time, Valencia has reached economic highs and endured financial hardship and through it all, the region became united. Today, Valencia is a flourishing, modern corner of Spain. Yet underneath its contemporary appearance, its regional identity remains strong.

Valencia

If you mention the name Valencia to a Spaniard, you might be asked to specify which Valencia you mean. Perhaps you're talking about the city itself, but you might also be referring to the province or the region. There's no need to scratch you're head over that—it can easily be explained. The region of Valencia (or rather, the community) is a big slice of Spain that begins at the border of southern Catalonia and winds 280 miles down the coast until it hits Pilar de la Horadada in the south of Spain. Three provinces lie within that land: Castellón in the north, Valencia in the middle, and Alicante in the south. Valencia City is the capital of the region and the middle province; the other two provinces are named for their capital cities.

Of the approximately four million people living in the Community of Valencia (La Comunidad de Valencia), 753,500 of them live in Valencia City. The region's overall population is still about 95 percent Spanish and a lot of those people live in the same towns that they were born in. That fact might surprise you when you're touring some of the flashier resort towns catering to northern Europeans. In such places the masses of foreigners seem to eclipse the local population, but in many cases those English- or German-speaking folks are only on vacation.

THE LAY OF THE LAND

The region's terrain is fertile and a wide variety of fruit and other crops are all grown locally. La Albufera, a freshwater lagoon south of the city is rich with wildlife and it's also the largest rice-producing region in Spain. West of the coast lies a large, bountiful plain that yields an abundance of oranges and even further west, the land juts up into pine-covered hills where almonds grow. Some coastal towns have large *salinas* (salt flats)—those have made mighty contributions to the local economy over the years. Although the coast is known for broad stretches of beach, don't assume that if you buy a house on these waters you'll find golden sands outside your front door. In some places, the surf crashes onto rocks or even cliffs. Although the seaside is more varied than some real estate agents might suggest, all of it is breathtaking in its own way.

Wherever you go in Valencia, the sun will shine a lot—about 320 days a year—and that perk coupled with the sea and sand bring in more than 4.5 million visitors annually. (Forget about almonds and salt—the chunk of tourist change that comes in with all those vacationers is a vital piece of the economy.) Yet for all that sun, July and August days will

© Nikki Weinstein

On the beach in Valencia

The Ciudad de las Artes y de las Ciencias complex shows off Valencia's modern face.

rarely scorch. The region of Valencia remains temperate year round—the average temperature is 85°F and winter lows average a blissfully mild 40°F. Naturally, the higher the elevation the chillier the weather, but even inland the mercury only dips a little ways into the 30s in December and January.

Local Language

Like Catalonia to the north, Valencia is officially bilingual and people speak both Spanish and Valenciano—a dialect of Catalan. However, Valencia's brand of regionalism isn't fraught with the same tension as in Catalonia or Basque Country. Valenciano is the second language and Spanish is the first. A small, vocal faction feels passionate about promoting Valenciano and people of that mind want the dialect treated as an official language complete with grammatical rules and a body of literature. On the other side is an equally vocal group that is happy to regard Valenciano as a dialect, albeit an important one. For such people, the issue is less critical. As a foreigner, it's not crucial that you learn Valenciano, although you will mix more easily with the locals if you do.

It Must Be Something in the Water

You don't have to look hard to find paella in Spain—restaurants throughout the country are more than happy to ply tourists with mediocre platters of yellow rice crammed full with sausage, shrimp, chicken, squid, and soggy vegetables. However, it is difficult to find paella cooked so well that at first bite you suddenly understand where the country's staple dish won its outstanding reputation. The preparation and consumption of paella is passionately debated (and has probably even sparked a couple of bar brawls). But there is one thing everyone can agree on: to find a good paella, you must go to Valencia, where dish originated. Many Valencianos contend that the water holds the magic while others say the locals chefs do, but both sides agree that Valencia is the only place to eat paella. That's the golden rule but it's not the only one—there are a couple more to know, and a little history to boot.

When the Moors occupied Valencia in the Middle Ages, they introduced rice, oranges, and a complex system of irrigation canals that are still used today. Those oranges led to groves which workers had to tend to. Come lunchtime, they'd fuel up for the afternoon's labor on paella—it was cheap, filling, and it didn't taste half bad.

Much later, seafood was added to certain paellas—some say to justify the in-flated prices restaurants charged for the dish. Others explain the change as culinary evolution, plain and simple. Either way, the new ingredient gave birth to a new rule: if a paella has meat and poultry it shall not have seafood.

Seafood or no seafood, it's still a paella. The word does not refer to just one specific dish but to a number of them, all cooked in a *paellera*—a broad, flat, metal pan. Among the more popular paellas is *arroz negro,* a deep-black version filled with squid and cooked in squid ink. Another favorite is *arroz a banda,* rice simmered in fish stock. One type of paella forgoes rice altogether and replaces it with short, flat noodles called *fideuás.*

Although paella has moved away from its humble origins over the years and is now held in high regard by true gourmets, one tradition has stuck. It's generally agreed that paella should be eaten for lunch and never for dinner, simply because it's too heavy for the evening. Of course, the endless debates rage on. Should paella always be eaten outside? Cooked over a wood stove? Must conversations while enjoying the dish cover traditional subjects such as sports and business? I wouldn't presume to guess at the answers—you'll have to go and find out for yourself.

VALENCIA CITY

Valencia's Mediterranean climate and gorgeous, ocean views stand for a lot, but residents also enjoy the city's range of sports facilities, nearby golf courses, local theaters, and handful of cinemas—a couple of which show films in the original language.

Valencia is too far from both Madrid and Barcelona to be a commuter town and most the people who live there work locally. That, however, might change soon. The city is the railroad center of eastern Spain, and its capacity will be increased tenfold as soon as the track is complete for the high-speed train to Madrid. When that route opens, the commute to the capital will be cut down to less than an hour and a half. True, that's not short, but it might be short enough for some who want to leave their work in the big city behind and return home to a quieter, coastal locale. Construction on the railroad has been stepped up there's a good reason for the rush. The America's Cup is coming to town in 2007 and that's a mighty big coup for the city. The event will be held in Valencia and the race is sure to bring in a load of tourists, a few up-market hotels, and of course the sailors competing in the world's most famous regatta event. The combination the America's Cup and the shorter commute time to Madrid will undoubtedly drive real estate prices up, although there's no telling by just how much.

The port is one area that's sure to see a few changes. The harbor has expansive beaches and the best paella restaurants in town, yet it's currently underutilized despite recent renovations. Right now, the port is not the city's hub but the preparation for the America's Cup might change all that; the area will very likely be revamped. However, Valencia does have a core and it's plenty alluring.

Where to Live

The undisputed heart of the city is the oldest part, the historic center, a large oval plot of urban land that is flanked on one side by the Jardines del Turia. The gardens were once the river Turia but it has since been been filled in and transformed into a verdant municipal space with paths for strolling and beautiful landscaping. The other borders surrounding the neighborhood are the ring roads Calle de Colón, Xátiva, and Guillem de Castro.

Within the larger neighborhood, you'll find the Plaza del Ayuntamiento, Plaza de la Reina (or Zaragoza), Plaza de la Virgen, and Barrio del Carmen—the most historic of all the city areas and a place that valiantly defies its age with a booming nightlife. The cathedral lies between Plaza de la Virgen and Plaza de la Reina. It is a majestic monument that shows off Valencia's history with its mix of Romanesque, baroque, and Gothic styles. Just off of the Plaza del Ayuntamiento, is the Mercado Central (Central Market), an iconic building that opened its doors in 1928 and since then, has pulled in hordes of shoppers in search of edibles as basic as fruit, meat, and vegetables, and as adventurous as eels, snails, and barnacles. Baroque is the most dominant style of architecture in the city center—building facades are ornate and in many cases, stunning.

The neighborhood is well serviced with buses and metro lines. Apartments in this part of town are reasonably priced given that Valencia is one of Spain's largest cities. A two-bedroom apartment in the old part of the city rents for about €300–400 ($375–500) a month. And to buy, you can expect to pay €110,000 ($138,000) or more. If you want to step outside your front door into the center of the action, Barrio del Carmen is the place for you but be warned, the street noise is perpetual. However, if you want the magic of old town with a little less noise, seek out an apartment around the Plaza del Ayuntamiento.

Just a word of caution: Valencia City's two biggest drawbacks are most related to the center of town. Valencia has one of the highest crime-rates in Spain, and the biggest problems are pickpockets, car theft, and drug-related crimes. Noise is a constant problem (but what else would you expect from a city that so famously adores firecrackers?). Valencia has earned the debatable honor of being one of the world's noisiest cities, and the majority of that din emanates from the town's center.

People who want an urban location but with a little peace and quiet often choose the neighborhoods north of the city in Los Monasterios—a housing development near Puçol and about a half-hour from the city center. Because the community is perched on a hill and has magnificent sea-views, Los Monasterios has a distinct advantage in Valencia, which is generally flat land. The community homes are detached and fairly new—about 25 years old. It's both metropolitan and serene and for that reason, it's a popular location with families. Parents with young children often live there for the proximity to the American school, although many families do opt for public education. Prices in Los Monasterios tend to be some of the highest in the city. A four-bedroom house can sell for €400,000 ($500,000) and rentals begin at about €1,200 ($1,500) a month and move up from there.

Although a few of Valencia's international schools are in the city proper, most English-language schools are in the metropolitan outskirts. The small towns surrounding Valencia function as city suburbs and you can find beautiful villas with mountain views, orange groves close by, and in some cases, with metro access to the city center. Rocafort is about 15 minutes from the city center, about 20 minutes from the beach, near golf courses, and it's also the location of a British elementary and primary school. The town itself is fairly decadent—villas are the most common style of home and in many cases they have swimming pools. A two-bedroom home begins at around €130,000 ($163,000) and goes up from there. Rent on a home would cost about €1,200 ($1,500). Campo Olivar, a section of Rocafort, also pulls in scores of foreign families, many of them wanting to be local to the English school. Orange groves and scenic hills are close by, but despite the natural views, make no mistake about it—this place is a lavish suburb. The town has plenty of amenities but Valencia's city center is just five miles away. Homes in Campo Olivar rent for about €900–1,200 ($1,125–1,500) per month. Purchase prices begin around €220,000 ($275,000) and increase from there. Rocafort's biggest drawback is that it's not connected to Valencia by metro. However, Liria is.

Liria, 15 miles northwest of the city and about six miles from Rocafort, was originally a weekend retreat but in recent years it's become a coastal suburb to Valencia. Summer resorts are close, but not too close for comfort. The area has about 18,000 residents and it's surrounded by scenic, low hills. The metro connection to the city is a tremendous boon and buses also serve the area. Homes in the area are all detached and they're mainly villas. Two-bedroom homes begin selling at around €120,000 ($150,000). Three-bedroom places can be had for as little as €140,000 ($175,000) and as much as €200,000 ($250,000). Sprawling homes with four or more bedrooms begin at about €200,000 ($250,000) and can sell for much more, depending on extras such as pools and gardens.

Real Estate Agents: Valencia City
You'll find plenty of real estate agencies to help you with your search for a home, but most relocation companies are based elsewhere. Still, the ones below will help with people moving throughout the country including Valencia, and they're some of the best around.

Valencia Property S.L.
Calle Valencia, 57
46185 La Pobla de Vallbona
Valencia
tel. 609 878 154
fax 96 166 28 92

Valencia Inmobiliaria
Avenida Antiguo Reino de Valencia, 2
46005 Valencia
Valencia
tel. 96 335 64 64
fax 96 335 64 64

Villas Valencia
Apartado, 37
46119 Naquera
Valencia
tel. 96 168 00 25
fax 96 168 21 44
www.villasvalencia.com

Getting Around
When you see people cruising through the city on their bicycles, don't misunderstand. The city has an excellent method of public trans-

© Nikki Weinstein

Candy for sale in a Valencia window

portation. Those on foot or two wheels simple choose to take their time. If you're in a hurry, you can take the metro, tram, or bus.

The buses, all run by the Empresa Municipal de Transportes, run until about 10 P.M. Monday–Wednesday, 2:45 A.M. Thursday–Sunday. Tickets cost €0.80 ($1). A BonoBus ticket goes for about €5 ($6.25) and buys you 10 rides. Spring for the €6 ($7.50) Bono10 and you can make connections on each of the 10 rides as long as you pick up the next leg of your journey within 50 minutes of first using your ticket.

You can also take the high-speed tram or the metro. The former serves the city particularly well, while the metro runs throughout the city and the suburbs. One ride costs €1 ($1.25) for most limited zones, and to travel a further distance you might pay as much as €3 ($3.75). Regular riders can enjoy discounted fares on month-long passes known as Tat cards. You decide the zones and the zones determine the price, but you can expect to pay at least €53 ($66).

THE COSTA BLANCA

If you find this sweep of Spain magnificently alluring, you won't be alone—the Costa Blanca (the White Coast) is one of Spain's most heavily trafficked shores. Of the 750,000 people who live there, 52,000 of them are foreigners (and many are also retirees). People coming from elsewhere usually settle in the resort areas; the only place that attracts more foreigners is the Costa del Sol. So exactly why do folks come in droves? The weather is one part of the reason. The sun shines for about 320 days a year and yet it's rarely too hot. The World Health Organization named the coast's climate one of the healthiest in the world. Moreover, the crime rate is low, the number of amenities is high, and have I mentioned that the coast is absolutely gorgeous?

Along the 63 miles of coast between Valencia City and Alicante City, the sand is bright and soft, the light is clear, and whitewashed homes dot the region—perhaps that's why this expanse of land was dubbed the White Coast. Both the hilltop towns that glint in the sun and the enchanting ones clustered around coves could easily seem like a touch thought up by the board of tourism to make the most of the area's name. Of course, the homes have white exteriors to deflect the summer sun, but, whatever the practicality of the reason, the effect is indeed picturesque.

If you're planning on living in your home year-round, it's worth seeking property that's a little inland—even in coastal towns. The further a

Landing a Steal

If you're looking for property in the Valencia region, people will scare you silly with horror stories about the province's land-grab law. While the tales are not fiction, you can avoid falling into a trap with a little knowledge about how the law works.

In 1994, the province passed the Ley Reguladora de la Actividad Urbanística, or LRAU. At the time, the law seemed like a fine idea—its purpose was to promote development while ensuring sufficient amounts of facilities, public services, green spaces, and roads in urbanized areas. Unfortunately, the statute was written in a way that allowed for widespread abuse.

Land is classified as either rural or urban, and a property developer can request a change in a plot of land's status without the consent of the owner. While that detail isn't so crazy, the real problems lie in what reclassification allows. Once land has been reclassified, developers can purchase land from owners by paying amounts far below market value. *That's* what hurts. Some people have been forced to sell their land for scant compensation.

So what can you do to hang onto your land or sell it at market value? If there's a particular property that you have your eye on, find out what the official status of the land is. It will either be listed as urban, developable, or rural. If it's already urban or developable when you buy it, the price will be higher but at least you won't risk having your land taken from you. However, if it's rural land that you're after, you'll be vulnerable. You can find out what plans are in the works for the area and if none are, there's a good chance that your property will remain untouched—but you won't have a guarantee. You also should speak to a lawyer before buying property to find out what you can do to protect yourself and your investment.

home is from the ocean, the lower the price. However, if you'll be renting out your home for part of the year, it's wise to buy closer to the water since most tourists will seek out that perk when looking for accommodations.

The N-332 runs down the coast and hits a few of the better towns as it meanders south. The A-7 toll road also snakes down the coast just a little bit inland from the coast. While the beach towns will all be swarming with people in the summer months, things slow down considerably during the rest of the year and a few small towns have managed to retain their pristine beauty. Jávea, Moraira, and Altea are among the more attractive areas that offer services such as good medical facilities, hospitals, sports centers, and cultural outlets either locally or nearby. Additionally, all the towns are close to both the airports in Valencia and Alicante. All three are expensive, but you will get what you pay for. Further inland, you'll find Benitachell—a quieter village just north of Moraira that attracts plenty of foreigners, too.

Aside from Valencia, Alicante is the biggest city in the area, and with a population of 277,000. Several years ago Alicante was a sleazy port town, but gentrification hit the area and the result is welcome. For its relatively small size, Alicante is a vibrant town with a youthful atmosphere. Although plenty of tourists visit, the city is unquestionably for the locals.

Where to Live

With a population of 23,350, **Jávea** (or Xàbia in Valenciano) is one of the more sizable small towns on the Costa Blanca, yet it retains an intimate air of seclusion. Perhaps that's because it's tucked in between Cabo de la Nao and Cabo de San Antonio and it's sheltered by Mount Montgó lying to the west. Its enticements include a scenic old port, a marina that can hold about 300 boats at a time, an old quarter, and a long expanse of beach. Throughout the town you'll find galleries, restaurants, and a theater, and even a launderette. (Finding one of those in Spain is about as good as spotting a bald eagle, though mainly travelers take advantage of it since most homes have washing machines.) Sailing, scuba diving, and other water sports are widely available, too. The old town is a medieval tangle of streets and white homes. If you're a tennis buff or an avid golfer, you'll be able to get your athletic kicks locally, and the nearby walking trails are another boon for the healthy.

> *If all the little towns along the Costa Blanca were contenders in a beauty contest, Altea would win hands down.*

Jávea is expensive but the prices of properties further inland are lower. Throughout the town, you can find apartments, townhouses, and villas. Monthly rent on a two-bedroom apartment ranges from €400–900 ($500–1,125). To buy an apartment, expect to pay no less than €100,000 ($125,000) on the low end, and €200,000 ($250,000) for a decent, two-bedroom pad. Villas and town houses begin around €150,000 ($188,000) and the sky is the limit. Some palatial homes can easily top the million-euro mark.

People come to **Moraira** for numerous reasons—the beach access, the quaint atmosphere of the fishing village, or to live in a town that's protected from cold, winter winds by hills that also funnel in gentle, summer breezes. The town's fishing harbor is still active, and the local fishing market still bustles with the activity of business. For such a small town— the population is just 9,100—Moraira has a lot to offer, from a stunning old quarter and a range of restaurants, to idyllic beaches nestled into coves. In addition to the abundance of water sports and good eateries, Moraira has plenty of shopping opportunities and you can browse boutiques or stock up in a number of food stores. Some of these cater to gourmands, and others satisfy foreigners cravings for a taste of home.

Strict zoning laws keep the town unspoiled. Rather than high-rises, you'll find townhouses, apartments, and villas. However, the price of a little peace, quiet, and beach is steep. Monthly rent on a two-bedroom will begin around €600 ($750). Purchase prices on a two-bedroom start at €130,000 ($163,000) and that will buy you something modest. At about €200,000 ($250,000) things begin to get posh and one-bedroom apartments with pool access, prime buildings, and beach access can cost upwards of €600,000 ($750,000). Rent for such places typically runs about €800–1,000 ($1,000–1,250) per month.

If all the little towns along the Costa Blanca were contenders in a beauty contest, **Altea** would win hands down. The village appears to be floating on a hilltop hovering over the ocean. The local beach is predominantly pebbles, but before you complain take note: those rocky shores have managed to deter some of the serious beach bums. In the process, Altea has remained as exquisite as ever while the more destructive effects of tourism have all taken their toll in Benidorm, just over the hill from Altea.

With a population of 15,600, Altea has a disproportionate number of local services and cultural opportunities. Perhaps that's because the town was an artisan's haven in the 1960s. Some of the bohemian flavor remains today—Altea's art center, concert hall, and numerous galleries are part of the town's draw.

You'll have a choice between settling into an apartment or a villa. Rent on a two-bedroom apartment is about €600 ($750). Purchase prices on a two-bedroom apartment begin at about €130,000 ($163,000) on the low end. An apartment that's in between low-end and decadent will be priced around €200,000 ($250,000) and the sky is the limit. Rent for villas will be €800–1,000 ($1,000–1,250). If you want to buy a villa, you can expect to put up at least €200,000 ($250,000), and you'll undoubtedly shell out a lot more for a rambling pad with all the frills.

Although **Benitachell** is just a five-minute drive from the beach, it's considered an inland town, and almond trees and pretty hills lined with scenic walking trails add to the town's charm. The town is every bit the low-key resort area that the beachfront towns are, but the people who move to this plush village are usually attracted to a place with a more Spanish flair than a foreign one. Still, golf courses, restaurants, and cultural outlets catering to foreigners are all a short drive away and some of those same things are even local. Rent on a two-bedroom apartment will set you back about €500–800 ($625–1,000) a month. To buy a similar place would cost a minimum of €130,000 ($163,000) and might cost three or four times that amount depending on the how deluxe it is. Villas rent for about €1,300 ($1,625) a month and cost about €200,000 ($250,000) at the low end and can be much more expensive.

With a population of 277,000, **Alicante** is the second biggest city in Valencia province. The local history spans about 3,000 years and not surprisingly, you'll find an antique charm in El Barrio, the old quarter, where a lovely web of streets play host to a mix of architectural styles. The Cathedral of San Nicolás was built in the Renaissance fashion yet its alter is baroque, and the 14th-century Church of Santa María has a Gothic nave with an 18th-century baroque facade.

Yet with all the contemporary bars and clubs that clutter El Barrio, Alicante also has a youthful vibrancy—one that seamlessly mixes into a historic setting. The pedestrian promenade, Paseo Explanada de España, is a lovely, marble boulevard lined with palm trees. It runs parallel to the harbor and is full of lively cafés. The beach stretches on for five miles and teems with people in the summer months.

Although fewer foreigners live in Alicante than along the Costa Blanca, the city is chock full of amenities including sports facilities, concert halls, theaters, and a broad selection of stores, boutiques, and food markets. However, if you need to stock your cabinets with the culinary comforts from home, you'll find that it's easier to come by foreign foods along the Costa Brava than it is in Alicante.

Seafront properties along the Playa de San Juan are among the city's most desirable homes, as are any lodgings in the city center. Monthly rent for a two-bedroom will cost you at least €500 ($625). To buy a two-bedroom, expect to pony up €100,000 ($125,000) and for prime digs you might pay three times as much. Rent on a villa begins around €800–1,000 ($1,000–1,250) and to buy a luxury home you'll pay about €300,000 ($375,000) or much, much more.

Real Estate Agents: The Costa Blanca

Some agents in the Costa Blanca specialize in certain areas and others cover the whole coast, but there's one thing to be sure of: you won't have to look far to find an agent who can help you find a house or apartment. Property is big business in these parts, and plenty of people are looking for a slice of that pie. Many such agencies are reputable ones—here are a couple of them:

BTB Grupo
Residencial La Plaza—Local 11 y 12
03730 Jávea
Alicante
tel. 96 579 14 00
fax 96 579 30 75
www.btb.es

Molino Villas Servicios
Inmobiliarios S.L.
Centro Commercial Kristal Mar, 18C
03724 Moraira
Alicante
tel. 96 649 23 35
fax 96 649 20 12

Getting Around

Although the train service running through the southeast is excellent and you can get around most of the small towns on foot, you'll need a car if you want to be truly mobile. You'll *definitely* need one if you live on the outskirts of town. Thankfully, cars are easy to park in the towns along the Costa Blanca. Many of villas have private garages as do some of the apartment buildings. But you can also park your car on the street without worrying about theft as you might in a city.

The Balearic Islands

Cruise into those Mediterranean waters by boat and you'll find the Balearic Islands (Las Islas Baleares) 120 miles off the Costa Blanca shoreline. Although they're not part of the Comunidad de Valencia, the isles have two key features in common with the mainland community: both areas rely on dialects of Catalan, and they share a climate that's mild and balmy. The islands draw upwards of 10 million tourists annually for good reason: they're bursting with dramatic landscapes, pine forests, gorgeous Mediterranean beaches, and craggy cliffs. Moreover, the area has—against all odds—fended off some of the more ruinous effects of mass tourism and maintained its historic towns, which are often complete with Gothic cathedrals, plazas, and fountains and surrounded by almond and citrus trees as well as olive groves. Today, tourism is the biggest industry of the islands, and agriculture is a distant second. The islands' populations total 869,200. Of these, 700,800 residents live on Majorca—the largest of the islands.

Foreigners have loved these ocean gems since long before our time. The first island settlements date back to 500 B.C., and Phoenician traders made regular stops when the Balearics were home to booming, Mediterranean ports. In subsequent years, the islands were raided or invaded by a host of people including the Carthaginians, Romans, Moors, and Turks. In the 3rd century, the Catalonians moved in and when they arrived they brought their language—something that proved to be a lasting legacy. In 1713, Menorca (the second-largest of the islands) was given to the British in the Treaty of Utrecht, and the empire's rule lasted until 1802. However, foreign invasion didn't end just because other countries stopped planting their flags on the islands' soil.

© Nikki Weinstein

Valencia's bakeries tempt those who stroll by.

Long before expatriation was commonplace, people in privileged positions sought out homes on the Balearic Islands for their verdant charms and enticing sunshine. Chopin and his sweetie, George Sand, lived on Majorca for years, as did the poet, Robert Graves, who brought his family over from England to settle in Majorca in 1944.

Tourism hit the islands in a big way in the 1950s, when fashionable celebrities and the ultra-rich began enjoying the islands' charms. Soon, scores of resorts opened up and the Balearic Islands became known as more than a sexy playground for those who grace the society pages—they became a place for regular joes in search of a package vacation. High-rises sprang up alongside heavenly beaches, souvenir shops opened their doors for business. . . They built it, and oh my God, did they come; they came by the thousands.

> The islands draw upwards of 10 million tourists annually for good reason: they're bursting with dramatic landscapes, pine forests, gorgeous Mediterranean beaches, and craggy cliffs.

Today, development is strictly regulated and real estate is pricey—even off of the coasts where a modestly sized apartment can fetch millions of euros. The coast has one of the highest standards of living in Spain and some homes are so costly that most Spaniards simply cannot afford them. The result of that economic detail has had a big impact on the culture of the islands. A fifth of the property in Majorca is foreign-owned. However, many homeowners rent out their pads to vacationers and spend only a few weeks there each year themselves. One of the reasons might be that while the islands are breathtakingly beautiful, year-round life there can be too claustrophobic for some. Regardless of the reason, the result of the ever-shifting population of foreigners is significant; although the islands have a huge community of foreigners, it's also a relatively transient one.

THE LAY OF THE LAND

The four largest islands—Majorca, Menorca, Ibiza, and Formentera—combined with the smaller islets comprise 3,125 square miles of land surrounded by sapphire, Mediterranean waters. The first three of the islands are the most populated, and of the main islands, Majorca is the largest by far. Its 2,260 miles of landmass includes the island's only city, Palma de Majorca (or "Palma," if you're in the know). With a population of 334,000, the city is more than a bustling point of departure and entry into the islands. Its old quarter is a charming blend of Gothic architecture, baroque touches, and extravagant, ultrachic stores. Of course, the city is also packed with shops selling cheap, tourist trinkets that cater to the boatloads of day-trippers who come trundling through town on their way to the seaside and the clubs. The beaches (the Mecca sought out by all the sun-seeking pilgrims) are a short distance away and people take buses to reach them from Palma.

The city lies on the south side of the island and on a pretty bay. Not far from the northwest coast, the land rises up into the Serra de Tramuntana, a mountain range full of walking trails whose highest peak reaches 4,740 feet. The eastern coast is crammed with tourist developments that have sprung up in order to make good on the expanse of fine-sanded beaches. The center of the island has a broad, fertile plain.

While Majorca is a steady party in its most populous areas, Menorca is relatively quiet and the few foreigners who live there seek out halcyon days in a remote locale. In 1993, UNESCO ordained the lesser-traveled island a Biosphere Reserve, and indeed much of its physical splendor has been maintained. Mahón, the capital, is on the eastern part of Menorca. The small town has just 23,200 residents. The north boasts green hills and craggy coastlines, while the southern portion of the island is the flattest, least interesting part, although the beaches there are lovely.

Ibiza—a name that's long been synonymous with carnival—has been both blessed and cursed. Its blessing comes in the form of a spectacular countryside marked by deep-green pine trees, scrubby hills, patches of olive, almonds, and fig groves, and a dry climate with little rainfall. However, Ibiza's curse lies in what happened when so many hundreds of thousands came to enjoy the island's charms. The Balearic Islands' famous club-culture is most visible on Ibiza, and the drugged-out travelers impact the island's vibe. However, Ibiza City (the capital) is more than a mere resort town.

Local Language

Although Spanish is spoken across the Balearic Islands, dialects of Catalan are also spoken and on each island the language varies. However, the variance is slight enough so that each strain of Catalan is understood throughout the area; someone from Ibiza can understand the Catalan spoken in Majorca, and were a person from Menorca to speak with someone from Formentera, both versions of Catalan would be decipherable. Some of the television and radio stations are bilingual, and the government has made strides in working Catalan into the local school system. You won't need to speak any Catalan at all, but if you choose to ignore it altogether, you'll likely spend less time with locals.

WHERE TO LIVE

Majorca

Palma de Majorca is the most popular place of residence among the whole cluster of islands, and the city is breathtakingly beautiful. The mix of Gothic architecture, baroque touches, cobblestone streets and broad avenues enchants visitors, and the local yacht club is considered Spain's most prestigious—a reputation helped by the fact that it's the home of King Juan Carlos's annual regatta event. As with most everywhere in the Balearic Islands, the towns will be teeming in the summer months, and the activity will slow down (not considerably, but noticeably) in the off-season.

Those who live in this part of the island usually choose it for its wealth of English-speakers, range of cultural activities, sports (golf, sailing, and horseback riding just to name a few), excellent restaurants, galleries, plays, and musical performances. Doctors and the like are also available and plenty more work in the resorts scattered around the island, so no matter where you live, you'll be a short drive away from what you need. One additional benefit to living in Palma is proximity to a handful of international schools.

Homes in and around Palma de Majorca do not come cheap. The most notorious houses are grand, sandstone villas that have been around for decades. Prices are high for two reasons: the market, and the restoration, which requires specialized craftsmen that charge big bucks for their services. The cheapest homes are the ones in need of restoration but don't be fooled—the additional money that you'll have to pony up for renovations will offset the lower price. A two-bedroom apartment in the old part of town will rent for about €800–1,000 ($1,000–1,250) a month. Purchase prices begin at about €175,000 ($219,000) on the *very* low end, and there is no limit on how much property might cost.

Although expatriates usually congregate in the resort areas such as Calvià, Bay of Palma, Peguera, and Santa Ponça, a few towns are on the less-trodden path. The northwest part of the island is the least visited, and although it pulsates with tourist activities in the summer months, the noise dies down to a low-level buzz during the rest of the year. It was in this lush landscape that Robert Graves set up house, and a few have followed in his footsteps. The town of Andratx is nestled into a valley replete with almond and pine trees. You'll likely be beguiled by the its attractions (that is, as long as you can ignore that Andratx sounds unnervingly like Anthrax). Nearby Port d'

Andratx is a haven for the decadent class, and both towns have cap-italized on the fact that their beaches are not the island's most beau-tiful; that small point keeps some of the sightseers away. Yet all the services you might want including spa treatments, golf, and excellent restaurants are nearby. The luxury of escaping the party atmosphere elsewhere on the island does not come cheap. A two-bedroom apart-ment in Andratx rents for about €800–1,000 ($1,000–1,250) and if a sea view is included the monthly fee will rise. To buy those prop-erties, expect to shell out €175,000–220,000 ($219,000–275,000). The monthly rent for a villa begins at about €1,400 ($1,750), al-though it can be far pricier than that. Buying a villa will set you back about €800,000 ($1 million).

The northeast section of the island also has a few big-name resorts, all of which offer not only decadent spa treatments and sports, but doctors and food markets selling a diverse range of products. If you choose to live in one of the smaller towns near a resort such as Alcúdia or Portopetro (on the east coast), you'll be able to disappear into a relatively pastoral setting while being conveniently close to the amenities offered by resorts. A two-bedroom apartment's monthly rent will run you about €800–1,000 ($1,000–1,250) and to buy an apartment you'll have to pay about €200,000 ($250,000) or more. The more attractive villas rent for about €1,400 ($1,750) per month, and they can go for even more. They'll sell for €500,000 ($625,000) on the bottom end, and they can be quite a bit pricier.

Menorca
Menorca is as quiet and remote as Majorca and Ibiza (especially Ibiza) are frantic. If you need a lot of activity and culture, then this island isn't for you, but if you want to disappear into a patch of countryside, setting up house in Menorca might be ideal. Moreover, you won't have to give up the comforts of home or even some luxuries. This is hardly a deserted island; it only appears that way when compared to its siblings Ma-jorca and Ibiza. The capital, Mahón, has a British school as well as good medical facilities, a choice of restaurants, and some shopping opportunities. However, you'll have to do without certain extras such as private hospitals or seeing undubbed movies.

Mahón is a charming little city and thanks to the island's history, you'll see hints of Britain in the architecture, some of which is Geor-gian. Rent on a two-bedroom apartment in the city will begin around €600 ($750) and can get much pricier. Two-bedroom price tags usually begin around €150,000 ($188,000). A villa will rent for about €900 ($1,125) or much more. Buying the same sort of place costs at least €450,000 ($563,000). Prices are tad cheaper in Ciutadella, the former capital and a place with a rustic, old town and captivating harbor.

You can avoid the towns where resorts eclipse the local culture, such as Torre Del Ram and Cala En Blanes and instead choose to live in a more authentic place such as Fornells—a town on the north part of the island. Fornells is situated on a tranquil bay. It boasts a lovely old town and harbor. Yet the local resort creates an upscale market and brings in daily conveniences, so you'll have the best of both worlds.

Ibiza

Ibiza is the island known around the world for its all-night culture. For this very reason tourists flock to it while some potential residents shy away. For some, a constant party in a gorgeous locale is paradise but for others it's constant punishment. Most of the tourists seeking the island's famous nightlife head to San Antonio or other resorts but many residents look elsewhere when seeking a home. They want a place close to the party (i.e., somewhere on Ibiza) but they want a little piece of home and hearth as well. About 6,000 of the island's 87,000 residents are foreign, and if you choose to become one of them, there's a good chance that you'll want to live in Ibiza City. Most of the resorts in the island are *just* resorts, but the island's capital is a real town and a resort, too. It's situated on a harbor and it has a beautiful, ancient walled-in town, whitewashed architecture, and cobbled lanes. Yachting is big fun in Ibiza City and the marina shows off a host of sleek sailboats. In addition to the clubs, you'll find top-notch restaurants, sporting activities (on land or in water), and great shopping—especially during the summer months. Property in such a plush place is costly and you can expect to pay about €800 ($1,000) or more for a two-bedroom apartment, while the same sort of home can fetch about €220,000 ($275,000) and upwards. A villa might be rented for €1,400 ($1,750) a month, or can be bought for €450,000 ($563,000) on the low end and a couple million euros on the high end.

REAL ESTATE AGENTS: THE BALEARIC ISLANDS

Some of the agents on the Balearic Islands work in specific sections, while others work throughout the whole of the islands. Here are a few that have developed good reputations.

Mallorca Domizil
Enrique von Goetz
Isaac Peral, 41
E-07157 Puerto de Andratx
Majorca
tel. 971 67 47 67

M.I.A. Mallorca Property
Calle Hostalets, 1
E-07181 Portals Nous
Puerto Portals
Majorca
tel. 971 67 90 25
fax 971 67 92 35
www.realestatemajorca.com

Terramares
Apartado, 63
07710 Menorca
tel. 902 15 20 03
fax 902 15 20 03
www.terramares.com

GETTING AROUND

The only train transportation throughout the Balearic Islands is in Majorca, and the train is just a notch up from the one in Disney World. In other words, it's a good idea to have a car on the islands. Ferries between islands and to the mainland take cars (for a fee) and you'll find it enormously useful—almost necessary—for getting around.

Ferry services to the Costa Blanca, Valencia, and Barcelona run frequently through the summer, while in the off-season the boats come and go more sporadically. Each of the main islands has its own airport with connection to Spain and several European capital cities.

Andalusia

When people conjure up an image of Spain, it's usually Andalusia (Andalucía) that springs to mind—sprawling green pastures that bump up against the horizon, sleepy cities where Moorish flourishes mingle with Gothic architecture, orange trees, olives groves, flamenco guitar, whitewashed towns, and the iconic tradition of the *corrida de toros* (bullfight). Andalusia today is much more than all that—Seville and Granada in particular are urban centers complete with active business districts, a multitude of restaurants, and modern buildings surrounding the historic quarters. Yet the fact remains that the long-preserved traditions of Andalusia are still patently felt and that's part of the draw for those who make their homes here.

If the culture doesn't win you over, the climate and landscape will. Andalusia has about 320 days of sunshine a year and well over a hundred miles of coast where you can soak up all those rays. Inland, you'll find a sprawling fertile plain, dunes and wetlands in the Coto de

How the *Oeste* Was Won

If you struggle to believe that Almería's desert compares to the ones in the western United States, you don't have to visit the place for confirmation. You can just watch *A Fistful of Dollars*. The famous western was shot in Almería, and that's not the only big-budget, Hollywood production that was set in Spain's arid badlands. *The Good, the Bad and the Ugly* and *The Magnificent Seven* were also staged in the dry, rocky desert, as were dozens of other American westerns from the 1960s and 1970s.

Clint Eastwood, Raquel Welch, Henry Fonda, and Charles Bronson took the starring roles, the Native Americans were played by Romas, and Spaniards fill the credits as extras. Weird? You betcha. But even more bizarre are the relics that were left behind.

Mini Hollywood is a cluster of three sets and if you long for a taste of home (assuming your home was Buffalo Bill's American West), you can tour the constructed towns. Tipple in the Tombstone Gulch saloon wile cancan girls kick it on the stage. Watch the epic shooting of Jesse James—staged multiple times a day by gun-slinging actors in full cowboy regalia. And don't miss the U.S. cavalry frontier fort, and the Native American wigwams.

As strange as Almería's film history is, it's worth nothing that the American westerns shot in Spain are not the only polyglot aspect of the genre—many of the movies were directed by Sergio Leone—an Italian. It's good to know that the lore of the American West is enjoyed the world over and who knows . . . perhaps future westerns will begin adding the word Hee-Haw in Esperanto.

Doñana (a national park that hosts millions of migrating birds), and Europe's one and only desert. Andalusia is also home to a series of mountains, including the impressive Sierra Nevada range outside of Granada, where you'll find Iberia's highest peak, Pico de Mulhacén. All that splendor spreads over about 558,000 square miles and eight individual provinces—Almería, Granada, Jaén, Málaga, Cádiz, Córdoba, Huelva, and Seville.

The coasts attract the bulk of foreigners who move to Spain, especially the notorious Costa del Sol, which is jam-packed with spas, golf courses, marinas, and villas. However, the cities' enchanting way of weaving history and modernity together have attracted their share of expatriates, too, and you'll enjoy yourself there if you're looking to settle into an authentically Spanish place.

Seville

In the 16th century, Seville (Sevilla) was *the* place to be—it was the point of entry and departure to and from the New World, and the city still retains that grandeur. With a population of 702,000, Seville is

Spain's fourth-largest city and one with a discernibly elegant air to it; it's not unusual to see old men in three-piece suits lingering over their morning coffee in cafés. Don't misunderstand, there's nothing reserved about the city. Seville is Don Juan's Spain, it's Carmen's country, and it's a place where women in jewel-colored dresses step into plazas, stamp their feet, raise their hands, and show you how flamenco is really done. That such events still occur in the midst of modern-day activity is the true marvel of the city, and the key to Seville's appeal. The grand city, full of whitewashed homes with balconies hanging over shaded plazas, is also a business center devoted to shipbuilding, food processing, construction, cigars, pottery, silks, and a whole lot of tourism. Outside of the city center, you'll see the high-rise buildings to prove that commitment to commerce. The city's contradictions are conspicuous, and they're not always so romantic—Seville is the center of an agricultural region with an unemployment rate of 40 percent. It's the heart of Andalusia—a place that's as beleaguered as it is beautiful.

> *In the 16th century, Seville (Sevilla) was the place to be—it was the point of entry and departure to and from the New World, and the city still retains that grandeur.*

THE LAY OF THE LAND

Seville is in the southwestern part of Andalusia, an inland city surrounded by farms that grow olives, almonds, fruits, and vegetables. You'll notice more olive groves than anything else, though. About 40 percent of the world's olive harvest comes from Spain and the region is the country's main producer. The nearby hills are gentle and the sun is strong. Summer temperatures are on average in the mid-to-high 90°F range, although winter is a far gentler season, when the temperature rarely dips below the mid 40°F range.

Seville is 60 miles northeast of Cádiz. The Guadalquivir River bisects Seville into two sections with most of the city's cultural and historic treasures on the eastern side (although the western side offers some decent apartments). The Avenida de la Constitución runs through the center of town—it's a broad avenue lined with banks, shops, and offices, and it cuts a modern line through a patch of historical landmarks. Head to the northern end of the avenue and you'll reach Plaza Nueva, the border to the city's premier shopping district. South of Plaza Nueva you'll hit the cathedral, the Alcázar, and Barrio de Santa Cruz (a.k.a. the Jewish quarter)—a mess of twisting, narrow streets dotted with plazas filled with flowers. This small district is the loveliest piece of Seville.

© Nikki Weinstein; © Jessica Chesler

Andalusia's beaches are magnets for tourists and foreign residents alike.

Seville's bullring can be viewed from the top of La Giralda tower.

WHERE TO LIVE

The city is filled with old buildings that are as beautiful as they are dilapidated, yet you can also find historic places that have been beautifully renovated. Not surprisingly, newer buildings have appeared as the city has grown, and Spaniards typically dive for the modern digs while young foreigners are all too pleased to snap up a vacancy in Barrio de Santa Cruz. Go figure. There's one thing that's for sure: most people in Seville want an urban experience, and they'll often choose apartments over houses. That goes for families and 20-somethings alike. To find a place, you can look through the classified ads in the paper, speak to real estate agents, or check out El Cambalache (www.elcambalache.com), which publishes listings.

The center of town is the commercial district. It's conveniently located to all parts of Seville, the best shopping will be right outside your front door, and theaters and cinemas are nearby. Add the fashionable Calle Sierpes and stately old buildings to the mix, and it's no shock that people like living around here. You can expect to pay about €500 ($625) a month to rent an apartment, and about €200,000 ($250,000) to buy one.

You'll pay about the same prices for aged charm in Barrio de Santa Cruz but be warned: what you gain in atmosphere, you *might* lose in quality. Aged charm is just another way of saying "old," and while some buildings are in prime condition, others are not. You might not know your apartment's defects until you discover maddening wiring problems after moving in. If you want to live in Santa Cruz, be sure to inquire about the possibility of installing DSL and phone lines if you want those things in your home. Plenty of the apartments are in great shape and renovated to 21st-century standards, but you can't bank on it.

Barrio Triana on the west side of the river is sometimes described as a less polished part of town, but in fact it's a handsome area. Its reputation is likely due to the fact that it's not a tourist zone, and it used to be where the city's Roma population lived. Gentrification moved in and the area's former residents moved out, but the neighborhood hasn't lost all its traditions. Triana has long been a center of glazed tile production, and the fruits of the local labor are handsomely displayed on the surrounding buildings. Today, the area is a decidedly residential part of town with older buildings, restaurants, and markets all nearby. The prices are about equal to those in the center—that means that a two-bedroom apartment will rent for about €500 ($625) a month, and it will sell for around €200,000 ($250,000).

Nervión is one of the most sought-after neighborhoods. (Hmm. Perhaps that's because an El Corte Inglés department store is conveniently located in the neighborhood.) The commercial district is on the east side of town, a half-hour walking distance from the center, and it attracts families more than anyone else. You'll find apartments in bulk but a few houses as well. Apartments with two bedrooms go for at least €600 ($750) per month, and they sell for about €240,000 ($300,000). A modest house will run you about €800–1,000 ($1,000–1,250) a month, and you can buy one for about €300,000 ($375,000).

REAL ESTATE AGENTS: SEVILLE

Real estate offices are scattered throughout Seville, but here are a few that are well liked.

Inmobiliaria Estadio
Avenida Luis de Morales, 22
Piso 3, 3B
41018 Seville
Seville
tel. 95 453 75 28
fax 95 453 88 77

Vallehermoso Grupo
Avenida República Argentina, 25
41011 Seville
Seville
tel. 95 427 80 85
fax 95 427 16 52

Idonea Inmobiliaria
Madre Rafols, 8
L-2
41011 Seville
Seville
tel. 95 427 92 16
fax 95 428 17 94

GETTING AROUND

The traffic in Seville would make the Dalai Lama beat on the horn and start sputtering in rage, so if you plan on using your own wheels to get around town, be prepared for frustration. Another note of caution for car owners: be careful with street parking as the city is known for break-ins. While renting a parking space is an additional expense, it might just be a worthwhile one. Fortunately, a car is only necessary if you'll be using it to get around outside of the city. Within Seville itself, you'll find a good system of public transportation, plenty of taxis, and your own two feet can get you far—the city is compact.

Granada

Granada shares some of its culture with Seville. For example Moorish history is deeply felt in both places. However, Granada is much smaller, it exudes a more intimate air than Seville, and it's a different sort of beautiful. Back in the 11th century, Granada was the seat of the grand, Moorish empire and an important part of the Spanish one, and the city still displays relics from those glory days. However, you'll find a discernable wear-and-tear to the city's face, and yet it's the chipped paint and crumbling old walls that give the plazas, fountains, and whitewashed Moorish buildings half their charm. It's often said that Granada is a romantic city, and there's no doubt that the slight dilapidation bolsters that image.

> *The Sierra Nevada mountains stand guard over the city, and on most days, even when the sun bakes the streets with a heat fierce enough to send everyone scrambling for shade, peaks with snowy summits can be viewed in the distance.*

The Sierra Nevada mountains stand guard over the city, and on most days, even when the sun bakes the streets with a heat fierce enough to send everyone scrambling for shade, peaks with snowy summits can be viewed in the distance. Yet the mountains pale in comparison to the largest presence in the city—the Alhambra. Some say that the old fortress is the most beautiful building in all of Spain, and it's difficult to argue the point. The enormous red edifice sits high on a hill, and until you lay eyes on its detailed stuccowork and gurgling fountains for yourself, you might believe that people are exaggerating when they say that the place is the stuff of fairy tales. The Moors' architectural flourishes don't end with the Alhambra. They're visible throughout town, from latticed windows to curved archways.

Yet step away from the historic district and the maze of narrow streets that make up the Albaicín, the old Moorish quarter, and you'll find traffic jams and high-rises that are entirely 21st-century. With a population of 243,000, Granada is a decent-sized city, its university helps provide a good dose of fun, and bars and clubs can remain packed until the early hours. Even if Granada's most glorious era is in the past, the contemporary city still offers plenty.

THE LAY OF THE LAND

Although Granada is inland, it's close to the coast, although you'd never know it with the Sierra Nevada mountains looming in the distance. Just south of the mountains you'll find the valleys of Las Alpujarras, an ideal spot for rustic day trips. As is the case throughout Andalusia, the weather is mild. On summer days the temperatures will rise to 95°F, and winter temperatures rarely drop below the mid-40s.

© Nikki Weinstein

Andalusia's arid climate is perfect for cacti.

Granada is laid out amorphously with a dense cluster of streets in the city center. The two central streets, Gran Vía de Colón and Calle Reyes Católicos, merge at Plaza Isabel La Católica. At that point, the main avenue continues its beeline for Puerta Real in the southwest. To the northeast the same street runs up to Plaza Nueva, near the Alhambra, the Albaicín, and the narrow Darro River.

WHERE TO LIVE

You'll find some beautiful housing throughout the city, and you can end up with a spacious house for a modest amount of cash. None of the city's neighborhoods are exactly swanky, so you can settle into a large pad with all the trimmings for a fraction of what you'd pay for an equivalent place in Madrid or Barcelona. You'll even pay less than Seville prices.

The Albaicín is easily the best neighborhood in the city. The Darro River flanks the area to the south, creating a natural border. Increasing numbers of foreigners have discovered Albaicín's appeal, and slight price increases reflect that. The neighborhood is the historical heart of Granada, it was first settled by people in the 7th century B.C., and the Moorish Zirid Berber dynasty put their fortress in the same spot when they arrived in Granada in the 11th century. The houses are antique structures with the sort of charm that can only be amassed over centuries. In most cases, you'll find structures that share an outside wall and have two or three floors inside, and possibly even a balcony.

It's impossible to name any one type of person who wants a piece of property in the Albaicín. The area attracts 20-somethings in Granada for a short period and retired couples who have no intention of moving anytime soon. However, nothing is perfect. The hills are steep and even though you're guaranteed thighs of steel if you walk the slopes daily, you may not want to do that. On the other hand, you can find quite a bit within the perimeters, including a health center and food markets. You'll have to forego peanut butter and aisles of cereal, but you can buy fresh fish, vegetables, fruit, meat, and cheese at individual stores. Cafés, restaurants, and tapas bars can be found in the area and lining the streets at the bottom of the hill. For other needs such as banking and hospitals, the city center is about a half-hour away on foot. To rent a two-bedroom home in the Albaicín, expect to pay about €500 ($625) a month, and at least €250,000 ($313,000) to buy.

Barrio de Realejo, a 10-minute walk from Plaza Nueva, is also an attractive neighborhood and one that pulls in families, expatriates, and artists alike. Excellent tapas bars line the streets, as do cafés, a few restaurants, and grocery stores. The apartments in Barrio Realejo are spacious and cheaper than the homes in Albaicín, and the neighborhood is a mere 10-minute walk from the center of town. You can buy a two-bedroom place for €150,000 ($188,000) on the low end, and about €200,000 ($250,000) will fetch you something gorgeous. To rent for an equivalent place, expect to spend about €400–500 ($500–625) a month.

Plaza Bib-Rambla, in the commercial center and near the cathedral, is in the middle of the city's commercial zone, and it's the part of town where you'll find the most banks, a good number of restaurants, and some markets. However, don't be fooled by all the hotels, people do live there, too. A two-bedroom apartment in the area rents for about €450 ($565) and the same sort of unit will sell for about €200,000 ($250,000).

REAL ESTATE AGENTS: GRANADA

You can stick to the classified ads or you can go with a real estate agent. Below, you'll find a couple of companies that have won kudos from former clients.

Inmobiliaria Generalife
Doctor Olóriz, 14
2 Izquierda
18012 Granada
Granada
tel. 958 80 43 14
fax 958 80 43 16

Inmobiliaria Los Portones S.L.
Plaza Trinidad, 2
1A
18001 Granada
Granada
tel. 958 26 70 01
fax 958 25 63 54

GETTING AROUND

Owning a car in Granada is much as it is in Seville—a luxury, not a necessity. The city has a solid network of buses and you'll be able to walk most places without even breaking a sweat. However, a car is an excellent perk if you expect to spend time visiting nearby areas without relying on mass transportation.

The Costa del Sol

If you want sun, surf, and sand, you can find all that and an easy, laid-back lifestyle along the southern coast. However, let's get straight to it. This is the Boca Raton, Florida of Spain, and people do not move here for Spanish culture. They crave the climate and the way of life. In the 1950s, Spain made a name for itself as a resort hot spot thanks to the now famous strip of land that stretches from Nerja in the eastern part of the region to Sotogrande in the southwest (about 100 miles). The area is unquestionably the most built-up of all of Spain's shores, and if you look for a home there you won't struggle to find a community where English is widely spoken, golf courses abound (there are close to 40 in the area), and international schools offer British curriculums. The region attracts several million tourists a year and of the approximately 200,000 foreign-owned homes in Andalusia, a good many of them are here. The vast majority of expatriates come from England, Germany, and Scandinavia. About 1.5 million people live in the Costa del Sol and the population is growing fast.

Why the popularity? That one's a gimme. The sun shines about 320 days a year, the beaches are broad, the bars packed, the amenities good, and the area is an excellent place to tee-up and play a round of golf. Let's go back to that part about the services. In most cases, that term refers to the basics—DSL lines, health clinics, supermarkets and the like. In the case of the Costa del Sol, services means all that plus the latest and greatest variety of facials, mud wraps, stores hawking designer duds, massages (Swedish, hot stone—you name it, they have it), and access to exclusive golf clubs.

You can find small towns with pretty marinas, low-key tempos, and homes built in an authentically Spanish style. That said, you won't see more than a trace of the fishing villages that dotted this coastline until the middle of the last century. But what's arrived in the wake of those quaint towns can be picturesque in its own way. If you're surprised to learn that, then you must have been to Málaga— the Costa del Sol's epicenter, and a place where natural beauty has been irrevocably scarred by anonymous high-rises and cheaply built tourist digs. It's unfortunate that the town has become synonymous with the Costa del Sol, because Spain's sun coast offers more than what Málaga has to show.

While those who choose to live along the Costa del Sol enjoy excursions to the small, whitewashed villages in the interior such as Ronda and Mijas, most people beeline for the coast when choosing a home. The most popular spots are Almuñécar, Benalmádena, Estepona, Fuengirola, Málaga, Nerja, Marbella, Torre del Mar, and Torremolinos. Málaga's Pablo Picasso airport is the main point of entry and departure to the region and it might explain why Málaga is the coast's hub and the surrounding towns are the most urbanized in the area. As you move away from Málaga, the developments change— you'll see fewer cranes digging into the landscape, fewer high-rises, and more natural space.

La Costa de la Luz

While most foreigners gush about the Costa del Sol, the Andalusian seaboard that captivates the Spanish is a little bit further west and a lot less known—the Costa de la Luz. While the shores are hardly untrodden, they are still unspoiled enough to explain their name—the coast of light.

When you hit the Tarifa—the southernmost tip of Europe—you'll have left the Mediterranean behind and entered a place where the Atlantic laps the shores. Between that point and the Portuguese border, you'll pass through some of Spain's less developed beaches and you should catch them while you can. Construction has been stepped up and this place might not be pristine for much longer.

A few people have stopped by this length of land for vacations and been so smitten with the area that they've stuck around and made it home. However, the local amenities don't compare to those in the nearby Costa del Sol. For that reason, this location is currently considered a prime living one to only a select few—yet that is changing as development along the coast increases.

Tarifa tops the list of the area's highlights. The town is the absolute tip of Spain's hulking landmass. It juts out into the ocean and from the beach you can see clear to Tangier when the weather is right. The *legvante* (east wind) and *poniente* (west wind) vie for control and thrash the city in a torrent of air that attracts windsurfers and kitesurfers from all over the world. While things pick up in July and August, the rest of the year is relatively slow and that's the perfect time to visit the town and enjoy a stroll through the walled-in old city where gem-colored blooms tumble over whitewashed walls.

Los Caños de Meca is a tiny village with just one street and a lighthouse. It's flanked by pines on all sides but the Atlantic one, and its white-sanded beach is marked by a network of coves. This place used to be a hippie mecca, and maybe the former residents left their vibe behind because it still feels real mellow. You will find tourists here but they'll likely to be Spaniards—inexplicably, Los Caños de Meca hasn't become a well-known entity with foreigners.

The crown jewel of the coast is a little further inland—the Coto de Doñana national park. With both dunes and wetlands, the area makes up one of western Europe's largest road-free areas. The region is protected for good reason—it's downright stunning. The delta waters flood the place in the winter and drop dramatically during spring, leaving marshes and cork oak trees in their wake, and providing an ideal resting spot for thousands of birds exhausted from their spring and autumn migrations.

The coast is an attractive location for day-tripping but with all its charms, it's really no surprise that increasing numbers of people are buying homes and moving in. Perhaps after just one visit, they saw the light.

The view towards Africa from the Costa de la Luz

© Nikki Weinstein

THE LAY OF THE LAND

It wasn't dubbed the sun coast for nothing, and in a place with sunshine almost year-round, the land is bound to be a little dry. That said, some areas are surprisingly verdant thanks to a complex network of irrigation systems. You'll also find patches of forests with pines and cork oaks, which adds welcome contrast to the more arid sections of land.

Behind the coastal towns you'll find small mountain ranges; the Sierra Bermeja looms behind Estepona, Sierra de las Nieves provides Marbella with dramatic scenery, and the Axarquía range edges the eastern part of the region. Best of all, the climate is balmy just about all the time. Winter temperatures almost never dip below the high 40°F range, and summer highs max out in the mid-to-high 80s.

WHERE TO LIVE

All of the shore towns attract their share of people, but most expats try to avoid the concrete resorts and instead settle into pretty, more subtle places that blend into the surroundings. The most attractive and least ravaged villages are Nerja, and Estepona, while Marbella—the Madison Avenue of the coast—also lures plenty of people. Fuengirola scores big with foreigners, too, and while the town isn't exactly beautiful, it offers more affordable housing than the most pristine resorts. Nerja and Estepona have maintained warm atmospheres despite the fact that they're very much on the tourist trail, and Marbella has become so fabulous (you'll find some of Europe's most expensive real estate along its "golden mile"), that it's nearly impossible *not* to fall for its glamour.

Nerja

How can you not adore a town with a plaza named Tutti-Frutti? Yet the weirdly named square is only the beginning of what Nerja has to offer. The town is huddled into the foothills of the Almijara range, and it has a tiny old quarter marked by streets so narrow that some cars simply can't use them. The historic part of town spreads north of the Balcón de Europa, a place where you'll catch some of the finest views in Spain. Oh, and did I mention the sea? The beach is attractive and broad enough to contain the masses that plop down on its sandy expanse in the summertime (yes, visitors *will* come—tourism has not completely passed this town by). However, the most attractive beach in town is Burriana, located on the east end of town.

With a population of 15,000, Nerja is small enough to feel quaint and large enough to offer the basic amenities you'll need. Thanks in particular to the population of British residents, you'll find markets stocked to foreign tastes as well as a range of bars and clubs, some of which will undoubtedly make you think of merry old England. The restaurants serve everything from grilled fish à la down-home in Iberia to pizza to nouvelle cuisine. Burriana's outdoor paella-fest has become de rigueur for locals and residents alike.

Although the seafront and western part of Nerja have the monolithic apartments blocks so frequently seen along this coast, further back from the water you'll find villas and other styles of homes that blend more seamlessly with the environment. Should you want to rent a two-bedroom villa, expect to shell out at least €900 ($1,125) a month on the low end. If you want to buy an equivalent property, it will go for no less than €320,000 ($400,000). Apartments cost a good deal less and you can expect to pay about €500 ($625) for a modest, two-bedroom place. Purchase prices for apartments begin around €150,000 ($188,000).

Fuengirola

You will not see Fuengirola's charms when you look the unexceptional blocks of hotels and apartments lining the beachfront, but if you scratch the town's surface you'll find that it does indeed have its attractions. For one thing, five miles of broad, sandy beach flank the municipal area, and a scenic promenade (recently widened as part of a landscaping drive that's still ongoing) adds to the natural beauty. What's more, the town has long been a popular holiday spot with the Spanish, and increasing numbers of foreigners are catching onto the town's enticements. The international combination has given Fuengirola a cosmopolitan flair and you'll see evidence of that in activities offered around town. One prime example of that is the Salon Varietés, an expatriate group that stages theatrical productions in English through the year.

Although Fuengirola has scored points with people from northern locales, it rarely pulls in masses of folks on a 48-hour, hedonistic holiday. Those in search of a package vacation will head to Torremolinos or Málaga, while Fuengirola's more tranquil environment is ideal for families and retirees. The town's population is 43,000, and from health services to restaurants, all the amenities that you'll need and a few of those you'll merely want are on hand.

The town is compact and laid out along the five miles of shore. If you push back from the water line where the towering buildings stand guard behind the beach, you'll find a reasonably handsome old square and a few plazas that add a good dose of historic charm to the place.

Most expatriates look for homes on the east side of town in Los Boliches, and some sections such as Riviera del Sol seem to be almost entirely populated by British people. That can be a real plus if you want to move to Spain without so much as breaking a sweat, but if speaking Spanish is high on your list of things to do in Spain, you might want to steer clear of that neighborhood. A beachfront property will cost you a little more, but the going rate for rent on a two-bedroom apartment in town is about €500–800 ($625–1,000) a month. To buy, expect to pony up at least €130,000 ($163,000) and as much as €180,000 ($225,000).

Marbella

New York has the Upper East Side, Los Angeles has Beverly Hills, and the Costa del Sol has Marbella. The natural beauty might have been the first thing that grabbed people's attention (the good beaches and the picturesque backdrop of the Sierra Blanca mountains add a lot to the town), but when the Marbella Club Hotel opened its doors in the 1950s, the territory suddenly grew hot. Celebrities, oil barons, and filthy rich heirs and heiresses came from all over the world to lounge in the sand and smile for the paparazzi. However, when suburbs began to crop up in the 1980s, the déclassé stench of the upper-middle class drove the society set away. Even worse than the suburbs were the drug lords—Marbella had gone from a ritzy resort to a crook's retreat complete with gunfights in decadent mansions.

Along came Jesús Gil y Gil at the beginning of the 1990s, and when the right-wing politician was elected mayor, he decided to set things right. Perfect. Er . . . right? Not quite. The former mayor spent his time in office employing draconian methods to get rid of drug addicts, prostitutes, and the homeless in order to revamp the town. Although Marbella is lovely today and the moneyed class has returned, Gil y Gil ruled through a ruthless police force that would make even the staunchest supporters of law and order cry foul.

When €27 million of town council money somehow landed in the bankroll of the football club that Gil y Gil just happened to oversee, he had to take a brief holiday to prison. So Gil y Gil is no longer mayor, but the bottom line is this: Although organized crime has not completely disappeared, Marbella is once again pretty as a picture and it's a fun hometown if you can afford it. The residents number 98,900, and given the decadence of the surroundings and Marbella's healthy size, you can bet that you'll find everything that you need and most of what you want without traveling too far.

Although the marble walkways and flowerbeds—added as a result of Gil y Gil's efforts—are genuinely nice touches, Marbella's true crown is its old section, Casco Antiguo. Even with all the new construction that goes on around town, there's still a spot where you can drink a glass of wine with a view of whitewashed old alleyways and nearby mountains. Plaza de los Naranjos is the nexus of Casco Antiguo, and the many balconies that hang over the square do a lot to enhance it. You can live in an apartment right in the center of town, or move to one of the many developments in Marbella's outskirts. Those run the gamut from mid-range to high-end. The city's famed "golden mile" runs from the western border of Marbella to Puerto Banús port—the chic leisure center and marina about three miles west of Marbella.

If you choose to live in the center, you'll almost inevitably live in an apartment and you'll pay just a tad less than you would elsewhere. Some units are in high-rises, others in smaller buildings with just a few floors and a grand old door leading to the street. Health clinics, stores, and restaurants will be right in your neighborhood, and you'll be minutes away from the Puerto Deportivo, where the marina is packed with yachts and the bars, and clubs pulse with feverish activity until the wee hours of the morning. A two-bedroom apartment here rents for about €800–1,100 ($1,000–1,375) a month, and sells for approximately €300,000 ($375,000).

You'll find more spacious properties in the outlying communities, such as San Pedro, Nueva Andalucía, and Nagüeles on the west side of town. With sprawling estates and proximity to the city center, the area is also home to a British school that teaches students ages 3–18. A two-bedroom apartment rents for €800–1,100 ($1,000–1,375) a month, and you can buy the same sort of property for €400,000 ($500,000) and upwards. A two-bedroom villa will set you back at least €1,000 ($1,250) a month, and sales on such luxury digs begin around €600,000 ($750,000). The east side of town where you'll find Los Monteros and other such developments is slightly cheaper, but it's by no means a bargain. Rent on a two-bedroom apartment begins around €750 ($940) and sales start at €320,000 ($400,000). Naturally, villas cost more and for such a place, you rent will total at least €900 ($1,125) every month. You'll pay no less than €450,000 ($563,000) to become the proud owner of such a home.

If you want a house and a little bit of space, you can head outside the municipal limits. In fact, you can just move to paradise—it happens to be a mere 10-minute drive west of Marbella. El Paraiso (a.k.a. paradise) is a beachside community for the wealthy, and you'll get a lot for what you put down. You'll have an 18-hole golf course in the area, as well as a health clinic, lawn bowling, and a tennis club. Restaurants and supermarkets are also nearby. Villas typically come with all the frills and they're downright deluxe—you'll see that in the prices. Rent for a two-bedroom apartment costs a minimum of €800 ($1,000). Purchase prices begin at €250,000 ($313,000) and can go up to about €500,000 ($625,000). Two-bedroom villas will rent for approximately €1,100 ($1,375) a month, and to buy, you should expect to spend at least €475,000 ($594,000) or significantly more, depending on the property.

Estepona

The coast between Marbella and Estepona is crammed full of insipid enclaves of wealth that are more Spain-inspired than Spanish, but Estepona is a notable exception. While the town doesn't have the number of postcard-worthy views that Marbella has, it more than compensates with its culture and warm ambience. Estepona is one of the very few places along the Costa del Sol that is completely and authentically Spanish. For evidence of that (or just a good time), check out the daily fish market on the western end of the promenade where the local trawlers auction off their loot. That's no tourist show; Estepona has one of the largest fishing fleets on the coast and the spectacle of the auction ends around 7 A.M.—long before most day-trippers have had their morning coffee.

With 37,500 residents, the town is small enough to easily navigate. Development has been kept in check, so the beach, Playa de la Rada, has foregone colossal hotels in favor of a scenic promenade and a row of flowers and palm trees. Further inland, the historic portion of town is a car-free, cobbled network of streets with the aptly named Plaza Las Flores as its core. At the western edge of town, you'll find a decent marina and a lighthouse.

Almost as if to prove its devotion to culture—and Spanish culture in particular—the town has recently opened four new museums. One's a folk museum, another is devoted to archaeology, the third centers on paleontology, and the last is all about bullfighting (there's an active bullring right in town). However, you can't gaze at exhibits all day, every day—you also have to eat. Estepona has an impressive number of restaurants for its size, and the majority of them serve up traditional Spanish fare. You'll also find a decent amount of foreign foods in the supermarkets around town. (You'll be especially pleased about that if you're a sucker for English and German grub.)

The local culture isn't limited to water sports and discos—you can also take in live music or tour art exhibitions. Yet the town's entertainment is not geared towards the approximately 7,500 foreign residents who live in the town—you'll lack certain extras such as movies shown without dubbing. An additional drawback is that, while you'll have access to a number of health clinics, the nearest hospital is in Marbella.

It's hard to come by long-term rentals right in town, but if you manage to find one you'll likely pay about €500 ($625) a month for a two-bedroom apartment. The same sort of property sells for around €160,000 ($200,000). A villa on the outskirts of town will rent for €700 ($875) or more, and such a home can be yours for €350,000 ($438,000).

A few miles west of Estepona, you'll find one of the toniest resorts in Spain—Sotogrande, a *vedy, vedy* exclusive spot near the rock of Gibraltar (and technically located in Cádiz). The town comes complete with polo grounds, horseback riding, tennis, lots of yachts, and a British private school that teaches students ages 3–18. Children 11 years old and up can board there—it's the only school in Andalusia that accommodates boarders. The two golf courses in the area are highly regarded, and the Valderrama hosted the 1997 Ryder's Cup tournament. You're much likelier to find a home with four or more bedrooms than you are to find one with two, and the prices are steep. However, if you do get lucky and find an apartment with just two bedrooms, you'll pay at *least* €850 ($1065) to rent it, and you'll have to shell out about €375,000 ($469,000) or much more to buy it. Villas will rent for €1,100 ($1,375) on the low end. Buying such a place will cost you €500,000 ($625,000) at least and maybe even a few million euros more.

REAL ESTATE AGENTS: THE COSTA DEL SOL

You won't have to search for real estate agents along the Costa del Sol—you'll be fighting them off. The good news there is that with such a hot market, you'll be able to work with English-speakers. The bad news is that you'll have to be wary of swindles. Be careful and as always, check to be sure that your agent of choice is a licensed one. The following agents have won high marks with previous customers.

Passepartout Andaluz
Pasaje Brazales, Milenio A13
29649 Miraflores,
Mijas-Costa
Málaga
tel. 66 16 26 298
fax 952 939 087
www.passepartoutandaluz.com

Panorama
Edificio Centro Expo,
Búlevar Príncipe Aflonso Hohen-
lohe s/n,
29600 Marbella
Málaga
tel. 902 111 114
fax 952 822 111
www.panorama.es

1st Choice Properties
Casa Juanita
Camino de Estación
29639, Benalmádena Pueblo
Málaga
tel. 952 449 118
fax 952 448 774
www.1stchoiceprop.com

GETTING AROUND

Yes, Spain has an excellent public transportation system but don't kid yourself—life in the Costa del Sol will be much easier if you have a car. In most cases, you won't need to drive it to get around but you'll likely want to head to a town a few miles down the road to try a new restaurant or see a show, and doing that is much easier if you have your own wheels on hand. Villas often have garages attached and some apartment blocks also offer residents private parking spots, but if you need to leave your car on the street overnight you can rest assured that you're doing so in a relatively safe area.

THE CANTABRIAN COAST

© AVALON TRAVEL PUBLISHING, INC.

The Cantabrian Coast

I f you're looking for stunning, hilly landscapes, elegant marinas, rivers filled with trout and salmon, or opportunities to windsurf, canoe, or just lounge on a stretch of white-sanded beach abutting rough Atlantic waters, then the Cantabrian Coast is your ideal home. Add to the bargain the culinary treats that you'll be in for on a daily basis and you'll wonder why *everyone* doesn't live here. The decadent fare that's served in even the most nondescript tapas bars make this region Spain's kitchen—you simply can't eat better than you can along the Cantabrian Coast. That would be enough to lure in plenty of people, but there are more enticements. If you settle into this expanse of rural Spain, you'll find a culture of open people who are pleased to get out and socialize, and local festivals—born from wild, folkloric legends—that are numerous enough to fill a calendar.

The Cantabrian Coast runs along northeastern Spain from Galicia to Basque Country, and it includes Asturias and Cantabria. It's a cluster of regions and each of them is distinct. You'll find beautiful cities, industrial ports, and small villages. Not every spot is ideal for foreigners seeking a piece of gorgeous greenery and all the comforts of home, but plenty of places offer amenities and bucolic charm. The following section outlines a few of them.

Galicia

You probably don't think of Galicia when you think of Spain but don't worry—few people do. Although Spain's northwest corner happens to be one of the country's most beautiful spots (arguably the *most* beautiful) and Spain's patron saint is reputedly buried in the region, Galicia has only recently made it onto most foreigners' maps. The area is usually described as Spain's most feral land; deep, salty fjords serrate the brutish Atlantic coast, while further along the country's edge, broad stretches of white-sand beaches pull in summer visitors seeking cooler locales. Head to the interior and you'll find rolling emerald hills, stone homes with over-sized eaves, and small, farming towns where time appears to have stopped. Those who know Galicia well compare it the wild, western coast of Ireland and not merely for the similarities in the landscapes. The Spanish region traces its roots back to the Celts, and its past is peppered with myths and colorful legends that have blended with history over the years and helped shape modern-day culture.

So perhaps you're thinking that Galicia might be a great place to visit but you wouldn't want to live there, right? Not so fast. The region has fewer expatriates than other parts of Spain, but those numbers are on the rise. Statistics on foreigners living in Spain are dubious but it's safe to say between 30,000 and 45,000 foreigners call Galicia home, and those who do probably wouldn't choose to be anywhere else. However, chances are good that those expatriates are not going to woo you with overblown descriptions of their region's charms. People who settle in this lesser-known section of Spain aren't interested in fostering a foreign invasion—they'd prefer to keep their home quiet, green, and on the down-low. To their way of thinking, if the crowds bypass Galicia for points south, all the better.

Yet just because Galicia is lesser known doesn't mean it's unknown. Santiago de Compostela has long been a destination point for religious pilgrims and in recent years tourists, too. It's said that the remains of Santiago Apóstol (Saint James) are in the city's cathedral and the alleged grave has become Europe's second most important religious shrine. Intrepid visitors arrive in the city via the Camino de Santiago—Spain's answer to the

Appalachian Trail (with a dash of God)—and they usually travel on foot or by bicycle. Once they make it to Santiago de Compostela, they're smitten with the lovely, medieval town but it must be said that Galicia's magnetism is equal in points outside its darling city.

Pontevedra, La Coruña, and Lugo—small cities with big appeal—pull in their share of expatriates. Some go for the halcyon towns, several want to immerse themselves in a culture that they adore, and still others come to buy a sizable home for less money. In fact, Galicia's riches come cheap and property sells for less than anywhere else in the Spain. But that good news comes from an unfortunate reality—the region has historically been one of Spain's poorest, and that's still true today.

Although Galicia's economic situation has improved along with Spain's, it continues to lag behind the rest of the country. Salaries are about 15 percent below the national average, and in 2003, unemployment was about 1 percent higher than the median throughout the rest of Spain. However, you will find some pockets of prosperity in Galicia, especially in the coastal towns that turn into resorts during the summer months.

Unlike the beaches along Spain's southeastern coast, the northwest has a more Spanish flavor when it's packed with tourists. That's because the numbers of vacationers who come from the rest of Spain far exceed those who come from outside of Spain. Why the tourists choose Galicia is no mystery. The province's appeal lays in its cool, wet climate, great expanses of beaches, and beguiling culture—one with a still-palpable medieval feel and powerful links to the past.

Unlike Andalusia—a place heavily influenced by Moorish culture—Galicia's history links the region to the Celts. Although inhabitants lived in the region as early as 3000 B.C., the Celts arrived around 6000 B.C. In A.D. 50, the Romans arrived and they left their mark by dubbing the region Gallaecia. Later, the Visigoths and Normans came, too, and in the 17th century, the French took over for a brief time. However, it's impossible to talk about Galicia's history without mentioning the profound influence of Portugal. Galicia hovers over the smaller, Iberian country and the two places are in some ways intermingled. Evidence of that is most plainly seen in Galician, the regional language, which sounds a lot like Portuguese.

THE LAY OF THE LAND

Geography keeps Galicia isolated. The Miño River to the south creates a natural border between the Spanish province and Portugal, while the Cordillera Cantábrica Mountains buffer Galicia from Spain's broad, central plateau. Thus Galicia stands apart and looks out over the Atlantic

A woman strolls along a beach—one of 750 beaches along the Galician shoreline.

© Nikki Weinstein

Ocean. The province breaks down into four interior regions: La Coruña, Pontevedra, Lugo, and Orense—each is named for its capital city.

Both saltwater and freshwater act as Galicia's lifeblood. The coast runs on for 740 miles, and you'll find approximately 750 beaches along the shoreline. Galicia is home to half of Spain's fishing fleet and Vigo in Pontevedra can lay claim to Spain's most vital fishing port. However, Galicia's love affair with water doesn't end there. The region is known as the "land of 1,000 rivers" for good reason. The area's signature *rias* (estuaries) serrate the untamed, Atlantic coastline, and rivers snake through the lush terrain. Inland, agriculture feeds both the local culture and the economy, and on some particularly steep or tiny plots of land, you'll see plowing done by oxen rather than tractors. Wine is the most known (and perhaps the most adored) Galician product, and though the whites steal the spotlight, Galician red wines are also enjoyed.

You don't have to look down to find water in Galicia—it's all around. The region is Spain's rainiest and the drops mostly fall in spring and winter. Still, the region has nothing on England and the sun shines plenty, especially in the summer. Temperatures in winter average in the low to mid 40°F range, and hit the high 70s in the summer.

Local Language

Galicia's strong sense of regional pride is nothing like that of Catalonia or Basque Country, so the use of Galician—the regional language—is not laden with political overtones. While Galicia is bilingual and you will find street signs and the like written in the local tongue, you're more likely to hear Castilian spoken among residents in the bigger towns. Still, the more you push into the rural land, the more widespread Galician will become.

During the Franco years, the regional language was suppressed (Franco wasn't even softened by the fact that he himself hailed from Galicia), but in recent years, greater emphasis has been placed on Galician. Learning the language is not essential to living in Galicia, but it's a good idea to at least add some Galician phrases to your lexicon should you want to socialize with locals without asking them to amend their verbal customs.

Black Tide

If you were in Spain during the months following November 2002, you would have noticed banners hanging from buildings, signs in store windows, and buttons on coat lapels all reading *Nunca Mais* ("Never Again"). That protest referred to the oil spill off of the Galician coast—a disaster so tremendous that some parts of the shore were awash in oil more than a couple of feet thick.

When the *Prestige* tanker was left to sink 133 miles off of Galician shores, it was filled with 77,000 tons of fuel oil that was seeping into the surrounding waters alarmingly fast. More than a year later, the sludge was still leaking out of the vessel at a rate of 4.4 gallons a day. Thousands of soldiers and civilians rushed to a cleanup effort but even so, the devastation was profoundly felt. The government spent more than a billion dollars cleaning up the spill and the Galician fishing industry took a big hit when certain sections of water were deemed too contaminated for fishing.

By the next summer, the beaches looked clean, beach-goers were splashing in the waves, and the region's fishing industry was back in gear. If you didn't know better, you might have thought the whole event had never occurred. Unfortunately, some of the damage still lingers and globs of oil continue to come in with the tides.

In addition to the tens of thousands of birds that were killed or injured at the time of the disaster, residual chemicals from the spill could remain in the water for as long as ten years. What does that mean exactly? Fish eggs, crustaceans, and plankton might absorb some of the toxicity and harm those higher on the food chain. That might take a toll on the fishing industry, which relies on fishing hauls and harvesting goose barnacles, spider crabs, mussels, scallops, and other seafood.

Still, Galicia shows remarkable signs of recovery and things improved faster than anyone had guessed. There's every reason to think that Spain has seen the last of the damage—that is, so long as those buttons and signs were prophetic: never again.

WHERE TO LIVE

People looking for a city that pulses with activity at all hours will head to Madrid or Barcelona. Those who come to Galicia are looking for something a little more pastoral. That's not to say that you have to give up the basics that make life easy. If you choose your town wisely, you can find all of the amenities that you need and some of the extras, too. In small cities you'll also have plenty of luxuries in addition to basic services. However, you won't have all options that you'd have available in a huge, metropolitan area. You'll be able to find movie theaters (showing dubbed-over movies) and cultural activities in all the larger towns. When it comes to entertainment, Galicia is as Spanish as any region and the local festivals provide a good time for all. The culture is rooted in folklore, regional music (thank the influence of the Celts for the bagpipes), and wonderful celebrations of local produce. The fairs occur on an annual basis in small and large towns alike.

Although big cities will have their share of sports clubs, people often choose to head outside and make use of the gorgeous environment for exercise. From windsurfing to scuba diving, water sports are broadly available on the cost. Fishing in both the ocean and the rivers is a popular activity, and you'll also see people paddling the rivers in canoes and kayaks.

Santiago de Compostela

Of all the legends in Galicia, the one that founded Santiago de Compostela is by far the most notorious—and one of the most outlandish. As the story is told, Saint James's corpse was brought to Galicia by boat after he died in Jerusalem. Once on land, the apostle's body was carried 10.5 miles inland and buried in what is today Santiago de Compostela. When a hermit discovered the spot by following a star, the grave became both a symbol of Christian Spain as well as an important shrine, and the city's stunning, Romanesque cathedral was built on the site where Saint James's remains were supposedly found. Every year, thousands travel to the holy place, and viewing the cathedral is the obvious prize of the journey. But once they arrive, the visitors discover that the city itself holds the true magic.

With its rustic ambience and cobbled, ancient streets, Santiago de Compostela seems to shine in the distinct medieval hues of gold and stone. During the school year, the place is alive with the activity of university students—truth be told, were it not for the legend of Santiago de Apóstol, this would be known as a university town. During the summer months, the students might not be present in the same numbers, but tourists come in by the thousands. The old quarter is compact enough to navigate on foot, and it's as lovely as it is habitable.

The city's population numbers 90,000 and plenty of residents live in the center where narrow lanes and cobbled alleys are packed with restaurants, shops, cafés, and bars that fuel a lively nightlife. Throughout the city, you'll find that Santiago de Compostela is hardly medieval when it comes to the service industry. You'll be able to find a range of eateries, food stores, hospitals, and leisure activities. A two-bedroom apartment will rent for about €550 ($690). Buying a similar place will set you back about €200,000 ($250,000) or more. The old quarter is the most desirable spot in town, and the prices reflect that—while they're relatively inexpensive by Spanish standards, they're costly in Galicia.

With its rustic ambience and cobbled, ancient streets, Santiago de Compostela seems to shine in the distinct medieval hues of gold and stone.

Look outside the center and you'll find that the modern areas are filled with housing. Southwest of Plaza de Galicia, you'll find a smart, residential zone filled with shopping opportunities and comfortable homes, especially around the new town southwest of Plaza de Galicia. Prices are about the same as they are in the city center. Another neighborhood that wins favor due to lower prices and detached homes is Ponte Pedreña. The small area is about seven miles east of the city. Here, a two-bedroom house will rent for about €450 ($565) a month, and you can buy the same sort of property for about €140,000 ($175,000).

La Coruña

Flinty New Englanders will feel right at home in La Coruña—an attractive, maritime city situated on a piece of terra firma thrust out into Atlantic waters. Located in Rías Altas, the city is part of Galicia's most breathtaking sweep of land, one that includes emerald hills dotted with pines and eucalyptus, deep coves, and prominent capes. Just past La Coruña to the southwest, you'll find the Costa de Muerte (Death Coast). Its menacing name arose from the many ships that have, through the centuries, crashed into shore's rocks, but the coast is as gorgeous as it is tempestuous. Even with it's foreboding name, the Costa de Muerte is a worthy destination point.

Many of Galicia's towns link their beginnings to fabulous myths, and La Coruña is no exception. According to legend, Hercules founded the city. Versions of the story vary, but the gist of it involves Hercules—the Vin Diesel of the ancient Greeks—slaying one of his enemies in what is La Coruña today. A lighthouse was eventually built over the victim's body. Much as I'm loath to spoil a good story with facts, I feel compelled to add that the Romans built the Torre de Hércules (the lighthouse) in the 2nd century, and it is the oldest, working lighthouse in Europe. The landmark is just one of many elements that make this thriving northern city so appealing.

Until recently, La Coruña was the region's largest city. Vigo has recently surpassed it in population, with 235,000 residents, but La Coruña is a true metropolis by Galician standards. It's beautiful and it offers a comfortable lifestyle with a range of bars, restaurants, health services, and shopping opportunities all across town. Situated right on a port, the city is known as the City of Glass—not as a nod to local industry, but for La Coruña's iconic balconies, which are encased in glass. Weighty, stone buildings stand out against the city's crystal sheen, and the unlikely combination creates a fascinating display of contrasts.

Some of the best parts of town can be found on La Coruña's isthmus, which leads to a large headland. La Ciudad Vieja—the oldest part of the city—-sits on the southern tip of the headland, outshining the city's sprawling, industrial suburbs. The Plaza María Pita, La Coruña's heart and main square, is filled with stately arcades and it's also where you'll find the town hall. The Avenida de la Marina is another popular spot and one that grows lively with an active bar culture in the evenings. If you get lucky, you just might land an apartment with a glass-encased balcony in the neighborhood. The Plaza de Santa Bárbara is a little quieter (although none of the places are too noisy), and it's captivatingly pretty.

A two-bedroom apartment rents for about €500 ($625) a month, and to buy that same pad, you'd pay about €170,000 ($213,000). If you prefer to live in a detached house outside the city, you might consider Oleiros, a small beach town about five miles east of the city center. In Oleiros, you'll find detached chalets that rent for approximately €450 ($565) a month. Purchase prices start around €140,000 ($175,000).

Pontevedra

With a population of 70,000, Pontevedra is big enough to be considered a small city—one with a long, colorful, maritime tradition. Christopher Columbus's boat, the Santa María, was built and set sail from these waters, and perhaps that's why a local fable claims that Columbus was born in Pontevedra. (As of press time, the Italians had yet to comment.) Fishing is still a vital part of the local economy today, and mussel farms are scattered throughout the area.

In recent years, tourists have begun to visit Pontevedra in increasing numbers. The town is situated in the relatively tame, picturesque part of Galicia known as Rías Bajas, and Pontevedra springs up at the end of a beautiful *ría* (estuary)—one that shares its name. Additional tourist bait lies all around the city in the form of sun and sand—the nearby beaches are broad expanses with soft, light-colored sand. However, plenty of attractions lie within the town's borders, too. Sandwiched between green hills and the sea, the Lérez river runs alongside the town, helping to form the oblong metropolitan center. The roads Rúa do Arzobispo, Rúa de Michelena, Rúa de Cobián, Raffignac, and Rúa de Padre A Carballo further define the egg-shaped old part of town.

Pontevedra is spirited, prosperous, and its old-town is chock full of history. It should come as no surprise that hints of Portuguese culture emerge in some of the city's architectural flourishes—Pontevedra lies just a hair north of Portugal. The old part of the city is tangled of cobbled lanes, granite buildings, and a mix of architecture that includes baroque and neoclassical. There's a vibrant café culture, a selection of bars, a decent choice of restaurants to choose from, and the area isn't just for tourists—locals live in the old quarter, too. A two-bedroom apartment rents for about €450–500 ($565–625) a month, and prices begin around €170,000 ($213,000) for the same property in the center of town. Families in search of a detached home might look to Marcón, just slightly east of the city where prices are about equal to the city center.

If you want to be in the city but prefer a quieter residential zone, consider looking for a place in the new town. The stately city gardens, Jardines de Vicenti and Alameda, add a whiff of green to this territory that sits just west of the historic district. Prices in the new town are about equal to those in the old quarter.

The south side of town is another popular spot with residents, who find the conveniently located hypermarket and commercial center to be a real boon. But the town is small enough that it's not necessary to live near the conveniences; they're always accessible.

REAL ESTATE AGENTS: GALICIA

You won't find nearly as many English-speaking real estate agents in Galicia as you might on the southern coasts, but you will find a few. However, if your Spanish is solid you won't be lacking help when it comes to finding your home. Here are a few agencies that are well regarded.

BK Property
Arida, 174
36980 O Grove
Pontevedra
tel. 665 33 89 12
www.bkproperty.com

Portela
Cobián Roffignac, 4 Bajo
36002 Pontevedra
Pontevedra
tel. 986 85 28 94
fax 986 85 22 06

Inversiones de Galicia Sur S.A.
Marqués de Riestra, 9
36001 Pontevedra
Pontevedra
tel. 986 84 51 60
fax 986 85 76 68

GETTING AROUND

Even Galicia's larger towns are pedestrian friendly, although they also have decent bus networks. However, if you want to head off to the interior at a moment's notice to take in a cheese festival or go trout fishing (hey— it happens), it's a good idea to have wheels of your own. Galicia is rural and amenities and cultural opportunities are spread out. You can rely on the train or take a bus, but if you plan on moving outside your town on a regular basis, having a car offers flexibility that mass transit doesn't. So even if you don't use the car on a daily basis, Galicia is a place where it's good (though not absolutely necessary) to have one anyway.

Asturias and Cantabria

Let's get one thing straight. Asturias is the one and only piece of Spain that was never conquered by the Moors—and yes, it matters. Asturianos are proud of that history. It means the region was Spanish before Spain even existed, and that distinguishes it from the rest of the country, which locals see as the Johnny-come-lately Spain. Yet in many ways, Asturias is linked to the areas that surround it. The Celts kicked off the region's history, and that's something that Asturias has in common with Cantabria—the region to the east. In fact, Castro de Coaña has some of the country's most impressive Celtic ruins.

Both Asturias and Cantabria are situated on the Bay of Biscay and lining the water you'll find quaint fishing villages, a few of which have evolved into summer resorts, while others have grown into industrial ports. The interior is dotted with fertile pastures and rustic villages

The villages along the Cantabrian Coast charm visitors.

filled with pre-Romanesque churches, and the quaint stone homes so typical of the region. However, Asturias and Cantabria are both industrial, too, though you'd never know it to visit its natural treasures and pastoral towns. The combination of industry and farming culture create an odd combination, and while one spot might enchant you with its beauty, a neighboring area might strike you as a nondescript factory town.

Among the area's boasting points are the brown bears that still trundle through the forests. Although their population is on the wane, there's no other place in Spain where you'll find the creatures. The regions are also ideal for dairy farming—an unusual benefit in Spain where summer temperatures typically grow too hot for cows. However, the area's biggest draws are the Picos de Europa to the south and the coastal broad beaches and fishing villages. Those lures are attractive enough to have turned more than a few visitors into permanent residents. Those coastal towns thrive as summer resorts and remain quiet for the rest of the year—and that's just the way the locals want it.

THE LAY OF THE LAND
To the north, Asturias and Cantabria are flanked by the Bay of Biscay, and geography also lends a hand in creating natural boundaries to the region's

The Picos de Europa

They're not the highest mountains in Europe and they're not even the tallest ones in Spain, so how is it that the Picos de Europa get away with being dubbed *the* mountains of Europe? There's justice in that badge. The stalwart crags in Spain's north country managed to throw the advancing Romans for a loop and centuries later, the natural, limestone wall blocked the advancing Moors. They may be relatively small in stature, but the Picos de Europa are not to be reckoned with—they helped change the course of European history.

The mountains were christened by sailors who, when returning to Europe from far-flung lands, saw the peaks rising up over the horizon. At the sight of the snowy hills, the ships' crews knew that they were home. These days, the summits are part of one of Spain's largest natural parks, and those who visit the majestic site are nature enthusiasts, not sailors or marauding armies. Within the hilly territory, you'll find deep gorges, lakes, pastoral valleys full of dairy farms, and numerous opportunities to rock climb or hike.

The parks spans about 400 square miles and the highest of the mountains is 8,685 feet. While that's not *so* high when compared to other European peaks, the Picos de Europa manage to humble visitors. At high altitudes, you'll see scant flora and even animals find that section of park uninhabitable—perhaps because water is hard to come by as you climb closer towards the sky.

south. The Cordillera Cantábrica mountains burst up out of the land, and the most magnificent among them are the Picos de Europa. The highest of the peaks is Macizo Los Urrieles, which soars to 8,685 feet. The mountains' grandeur draws rock climbers and hikers from all over the country and some from elsewhere in Europe. In between the beaches and the mountains, you'll find a lush, green interior.

All those pastures and meadows need water to stay so green, and it's no surprise that Asturias and Cantabria see their share of rain. Winter is the wettest time of year but the sun shines a lot in summer when temperatures average in the high 70°F range. In winter, the temperature dips into the low-to-mid 40s.

WHERE TO LIVE

The area has a number of captivating small towns and summer resorts. The more popular among the latter is Ribadesella, which hosts an international canoe festival on the Sella river in August, and fills with visitors all summer long. Llanes is another favorite resort for those searching for a low-key stretch of sea and sand. However, for all the towns' winning points, they screech to a near stop in the off-season when they have fewer than 10,000 residents apiece. If you want proximity to the best of Asturias and Cantabria without depriving yourself of basic services (and

Yet at lower elevations, the Cares River courses through the verdant land and rippling lakes are scattered throughout the area. In those places, the park is crawling with critters. Deer, foxes, badgers, and wild boar are just a few of the animals that live in the woodlands, and the truly lucky catch sight of wolves and golden eagles. If you're especially fortunate (or jinxed, depending on how you view it), you'll catch sight of one of the few remaining brown bears that still roam the hills.

Most of the park's attention-grabbing monuments are the natural sort, but a few were made by human hands. One famous spot tells the story of King Pelayo and his statue now defends the entrance to the basilica in Covadonga. It was there (or thereabouts) that the king and a cluster of Christians defeated the Moorish army in 722 (or maybe a little bit before or after that). Don't let the fuzziness of the exact location and date throw you— the story of King Pelayo is one that Spaniards are deeply proud of and it's said that the improbable victory inspired the Christians to take back Spain from the Moors.

You might enjoying the park for its natural wonders or its historical ones. Likewise, your interest might be living in the shadows of those peaks or attempting to summit them. Regardless of what brings you to the Picos de Europa, you'll inevitably learn one thing right away— everyone does: this is a place where attitude trumps altitude.

human company), you would do better by living in larger town—one that offers its own set of diversions, a host of amenities, and enjoys proximity to the region's lush natural beauty.

Oviedo

Oviedo's advantages lie in the combination of what it has to offer culturally and its desirable coastal location. The Austurian capital city is the seat of culture and industry for the region. The city itself has a population of 200,000. You'll also find a large university that's been around since about 1600, graceful parks, and something of an old town. That section was badly damaged in the Civil War, and while it isn't quite what some cities offer in the way of historic districts, the pre-Romanesque structures, cafés, and bars are enough to add charm to an already handsome city.

Oviedo's main street, Calle de Uría leads straight from the train station to the city's old section by way of the Campo de San Francisco—a grassy park. The old town's collection of sites includes Plaza de la Constitución and the old Mercado El Fontán, as well as a cluster of small plazas and collection of newer bronze statues. However, the city's most eye-pleasing features are the pre-Romanesque buildings

Small towns like this one appear throughout Spain's northern coast.

scattered about, the greatest of which is Iglesia de San Julián de los Prados, a 9th-century church.

The city center is a sought-after spot—elegant and with plenty of attractive properties. If you settle in there, you'll find cultural activities, theaters, cinemas, and doctors nearby. A two-bedroom setup will set you back about €500 ($625) a month. Buying an equivalent apartment will cost approximately €220,000 ($275,000) for something midrange, and close to €300,000 ($375,000) for a more spacious place, luxurious place.

If you want to live in the city outskirts, you might choose one of the communities that puts you in close proximity to an English school. This is one of the very few international schools in Spain's northern regions, located about nine miles from Oviedo. The school teaches students from ages 3–18, and the families of students either live in the city center or in La Fresneda or Soto de Llanera.

La Fresneda is a 10-minute drive from the city, and it's a family district complete with a golf-course and tennis club. Minus the golf, Soto de Llanera (a 15-minute drive from Oviedo) is very similar, with homes priced like those in La Fresneda. A home will rent for €800 ($1,000) and upwards. Two-bedroom houses sell for around €180,000 ($225,000).

Santander

Although the fire that raged through Santander in 1941 reduced a good amount of the town center to ashes, it was rebuilt into an elegant city with fine properties, and an active port on a pretty marina. The capital of Cantabria, the city has been a popular resort since King Alfonso XIII took to vacationing here in the 1900s, and sun-seekers and surfers still flock to the city when the days grow warm. Yet whatever the season, Santander, which has a population of 170,000, is rich with bars, clubs, restaurants, movie theaters, and every other sort of diversion and convenience that you might want.

Although nearby San Sebastián is known as *the* chic city of the north, Santander has a good amount of grace and style with a hefty dash of festivities. Also like San Sebastián, the prices in town are higher than the average for northern Spain—the city is a trendy destination point. Each August, Santander hosts the Festival Internacional de Santander where you can hear music that ranges from classical to choir, and jazz to arias. The city's annual festival in July, the Semana Grande, turns into a solid week of wall-to-wall revelry.

Santander is laid out in a long, amorphous strip along the northern side of the Bahía de Santander, and it reaches out to the Península de la Magdalena. Just north of the peninsula, the Sardinero beach is one of the most chic spots to catch rays, and the town itself is a well-heeled suburb. The folks who live in the small town truly put the *dinero* (money) in Sardinero.

Residential areas are spread throughout the city, and should you want to settle in the town's center where the nightlife is most vibrant, you'll find two-bedroom apartments that go for about €500 ($625) a month. To buy a comparable place will cost you anywhere between €210,000–240,000 ($263,000–300,000). Homes in Sardinero are more expensive and, although the area does have some independent homes, most people live in apartments. A spacious place with a garage and near the beach will rent for approximately €700 ($875) a month. To buy you should expect to pay around €600,000 ($750,000).

REAL ESTATE AGENTS: ASTURIAS AND CANTABRIA

You'll struggle to find a real estate agent who speaks English, but it won't be a challenge to find good agencies. Here are a couple reputable ones:

Reinas
Avenida Galicia, 31 Bajo
33007 Oviedo
Asturias
tel. 985 96 31 44
fax 985 23 48 23
www.reinasgrupo.com

Re/Max Bahia
Calle Calderón, 19 Bajo
39002 Santander
Cantabria
tel. 942 31 15 31
fax 942 36 22 09
www.remax.com

GETTING AROUND

While both Oviedo and Santander have solid bus services that link the various neighborhoods in the city, a car is a vital asset for the same reason it is in Galicia. Although you can be self-sufficient and reasonably entertained in the cities proper, you'll inevitably take advantage of the offerings in the towns around you, and you'll probably do that on a regular basis. A car offers an indispensable amount of freedom—it allows you travel according to your whims rather than according to the schedules of the local buses and trains.

San Sebastián

San Sebastián has been the single most elegant resort town in Spain since members of the Spanish aristocracy began going there in the late 19th century to work on their tans. As anyone who's ever visited the bayside city will tell you, its appeal will hit you the moment you enter town and catch sight of the views. San Sebastián is a gorgeous coastal spot, located in Basque Country and all but kissing the southern border of France. It's known as Spain's most fashionable city, and the wide avenues and elegant shops bolster that reputation.

What's more, San Sebastián has long been a justifiably celebrated gastronomic hub. Spain's preeminent chefs use the bounty hauled in from the sea to produce culinary delights that are piled high in tapas bars throughout the city's old quarter.

If you want a taste of culture in between your meals, you'll have plenty to choose from. In addition to the local museums, cinemas, and theaters, San Sebastián plays host to a number of festivals, including an international jazz festival every July, and a two-week film festival that's put on every September. The latter is the Spanish answer to the Academy Awards, and in the past Lauren Bacall, Susan Sarandon, and Jeremy Irons have all walked away with prestigious prizes.

Lest you think that good times are always staid and formal ones, you should check out Regatta de Traineras—a boat race that takes place every September and turns the entire city into a population of hard-drinking bettors. The mid-February Carnaval also unites the city in riotous celebration, and every night in Parte Vieja—the historic old quarter—is a boisterous affair.

When you're not caught up in local festivals, the city will still engage you culturally and with a population of 181,100 people, there's plenty of activity year round. Additionally, those who choose to make this part of Spain home will be immersed in one of the country's most unique and engaging cultures. San Sebastián doesn't just happen to be in Basque Country, it is the very heart of Basque Country. You'll hear Euskara (Basque) spoken on the radio, find newspapers written in the regional language, and see the Basque flag fluttering in the breeze throughout town.

Some conjecture that the Basque people might predate even the first Indo-European invasions into Europe, but there's one thing that's known for sure—the Basque people's roots go so far back that no one quite knows where they begin. Regional pride is understandably strong, and it blends with politics in Basque Country. In fact, there's little distinguishing the two things. However, Basque Country's strong sense of regionalism has an unfortunate side, too. While the majority of locals do not support Euskadi Ta Askatasuna (ETA), the terrorist group that sometimes resorts to horrific violence in order to make its desire for independence from Spain known, some people do back the group. You will see pro-ETA graffiti plastered on buildings around San Sebastián.

ETA's revolutionary efforts are often played out in Madrid or in tourist resorts, but bombs are also set off in Basque Country. There's no doubt that ETA has left a ghastly trail of deaths in its wake—more than 800 people have died at the group's hands since ETA was formed in 1961. As grim as that sounds, you won't have to worry for your own safety much more than you would anywhere. The group's favored targets are the Spanish Guardia Civil, and members of Basque's Partido Popular—Spain's right-wing party. The best way to avoid involvement is to read the news and keep abreast of where violence occurs (the local autonomous police department is a target), and avoid such places. However, ETA's actions are not common enough to deem San Sebastián dangerous—it's largely considered safe.

> San Sebastián has long been a justifiably celebrated gastronomic hub. Spain's preeminent chefs use the bounty hauled in from the sea to produce culinary delights that are piled high in tapas bars throughout the city's old quarter.

THE LAY OF THE LAND

San Sebastián spreads into a crescent-shaped sprawl that wraps around the Bahía de la Concha, a body of water flanked by hills at both ends. A tower caps both rises and la Isla de Santa Clara—a tiny island—sits in the center of the bay. The sea isn't the only body of water that helps shape this town—the Urumea River runs through the city, dividing it into two parts.

The old quarter and the undisputed nucleus of the city is Parte Vieja, with Plaza de la Constitución at its center. The neighborhood sits at the foot of Monte Urgull, the hill on the east side of the bay. Parte Vieja is a mesh of aged streets filled with pedestrians and is blissfully car-free. Head south from Parte Vieja, cross the Plaza de Guipúzcoa and you'll reach the center of town, a zone of broad, graceful avenues full with designer shops and upscale restaurants.

The city itself is situated in the northern part of Basque Country, a land that's coastal in one area and green and hilly in others. The Basques have long depended on the sea, and you'll find numerous fishing villages outside of San Sebastián. Some of the interior towns are industrial (Basque Country is one of Spain's most productive regions), and others are agricultural ones. But overall the area has maintained its beauty de-

The lush countryside of a small Basque town near the border of France

© Nikki Weinstein

spite industrial pockets scattered across the landscape. As is the case throughout Spain's north, the weather is far more temperate than it is in the south. Winter temperatures drop to around 45°F. In summer, the mercury usually stops rising when it reaches the high 70s.

Local Language

Basque is entirely unrelated to any language in the world — at least, as far as scholars can surmise. That means that if you speak Spanish, dabble in Italian, and have traveler's French down pat, you still won't understand a lick of what anyone is saying if they're speaking Basque. The good news is that everyone speaks Spanish—often with each other, too—and so you won't be struggling to communicate. The bad news (at least for foreigners worried about language skills) is that emphasis has been placed on Basque in recent years, and increasingly more young people are working on mastering it.

If your stay in San Sebastián is a brief one, you can forgo learning more than a few words ("men" and "women" are handy ones if you want to use the correct public bathroom). However, if you're planning to stick around, you'll find that even attempting to speak Basque will endear you to the locals, and speaking it well can ease social situations.

WHERE TO LIVE

The city has some gorgeous homes. If you move into an apartment you'll be set up in style and have endless services and recreational opportunities right outside your front door. However, there is one thing to note: the prices in San Sebastián are rivaled only by those in Madrid and Barcelona. In other words, housing costs more than it does throughout most of Spain, and certainly the rest of the north. The prices remain lower than those in Paris, London, and other notoriously exorbitant cities, but you can expect to pay handsomely for your home.

Once you lay eyes on Parte Vieja, it won't surprise you to learn that the neighborhood is considered one of the city's finest. The buildings have a historic charm despite the fact that few of them predate 1813, when a devastating fire wiped out a good portion of the infrastructure. The local fish market nods to the city's roots and adds character to the already enchanting area. Residents of the neighborhood benefit from the wealth of nearby shops and the proximity to the center—the commercial district—where banks, markets, and the like can all be found in abundance. However, the greatest perk to living in this area is the opportunity to be immersed in the liveliest part of the city, one that offers constant excitement.

Fishing villages like this one line the coast in Basque Country.

That said, the crowds on the street can grow riotously loud on summer evenings, and that's something to consider if you're sensitive to noise. A two-bedroom apartment will rent for about €500–800 ($625–1,000), and the nicest units will go for even more. To buy an equivalent home, you can expect to shell out at least €200,000–500,000 ($250,000–625,000), and the very best units will top those figures by a lot.

The graceful center of town that lies south of Parte Vieja is an equally popular choice for residents and it's a more composed part of the city— one that will suit those sensitive to noise pollution. The area is San Sebastián's commercial center, and it's loaded with conveniences from markets to restaurants. Gyms, health facilities, and the like are all nearby and the apartments are elegant and spacious, so you'll get what you pay for.

Those who want to live it up in style move to Ondarreta, but it is the priciest spot in an already pricey city. The adjacent beach is known to be the best in town, and its broad, sandy expanse teems with sun worshippers and surfers in the summertime. Just off of the beach you'll find villas, apartment buildings, gardens, supermarkets, banks, and shopping opportunities. In 1889, the Miramar Palace was built by José Goicoa, a Basque architect, for Queen Maria Cristina. The tony summer residence set Ondarreta's reputation as an refined area, and judging from the prices of property, that reputation persists today. Many people go for the luxury apartments that rent for at least €1,000 ($1,250) a month and sell for upwards of €700,000 ($875,000).

REAL ESTATE AGENTS: SAN SEBASTIÁN
You'll see agencies throughout the city, but here are a few places that other people have liked working with.

Inmobiliaria Arrieta
Arrasate, 1
Planta 1
20005 San Sebastián
Guipuzcoa
tel. 943 42 35 12
fax 943 42 35 18

Inmobiliaria Easo
Bermingham, 25
1B
20001 San Sebastián
Guipuzcoa
tel. 943 27 76 11
fax 943 27 72 89

Inmobira
Prim, 30
1A
20006 Donostia–San Sebastián
Guipuzcoa
tel. 943 45 54 32
fax 943 45 78 29

GETTING AROUND
You don't need a car to live in San Sebastián, and you can take the bus and rely on mass transportation to reach places outside the city. However, a lot of residents do have wheels of their very own to make life easier. A wealth of small towns pepper Basque Country, and they're all easier to enjoy if you're not relying on buses or trains.

Resources

Contacts

Embassies and Consulates

Some of the following contacts will be useful when in the United States (the consulates are crucial for visa applications), and others will be handy when in Spain.

UNITED STATES
Consulate General of Spain in Boston
545 Boylston St., Suite 803
Boston, MA 02116
tel. 617/536-2506 or 617/536-2527
fax 617/536-8512
www.spainconsul-ny.org/boston.html
Jurisdiction: Maine, Massachusetts, New Hampshire, Rhode Island, and Vermont

Consulate General of Spain in Chicago
180 N. Michigan Ave., Suite 1500
Chicago, IL 60601
tel. 312/782-4588 or 312/782-4589
fax 312/782-1635
www.consulate-spain-chicago.com
Jurisdiction: Illinois, Indiana, Iowa, Kansas, Nebraska, North Dakota, South Dakota, Ohio, Kentucky, Michigan, Minnesota, Missouri, and Wisconsin

Consulate General of Spain in Houston
1800 Bering Dr., Suite 660
Houston, TX 77057
tel. 713/783-6200, 713/783-6205, or 713/783-6214
fax 713/783-6166

Jurisdiction: New Mexico, Oklahoma, and Texas

Consulate General of Spain in Los Angeles
5055 Wilshire Blvd., Suite 960
Los Angeles, CA 90036
tel. 323/938-0158 or 323/938-0166
fax 323/938-2502
Jurisdiction: California (Imperial, Inyo, Kern, Los Angeles, Orange, Riverside, San Bernardino, San Diego, San Luis Obispo, Santa Barbara, and Ventura Counties), Arizona, Colorado, and Utah

Consulate General of Spain in Miami
2655 Le Jeune Rd., Suite 203
Coral Gables, FL 33134
tel. 305/446-5511, 305/446-5512, or 305/446-5513
fax 305/446-0585
www.conspainmiami.org
Jurisdiction: Florida, South Carolina, and Georgia

Consulate General of Spain in New Orleans
2102 World Trade Center
2 Canal St.
New Orleans, LA 70130
tel. 504/525-4951 or 504/525-7920
fax 504/525-4955
Jurisdiction: Alabama, Arkansas, Louisiana, Mississippi, and Tennessee

**Consulate General of Spain
in New York**
150 East 58th St., 30th & 31st floors
New York, NY 10155
tel. 212/355-4080, 212/355-4081,
212/355-4082, 212/355-4085, or
212/355-4090
fax 212/644-3751
www.spainconsul-ny.org
Jurisdiction: New York, Connecticut, Delaware, Pennsylvania, and
New Jersey

**Consulate General of Spain
in San Francisco**
1405 Sutter St.
San Francisco, CA 94109
tel. 415/922-2995 or 415/922-2996
fax 415/931-9706
Jurisdiction: Alaska, California (except southern part), Hawaii, Idaho,
Montana, Nevada, Oregon, Washington, Wyoming, and American
possessions in the Pacific

**Consulate General of Spain
in Washington, D.C.**
2375 Pennsylvania Ave., N.W.
Washington, DC 20037
tel. 202/728-2330
fax 202/728-2302
www.spainemb.org/ingles/
consulate/English.html
Jurisdiction: Maryland, Virginia,
West Virginia, District of Columbia, and North Carolina

**Consulate General of Spain
in Puerto Rico**
Edificio Mercantil Plaza, 11th floor
of 1101

Hato Rey, PR 00919
Mail to:
Apartado Postal 9243
Santurce, PR 00908
tel. 787/758-6090, 787/758-6142,
or 787/758-6279
Jurisdiction: Puerto Rico, Culebra
and Vieques Islands, and Virgin Islands

SPAIN
United States Embassy
Calle Serrano, 75
28006 Madrid
tel. 91 587 22 00
fax 91 587 23 03
http://madrid.usembassy.gov

**U.S. Consular Agency La
Coruña**
Cantón Grande, 6-8-E
15003 La Coruña
tel. 981 21 32 33
fax 981 22 88 08

**U.S. Consular Agency Fuengirola
(Málaga)**
Avenida Juan Gómez "Juanito," 8
Edificio Lucía 1-C
29640 Fuengirola
Málaga
tel. 95 247 48 91
fax 95 246 51 89

**U.S. Consular Agency Palma
de Majorca**
Edificio Reina Constanza,
Porto Pi, 8, 9D
07015 Palma de Majorca
tel. 971 40 37 07 or 971 40 39 05
fax 971 40 39 71

U.S. Consulate General Barcelona
Reina Elisenda de Montcada, 23
08034 Barcelona
tel. 93 280 22 27
fax 93 20 52 06

U.S. Consulate General Las Palmas
Edificio ARCA
Calle Los Martínez Escobar, 3
Oficina 7
35007 Las Palmas
tel. 928 27 12 59
fax 928 22 58 63

U.S. Consulate General Seville
Paseo de las Delicias, 7
41012 Seville
tel. 95 423 18 85
fax 95 423 20 40

U.S. Consulate General Valencia
Dr. Romagosa, 1, 2, J
Valencia 46002
tel. 96 351 69 73
fax 96 352 95 65

Planning Your Fact-Finding Trip

TRAVELING IN SPAIN
www.budgettravel.com/spain.htm
www.okspain.org (the U.S. tourist
   office of Spain's official website)
www.red2000.com
www.spaintour.com (the tourist office of Spain's official website)
www.travelinginspain.com

GUIDED TOURS

Gastronomy Tours
Food & Wine Trails
707-A Fourth Street
Santa Rosa, CA 95404
tel. 707/526-2922
fax 707/526-6949
http://foodandwinetrails.com

Culinary Adventures
Viajes Solymar
Saturnino Calleja, 6
28002 Madrid

tel. 91 531 64 89
www.atasteofspain.com

Bike Tours
Easy Rider Tours
P.O. Box 228
Newburyport, MA 01950
tel. 978/463-6955
www.easyridertours.com

Bike Riders
P.O. Box 130254
Boston, MA 02113
tel. 617/723-2354
www.bikeriderstours.com

Euro-Bike & Walking Tours
P.O. Box 990
DeKalb, IL 60115
tel. 800/321-6060
www.eurobike.com

Art History Tours
Icscis Inc.
44 Vieux Chemin
Val-des-Monts
QC J8N 4A9
Canada
tel. 800/611-4789
www.painting-workshops.com

Horse-Riding Tours
Euro Adventures
Velazquez Moreno, 9
4th Floor, Office 409
Vigo, Pontevedra
36201 Galicia
tel. 986 22 13 99
fax 986 22 13 44
www.euroadventures.net

Making the Move

LIVING IN SPAIN
www.easyexpat.com
www.escapeartist.com
www.expatfocus.com
www.expatica.com
www.meetup.org
www.spanish-living.com
www.spanishreporter.com
www.soccer-spain.com
www.typicallyspanish.com

Language and Education

SPANISH INSTRUCTION IN SPAIN
You'll find literally hundreds of language schools throughout Spain—some are excellent, some are awful, some are affordable, and some are exorbitant. The following ones are recommended.

Elemadrid
Serrano, 4
28001 Madrid
tel. 91 432 45 40
www.elemadrid.com

Don Quijote
The booking number for Don Quijote (www.donquijote.org) is tel. 923 26 88 60 and the schools are listed in the following locations:

Don Quijote Barcelona
Gran Vía, 629
08010 Barcelona
tel. 93 412 48 49

Don Quijote Granada
Calle Azhuma, 5
18005 Granada
tel. 958 25 42 12

Don Quijote Madrid
Virgen de los Peligros, 9
Planta
28013 Madrid
tel. 91 360 41 33

Don Quijote Salamanca
Calle Placentinos, 2
37008 Salamanca
tel. 923 26 31 86

Don Quijote Seville
Conde de Ibarra, 2
41004 Seville
tel. 95 421 03 00

Don Quijote Tenerife
Avenida de Colón, 14
Edificio Bélgica
38400 Puerto de la Cruz
tel. 922 36 88 07

Don Quijote Valencia
Plaza Ciudad de Brujas
4 Entresuelo
46001 Valencia
tel. 96 353 33 10

International House
International House (www.ihspain.com)
has four locations throughout Spain—
call individual schools for bookings.

International House Barcelona
Calle Trafalgar, 14
08010 Barcelona
tel. 93 268 45 11

International House Madrid
Zurbano, 8
28010 Madrid
tel. 91 319 72 24

**International House
San Sebastián**
Mundaiz, 8

20012 San Sebastián
tel. 943 32 66 80

**International House
Seville**
Albareda, 19
41001 Seville
tel. 95 450 21 31

INTERNATIONAL
UNIVERSITIES
Here are a few particularly popular
schools:

Barcelona Business School
Paseo Sant Gervasio, 71
Pral 1A
08022 Barcelona
tel. 93 418 62 82
fax 93 434 11 63
www.bbs-edu.org

**European University
(Barcelona)**
Ganduxer, 70
08021 Barcelona
tel. 93 201 81 71
fax 93 201 79 35
www.euruni.edu

**Schiller International
University (Madrid)**
San Bernardo, 97–99
Edificio Colomina
28015 Madrid
tel. 91 448 24 88
fax 91 593 44 46
www.schillermadrid.edu

Health

PRIVATE INSURANCE COMPANIES

Here are a few of the most popular companies that insure foreigners living in Spain:

Adeslas
tel. 902 200 200
fax 902 205 205
www.adeslas.es

Asisa
www.asisa.es

AXA PPP
Phillips House
Crescent Road
Tunbridge Wells
Kent
TN1 2PL
United Kingdom
tel. 800 33 55 55
www.axappphealthcarc.co.uk

BUPA International
Russell Mews
Brighton
BN1 2NR
United Kingdom
tel. 1273/208 181
fax 1273/866 583
www.bupa-intl.com

IMG Global
407 Fulton Street
Indianapolis, IN 46202
tel. 317/655-4500 or 866/368-3724
fax 317/655-4505
www.imglobal.com

Sanitas
Calle Padilla
Planta 1, Bajo
28006 Madrid
tel. 902 400 232
fax 91 432 62 00
www.sanitas.es

SAFETY

You can find out the correct number to dial for any emergency by calling operator information at tel. 11818. Here are some additional numbers to be aware of:

Ambulance, fire department, and/or police: tel. 112

Ambulance: tel. 061

Fire department: tel. 080 or 085 (A few parts of the country use a different number. Upon moving to a new place, it's a good idea to dial tel. 11818 to find out the correct number in your area.)

Asociación de Asistencia a Mujeres Violadas (Association for Assistance of Raped Women): tel. 91 574 01 10

Comisión de Investigación de Malos Tratos a Mujeres (Commission of Investigation into the Abuse of Women): tel. 900 10 00 09

Finance and Legal Matters

You'll undoubtedly want some help tackling taxes, immigration, and buying property—here are some firms that can lend you a hand.

Cuatrecasas Abogados
Pg. De Gràcia, 111
08008 Barcelona
tel. 93 290 54 23
fax 93 290 55 84
www.cuatrecasas.com

Gomez Villares & Alvarez
Calle San Lorenzo, 27
5A
29001 Málaga
tel. 95 222 50 87
fax 95 222 09 06
www.gva-abogados.com

Graydon & Associates Chartered Accountants, S.L.
Centro Plaza, Oficina 4
Planta 1
Nueva Andalucía
29660 Marbella,
Málaga
tel. 95 290 63 70
fax 95 281 61 90
www.graydon-associates.com

Strong Abogados
Regina, 5
41003 Seville
tel. 95 422 95 97
fax 95 422 96 74
www.strongabogados.com

Windram Miller & Company
Jacinto Benavente, 17
2A
29600 Marbella,
Málaga
tel. 95 282 07 79 or 95 282 49 10
fax 95 277 84 68
www.windrammiller.com

Communications

You can mail, fax, get online, and call all over the world from Spain. Here are a few contacts that will help you do those things.

TELEPHONE

Telefónica (www.telefonica.es) will almost certainly be your phone company, and you can call to have a line installed by dialing tel. 1004, or visit one of their stores—they're scattered throughout the country.

INTERNET SERVICE PROVIDERS

Wanadoo
tel. 902 011 902
www.wanadoo.es

Auna
tel. 902 50 00 60
www.auna.es

Terra
tel. 902 15 20 15
www.terra.es

EXPRESS MAIL SERVICES

Although a handful of express mail companies service Spain, the listings below are the most commonly used services.

FedEx
tel. 902 100 871
www.fedex.com/es

UPS
tel. 902 88 88 20
www.ups.com/europe/es/spaindex.html

SEUR
tel. 91 205 95 00 or 93 263 26 22
www.seurinternacional.com

Travel and Transportation

BY TRAIN

If you're relying on trains to get around, you'll surely want to know fares and schedules. Just one company runs Spain's network of trains—**Red Nacional de los Ferrocarriles Españoles (Renfe)**. For fares and schedules, call tel. 902 24 02 02 or check www.renfe.es.

BY CAR

If you have a car, you'll want details on driver's licenses, insurance, and the law. The **Real Autómovil Club de España** (www.seguridadvial.org) can help you out. The organization has been around for about a century, and it's the Spanish answer to AAA; you can receive breakdown assistance, insurance, travel services, and more. The club's general information number is tel. 902 404 545.

Real Autómovil Club de España Barcelona
Calle Muntaner, 81
Bajos
tel. 93 451 15 51
fax 93 451 22 57

Real Autómovil Club de España Madrid
Calle de Eloy Gonzalo, 32
tel. 902 120 441

Real Autómovil Club de España Oviedo
Calle Foncalada, 6 Bajos
tel. 98 522 31 06 or 98 522 31 07
fax 98 522 76 68

Real Autómovil Club de España Seville
Avenida Eduardo Dato, 22
tel. 95 463 13 50
fax 95 465 96 04

Real Autómovil Club de España Toledo
Calle Colombia, 10
tel. 925 21 16 37 or 925 21 17 06
fax 925 21 56 54

Real Autómovil Club de España Valencia
G. V. Marqués del Turia, 79
tel. 96 334 55 22
fax 96 334 39 89

Real Autómovil Club de España
Valladolid
Calle Santa María, 21
tel. 983 39 20 99
fax 983 39 68 95

Prime Living Locations

MADRID

www.aboutmadrid.com
www.awcmadrid.org (The American Women's Club of Madrid)
http://incmadrid.com (The International Newcomers Club of Madrid)
www.in-madrid.com
www.madrid.loquo.com

BARCELONA AND CATALONIA

www.amersoc.com (The American Society of Barcelona)
http://barcelona.fawco.org (The American Women's Club of Barcelona)
www.barcelona-metropolitan.com
www.bcn.es
www.loquo.com

VALENCIA AND THE BALEARIC ISLANDS

www.costablanca-news.com
www.costablanca.org
www.thisisvalencia.com
www.valencia.loquo.com
www.balearics.com

ANDALUSIA

www.andalucia.com
www.andalucia.org
http://costadelsolnews.es
www.exploreseville.com
www.surinenglish.com

THE CANTABRIAN COAST

www.basquecountry-tourism.com
www.cd.sc.ehu.es/DOCS/book.SS-G/v2
www.dicoruna.es
www.galice.net
www.lavozdegalicia.es

Spanish Phrasebook

Pronunciation Guide

VOWELS

a — like "ah" as in "lava"; shorter than the English "a"

e — like "eh" as in "pet"

i — like "ee" as in "meet"

i in diphthongs **ia, ie, io, iu** — the "i" is like "y" as in "yellow"

o — like "o" as in "no," only shorter

u — like "oo" as in "moon," only shorter

u in diphthongs **ua, ue, ui, uo** — the "u" is like "w" as in "willow"

CONSONANTS

b, ch, f, k, l, m, n, p, s, t, and **y** — pronounced as in English

c — lisped as in "think"

d — lisped slightly like a cross between "d" as in "dog" and "th" as in "think": *idea* ee-DHAY-ah

g — a guttural sound like that in "loch"

h — silent (except when following a "c")

j — a guttural sound like "h" in "hero"

ll — sounds like the "y" in "yes"

ñ — like "ny" together as in "canyon": *muñeca* moo-NYEK-ah

q — pronounced like an English "k"; always followed by "ue" or "ui" (the "u" is silent)

r — slightly stronger than the English "r" and generally punched

rr — "r" said with accentuated roll

v — sounds more like a "b" than a "v": *Vasco* BAS-ko

w — used in words that have been adopted from other languages; in most cases, pronounced like an English "w"

x — like "x" as in "fax"; if it begins a word, it sounds like a "z"

z — lisped like "th" as in "thread": *cerveza* thair-BAY-thah

Numbers

zero — *cero*	10 — *diez*
one — *uno*	11 — *once*
two — *dos*	12 — *doce*
three — *tres*	13 — *trece*
four — *cuatro*	14 — *catorce*
five — *cinco*	15 — *quince*
six — *seis*	16 — *dieciseis*
seven — *siete*	17 — *diecisiete*
eight — *ocho*	18 — *dieciocho*
nine — *nueve*	19 — *diecinueve*

20 — *veinte*
21 — *veintiuno*
30 — *treinta*
40 — *cuarenta*
50 — *cincuenta*
60 — *sesenta*
70 — *setenta*
80 — *ochenta*
90 — *noventa*
100 — *ciento*

101 — *ciento y uno* or *cientiuno*
200 — *doscientos*
500 — *quinientos*
1,000 — *mil*
10,000 — *diez mil*
100,000 — *cien mil*
1,000,000 — *millón*
one half — *medio*
one third — *un tercio*
one fourth — *un cuarto*

Days and Months

Monday — *lunes*
Tuesday — *martes*
Wednesday — *miércoles*
Thursday — *jueves*
Friday — *viernes*
Saturday — *sábado*
Sunday — *domingo*
today — *hoy*
tomorrow — *mañana*
yesterday — *ayer*
January — *enero*
February — *febrero*
March — *marzo*

April — *abril*
May — *mayo*
June — *junio*
July — *julio*
August — *agosto*
September — *septiembre*
October — *octubre*
November — *noviembre*
December — *diciembre*
a week — *una semana*
a month — *un mes*
after — *después*
before — *antes*

Time

What time is it? — *¿Qué hora es?*
It's one o'clock. — *Es la una.*
It's three in the afternoon. — *Son las tres de la tarde.*
It's 4 A.M. — *Son las cuatro de la mañana.*
six-thirty — *a las seis y media*
a quarter till eleven — *a las once menos cuarto*

a quarter past five — *a las cinco y cuarto*
an hour — *una hora*
the morning — *la mañana*
the early hours of the morning — *la madrugada*
the afternoon — *la tarde*
the night — *la noche*

Greetings and Basic Expressions

Most Spanish-speaking people consider formalities important. Whenever approaching anyone with a question, do not forget the appropriate salutation—good morning, good evening, etc. The greeting *hola* (hello) can sound brusque standing alone.

Hello. — *Hola.*
Good morning. — *Buenos días.*
Good afternoon. — *Buenas tardes.*
Good evening. — *Buenas noches.*
How are you? — *¿Cómo está usted?*
Very well, thank you. — *Muy bien, gracias.*
Okay; good. — *Bien.*
Not okay; bad. — *Mal* or *fatal*
So-so. — *Más o menos.*
And you? — *¿Y usted?*
Thank you. — *Gracias.*
Thank you very much. — *Muchas gracias.*
You're very kind. — *Muy amable.*
You're welcome. — *De nada.*
Goodbye. — *Adios.*
See you later. — *Hasta luego.*
please — *por favor*
yes — *sí*

no — *no*
I don't know. — *No sé.*
Just a moment, please. — *Un momento, por favor.*
Excuse me, please (when you're trying to get attention). — *Disculpe* or *Con permiso.*
Excuse me (when you've made a mistake). — *Perdone.*
Sorry. — *Lo siento*
Pleased to meet you. — *Encantado/a.* (male/female)
How do you say . . . in Spanish? — *¿Cómo se dice . . . en español?*
What is your name? — *¿Cómo se llama usted?*
My name is . . . — *Me llamo . . .*
Do you speak English? — *¿Habla usted inglés?*
Is English spoken here? — *¿Se habla aquí el inglés?*
I don't speak Spanish well. — *No hablo bien el español.*
I don't understand. — *No entiendo.*
Would you like . . .? — *¿Quisiera usted . . .?*
Let's go to . . . — *Vamos a . . .*

Terms of Address

When in doubt, use the formal *usted* (you) as a form of address.

I — *yo*
you (formal) — *usted*
you (familiar) — *tu*
he/him — *él*
she/her — *ella*
we/us — *nosotros* (all males or mixed gender); *nosotras* (all females)

you (plural, formal) — *ustedes*
you (plural, familiar) — *vosotros* (all males or mixed gender); *vosotras* (all females)
they/them — *ellos* (all males or mixed gender); *ellas* (all females)
Mr, sir — *señor*

Mrs, madam — *señora*
Miss, young woman — *señorita*
wife — *mujer* or *esposa*
husband — *marido* or *esposo*
friend — *amigo* (male); *amiga* (female)

boyfriend; girlfriend — *novio; novia*
son; daughter — *hijo; hija*
brother; sister — *hermano; hermana*
father; mother — *padre; madre*
grandfather; grandmother — *abuelo; abuela*

Getting Around

Where is . . .? — *¿Dónde está . . .?*
How far is it from . . . to . . .? — *¿Cuánto hay de . . . a . . .?*
How many blocks? — *¿Cuántas cuadras?*
Where can I find . . .? — *¿Dónde puedo encontrar . . .*
the bus station — *la estación de autobuses*
the bus stop — *la parada de autobuses*
Where is this bus going? — *¿Adónde va este autobús?*
the taxi stand — *la parada de taxis*
the train station — *la estación de ferrocarril*
Suburban railway — *las cercanías*
the port — *el puerto*
the ferry terminal — *el terminal de los ferrys*
the airport — *el aeropuerto*
I'd like a ticket to . . . — *Quisiera un billete a . . .*
first (second) class — *de primera (segunda) clase*
roundtrip — *ida y vuelta*
single; one-way — *sencillo*
reservation — *reservación*
baggage — *equipaje*

Stop here, please. — *Pare aquí, por favor.*
the entrance — *la entrada*
the exit — *la salida*
the ticket office — *la taquilla*
(very) near; far — *(muy) cerca; lejos*
to; toward — *a; hacia*
by; through — *por*
from — *de*
the right — *la derecha*
the left — *la izquierda*
straight ahead — *todo recto*
in front of — *delante de*
beside — *al lado*
behind — *atrás*
the corner — *la esquina*
the stoplight — *el semáforo*
a turn — *una vuelta*
right here — *aquí*
somewhere around here — *por aquí*
right there — *allí*
somewhere around there — *por allí*
street; avenue — *calle; avenida*
highway — *la carretera*
bridge — *el puente*
toll — *el peaje*
address — *la dirección*
north; south — *norte; sur*
east; west — *este; oeste*

At the Gas Station

gas station — *gasolinera*
gasoline — *gasolina*
unleaded — *sin plomo*
fill it up, please — *llénelo, por favor*
(flat) tire — *neumático (desinflado)*
air — *aire*
water — *agua*
oil (change) — *(cambio) de aceite*
grease — *grasa*

breakdown — *avería*
My . . . doesn't work. — *Mi . . . no funciona.*
car battery — *batería*
radiator — *radiador*
alternator — *alternador*
generator — *generador*
tow truck — *grúa*
repair shop — *taller de reparaciones*

Accommodations

hotel — *hotel*
Do you have any rooms available? — *¿Tiene habitaciones libres?*
May I (may we) see it? — *¿Puedo (podemos) verla?*
How much is it? — *¿Cuánto cuesta?*
Is that your best rate? — *¿Es su mejor precio?*
Do you have anything cheaper? — *¿Tiene algo más barato?*
a single room — *una habitación sencilla*
a double room — *una habitación doble*

double bed — *cama de matrimonio*
twin beds — *camas gemelas*
with private bath — *con baño*
hot water — *agua caliente*
shower — *ducha*
towels — *toallas*
soap — *jabón*
toilet paper — *papel higiénico*
blanket — *manta; frazada*
sheets — *sábanas*
air-conditioned — *aire acondicionado*
fan — *ventilador*
key — *llave*
manager — *gerente*

Food

I'm hungry — *Tengo hambre.*
I'm thirsty. — *Tengo sed.*
menu — *carta*
to order — *pedir*
glass — *vaso*
fork — *tenedor*
knife — *cuchillo*
spoon — *cuchara*
napkin — *servilleta*
drink — *bebida*

alcoholic drink — *copa*
coffee — *café*
tea — *té*
drinking water — *agua pura; agua potable*
bottled carbonated water — *agua mineral con gas*
bottled uncarbonated water — *agua sin gas*
beer — *cerveza*

red/white wine — *vino tinto/blanco*
butter — *mantequilla*
milk — *leche*
juice — *zumo*
cream — *nata*
sugar — *azúcar*
cheese — *queso*
snack — *bocado*
breakfast — *desayuno*
lunch — *almuerzo*
daily set menu — *el menú del día*
dinner — *cena*
small snacks served with drinks — *tapas*
meal-sized version of tapas — *ración*
small filled sandwich — *montadito*
the check — *la cuenta*
eggs — *huevos*
bread — *pan*
baguette — *barra (de pan)*
salad — *ensalada*
fruit — *fruta*
watermelon — *sandía*
banana — *plátano*
apple — *manzana*
orange — *naranja*
lime — *lima*
lemon — *limón*
olives — *aceitunas*
onion — *cebolla*
beans — *judías*
lettuce — *lechuga*
potato — *patata*
fries — *patatas fritas*
tomato — *tomate*
carrot — *zanahoria*
fish — *pescado*
trout — *trucha*
cod — *bacalao*
tuna — *atún* or *bonito*

sea bass — *dorada*
sole — *lenguado*
hake — *merluza*
salmon — *salmón*
sardines — *sardinas*
shellfish — *mariscos*
squid — *calamares*
shrimp — *camarones*
prawns — *gambas*
king prawns — *langostinos*
crab — *cangrejo*
mussels — *mejillones*
octopus — *pulpo*
(without) meat — *(sin) carne*
chicken — *pollo*
pork — *carne de cerdo*
beef; beefsteak — *carne de vaca; bistec*
chop — *chuleta*
fillet — *pechuga*
loin — *lomo*
leg — *pierna*
bacon — *beicon* or *tocino*
sausage — *chorizo*
ham — *jamón*
paella — *paella*
omelette — *tortilla*
potato omelette — *tortilla española*
pie — *empanada*
fritters — *churros*
biscuit; cookie — *galleta*
ice cream — *helado*
cake — *pastel* or *tarta*
almond nougat — *turrón*
fried — *frito*
roasted — *asado*
barbecue; barbecued — *barbacoa; a la parilla*
grilled — *a la plancha*
oven-baked — *al horno*

Shopping

money — *dinero*
exchange bureau — *oficina de cambio*
I would like to exchange traveler's checks. — *Quisiera cambiar cheques de viajero.*
What is the exchange rate? — *¿Cuál es el tipo de cambio?*
How much is the commission? — *¿Cuánto cuesta la comisión?*
Do you accept credit cards? — *¿Se acepta tarjetas de crédito?*

money order — *giro postal*
How much does it cost? — *¿Cuánto cuesta?*
What is your final price? — *¿Cuál es su último precio?*
expensive — *caro*
cheap — *barato*
more — *más*
less — *menos*
a little — *un poco*
too much — *demasiado*

Making the Move

border — *frontera*
customs — *aduana*
immigration — *inmigración*
tourist card — *tarjeta de turista*
visa — *visado*
inspection — *inspección*
passport — *pasaporte*
profession — *profesión*

marital status — *estado civil*
single — *soltero/a* (male/female)
married; divorced — *casado/a; divorciado/a* (male/female)
widowed — *viudado/a* (male/female)
insurance — *seguro*
title — *título*
drivers license — *carnet de conducir*

Health

Help me please. — *Ayúdeme por favor.*
I am ill. — *Estoy enfermo/a.* (male/female)
Call a doctor. — *Llame a un doctor.*
Take me to . . . — *Lléveme a . . .*
hospital — *hospital*
drugstore — *farmacia*
pain — *dolor*
fever — *fiebre*
headache — *dolor de cabeza*
stomach ache — *dolor de estómago*
burn — *quemadura*
cramp — *calambre*
nausea — *náusea*

vomiting — *vomitar*
medicine — *medicina*
antibiotic — *antibiótico*
pill; tablet — *pastilla*
aspirin — *aspirina*
ointment; cream — *pomada; crema*
bandage — *venda*
cotton — *algodón*
sanitary pads — *compresas*
tampons — *tampones*
condoms — *preservativos; condones*
birth control pills — *píldoras anticonceptivas*
toothbrush — *cepillo de dientes*

dental floss — *hilo dental*
toothpaste — *pasta dentífrica*

dentist — *dentista*
toothache — *dolor de muelas*

Finance and Legal Matters

I'd like to open a . . . account, please. —
   Quisiera abrir una cuenta . . . , por favor.
checking account — *cuenta corriente*
savings account — *cuenta de ahorros*
I would like to withdraw money. —
   Quisiera sacar dinero.
I would like to deposit money. —
   Quisiera ingresar dinero.
deposit — *depósito*

mortgage — *hipoteca*
loan — *préstamo*
accountant — *contable*
lawyer — *abogado*
notary — *notario*
taxes — *impuestos*
value added tax — *IVA—impuesto
   sobre el valor añadido*
title deeds — *título de propiedad*

Communications

long-distance telephone call — *llamada de larga distancia*
I would like to call . . . — *Quisiera
   llamar a . . .*
collect call — *llamada a cobro revertido*
person to person — *persona a persona*
credit card — *tarjeta de crédito*
post office — *correo*

letter — *carta*
stamp — *sello*
postcard — *(tarjeta) postal*
air mail — *correo aereo*
registered — *registrado*
money order — *giro postal*
package; box — *paquete; caja*
string; tape — *cuerda; cinta*

Housing Considerations

I am interested in buying/renting a . . . —
   Me interesa comprar/alquilar un/a . . .
house — *casa*
villa — *chalet*
apartment — *piso*
terraced houses— *casas en hilera*
plot of land — *parcela*
real estate agent — *inmobiliaria*
real estate agency — *agente inmobiliario*
Are you licensed? — *¿Es autorizado?*

suburbs — *afueras*
private community — *urbanización*
Does it have a . . .? — *¿Tiene un . . .?*
yard — *jardín*
garage — *garaje*
swimming pool — *piscina*
parking spaces — *aparcamientos*
How many square meters is it? —
   ¿Cuántos metros cuadrados es?
Where is the town hall? — *¿Dónde
   está el ayuntamiento?*

Courtesy of Bruce Whipperman, author of Moon Handbooks Pacific Mexico.

Suggested Reading

Over the centuries, Spanish writers have compiled volumes on their country, and foreign authors have also had quite a bit to say about Spain. When it comes to the printed word, you can find endless amounts on just about everything Spanish—history, art, recipes, poetry, novels, and more. Here are a few particularly good books on the subject of Spain.

Fiction and Poetry

Bly, Robert, translator. *Times Alone: Selected Poems of Antonio Machado*. Middletown, Connecticut: Wesleyan University Press, 1983.

Burns, Jimmy. *A Literary Companion to Spain*. London: John Murray (Publishers) Ltd., 1995.

Cervantes, Miguel de. *Don Quixote*. London: Penguin Books, 2001

Hemingway, Ernest. *Death in the Afternoon*. New York: Touchstone Books, 1996.

Hemingway, Ernest. *For Whom the Bell Tolls*. New York: Scribner, 1995.

Hemingway, Ernest. *The Sun Also Rises*. New York: Scribner, 1995.

Marsé, Juan. *The Fallen*. New York: Little Brown and Company, 1979.

Simon, Greg and Steven F. White, translators. *Federico García Lorca: Poet in New York*. New York: The Noonday Press, 1988.

Vega, Lope de. *Three Major Plays: Fuente Ovejuna/the Knight from Olmedo/Punishment Without Revenge*. Oxford: Oxford Press, 1999.

Nonfiction

Buñuel, Luis. *My Last Sigh*, translated by Abigail Israel. Minneapolis: University of Minnesota Press, 2003.

Casas, Penelope. *Discovering Spain: An Uncommon Guide*. New York: Alfred A. Knopf, Inc., 1996.

Goodwin, Godfrey. *Islamic Spain*. New York: Viking, 1990.

Graves, William. *Wild Olives: Life in Majorca with Robert Graves*. London: Pimlico, 2001.

Hooper, John. *The New Spaniards*. New York: Penguin USA, 1995.

Irving, Washington. *Tales of the Alhambra*. Granada: Miguel Sanchez, 1932.

Lorca, Francisco García and Donald M. Allen, editors. *Federico García Lorca: The Selected Poems*. New York: W.W. Norton, 1988.

Michener, James. *Iberia*. New York: Ballantine Books, 1982.

Orwell, George. *Homage to Catalonia.* New York: Harvest Books, 1969.

Pritchett, V.S. *The Spanish Temper.* New York: Ecco Press, 1989.

Radford, John. *The New Spain.* London: Mitchell Beazley, 1998.

Schoenfeld, Bruce *The Last Serious Thing: A Season at the Bullfights.* New York: Simon & Schuster, Inc., 1992.

Schweid, Richard. *Barcelona: Jews, Transvestites, and an Olympic Season.* Berkeley, California: Ten Speed Press, 1994.

Index

WXYZ

Acknowledgments

I want to thank my family and friends for everything. Everyone I know and love in the United States has been extremely patient about the calls that I've made ridiculously early in the morning when I just couldn't wait any longer, so thanks big for that. (Your enthusiasm about having long conversations at 6:30 A.M. has been faked so well, and don't think that goes unappreciated.) I specifically want to mention my parents (all three of them), my brothers (the big one, the little one), Jessica, Diana, Frankie, Gary, and Greg—my e-pal who could relate. Special thanks also to Kathryn Ettinger, who did everything that an editor should, and more.

As to Spain, assistance and advice have come from a lot of sources, but a few people have been especially helpful to me and I'd be remiss not to give a big *gracias* for that—especially to Aitana, Izabel & Co, Irene, Juan, Rafa, and Sam.

U.S.~Metric Conversion

1 inch = 2.54 centimeters (cm)
1 foot = .304 meters (m)
1 yard = 0.914 meters
1 mile = 1.6093 kilometers (km)
1 km = .6214 miles
1 fathom = 1.8288 m
1 chain = 20.1168 m
1 furlong = 201.168 m
1 acre = .4047 hectares
1 sq km = 100 hectares
1 sq mile = 2.59 square km
1 ounce = 28.35 grams
1 pound = .4536 kilograms
1 short ton = .90718 metric ton
1 short ton = 2000 pounds
1 long ton = 1.016 metric tons
1 long ton = 2240 pounds
1 metric ton = 1000 kilograms
1 quart = .94635 liters
1 US gallon = 3.7854 liters
1 Imperial gallon = 4.5459 liters
1 nautical mile = 1.852 km

To compute Celsius temperatures, subtract 32 from Fahrenheit and divide by 1.8. To go the other way, multiply Celsius by 1.8 and add 32.

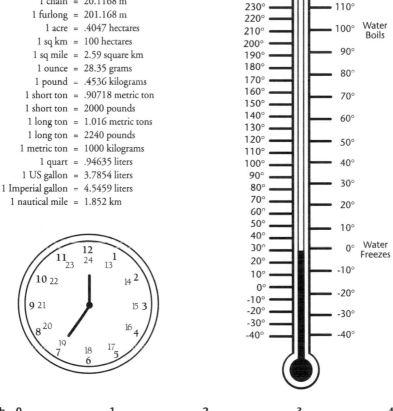

Fahrenheit   Celsius

230° — 110°
220°
210° — 100° Water Boils
200°
190° — 90°
180°
170° — 80°
160° — 70°
150°
140° — 60°
130°
120° — 50°
110°
100° — 40°
90°
80° — 30°
70°
60° — 20°
50°
40° — 10°
30°
20° — 0° Water Freezes
10°
0° — -10°
-10°
-20° — -20°
-30° — -30°
-40° — -40°

inch 0   1   2   3   4

cm 0 1 2 3 4 5 6 7 8 9 10

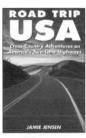

Living Abroad in Spain
Avalon Travel Publishing
1400 65th Street, Suite 250
Emeryville, CA 94608, USA
www.travelmatters.com

Editor: Kathryn Ettinger
Series Manager: Erin Raber
Cover design: Justin Marler
Interior design: Amber Pirker, Justin
 Marler
Copy Editor: Helen Sillett
Graphics Coordinator: Susan Snyder
Production Coordinator: Justin Marler
Map Editor: Olivia Solís
Cartographers: Kat Kalamaras, Mike
 Morgenfeld
Indexer: Rachel Kuhn

ISBN: 1-56691-666-6
ISSN: 1551-7128

Printing History
1st edition— November 2004
5 4 3 2 1

Avalon Travel Publishing is
an Imprint of Avalon Pub-
lishing Group, Inc.

AVALON
publishing group incorporated

Some photos and illustrations are used
by permission and are the property of
the original copyright owners.

Front cover photo:
© Esbin-Anderson/
Omni-Photo Communications

Printed in the USA by Edward Bros.

Keeping Current

Although we strive to produce the most up-to-date book that we possibly can,
change is unavoidable. Between the time this book goes to print and the time you
read it, the cost of goods and services may have increased, and a handful of the
businesses noted in these pages will undoubtedly move, alter their prices, or close
their doors forever. Exchange rates fluctuate—sometimes dramatically—on a
daily basis. Federal and local legal requirements and restrictions are also subject
to change, so be sure to check with the appropriate authorities before making the
move. If you see anything in this book that needs updating, clarification, or cor-
rection, please drop us a line. Send your comments via email to atpfeed-
back@avalonpub.com, or write to the address above.